Where (on Earth) did the
Enneagram come from?

FÁTIMA FERNÁNDEZ
CHRISTLIEB

Image research: Adelaida Harrison Lafuente

To Óscar

To Diego, Mariana and Andrea

To Óscar, Adrián and Andrés

Text © 2016 Fátima Fernández Christlieb
Translation into English: Dora A. Napolitano
Image research and administration for English version: Adelaida Harrison Lafuente

Original title: *¿De dónde demonios salió el Eneagrama?* 2016, Editorial Pax México

Cover illustration based on image from *Ars Brevis* [Logical Nova]/Ramón Llull [ms 993], published in 1432. Digital copy. Número de control: BVPB20070010624. Biblioteca Pública del Estado en Palma de Mallorca. © 2006 Ministerio de Cultura. Objeto digital 11000951, p.6. Tomado de la Biblioteca Virtual del Patrimonio Bibliográfico, http://bvpb.mcu.es/

Illustrations inside the book are referenced in the text.

ISBN: 978-607-29-0014-1

Printed by Lightning Source

Contents

List of figures

Acknowledgements

I would like to thank many people but in particular:

Óscar for his versatile, cheerful and profound support every day.

Adelaida Harrison, who went to great trouble to find the illustrations and diagrams needed for this book, and for her constant support since I started writing.

Carlos de León, because the seed he sowed with his explorations of so many traditions was formative.

Dora Napolitano, for her conviction that you cannot translate properly if you do not understand the original text. This English version exists thanks to her.

Thanks also to all those with whom I have taken courses and workshops on the Enneagram: in chronological order: Alfonso Ruiz Soto (1989), Ilse Kretzschmar (2004), Claudio Naranjo (2007), Rafael Ruiz (2008), Andrea Isaacs (2010), Ginger Lapid-Bogda (2011), Adelaida Harrison and Andrea Vargas (2012), Peter O'Hanrahan and Mónica Tinoco (2013) and Roberto A. Pérez (2015).

Introduction

Why I wrote this book

I am surrounded by people who, on hearing the word Enneagram, make a gesture of disdain or openly express their disinterest. They associate it with a technique for entrapping innocents and poorly informed folk or consider it one more product in the growing market of self-help manuals. In one sense, they are right. We are dealing with something that has often fallen into the hands of people who see it exclusively as a trivial game of 9 personalities or an easy way of earning money.

I met a young woman who, after giving up her secondary school studies, had started earning her living attaching artificial nails. Years later I encountered her again giving Enneagram consultations. "It's so much fun", she told me, "and it never fails, sooner or later all my clients get their number". Yes, they leave with a smile and a label, I thought. She, and those who listen to her, rarely have the elements necessary to see any further, and are unable to perceive that situating themselves in one of the nine personality types is no more than a mask that their ego adopts to survive in this world. The Enneagram goes much further than that. The determination of the ego is just a small part of it; a starting point, and that understanding is the basis for more complex interactions with the other types. Fixating on the ego, or one personality type, reduces the value of the Enneagram as a system of knowledge.

There is another group of people, especially in academia, who do not know and do not want to learn about the Enneagram. They have chosen their beliefs and although they are aware of obvious personality differences in those around them, they put them down to Hippocrates' four temperaments, to their genes or perhaps to certain events in their private lives. Most of my colleagues know who to get along with and how to behave, and they are very clear on the correct social actions in order to avoid problems and that is it. They would never think that the Enneagram has elements in common with the quantic theories of David Bohm or with some cutting edge theories in contemporary evolutionary biology.

Of course, it is not my intention to convince anyone of anything. I have written this book to answer questions that arose for me when circumstances placed the Enneagram before me. I needed to know where it had come from and if it was as serious as I at first perceived it to be.

It is not my intention in this book to explain what the Enneagram is from A to Z. Not at all. That has already been written in dozens of books. What you will find here is a history of how I believe this knowledge has been passed down and articulated through the centuries. Here are some of the answers that I had not been able to find for years: Where does this understanding come from? Who had the idea and when? How serious and verifiable is it? I believe I have found some answers in the course of this research. But note: I have set one foot firmly on the path to disentangling the real origin of the Enneagram, but I say *one* foot, the other has yet to join the first. More researchers are needed, not alone like me, but as a team, with a clear direction, reasonable funds, and a research deadline because we are dealing with a history without a precise beginning and which is continuously evolving.

It is only in the second half of the 20th century that the Enneagram opens up massively and the bibliography on the subject is now, in the second decade of the 21st century, both extensive and varied. If someone visits a bookshop today and skims a text about the Enneagram, they might be inclined to leave it quickly behind as one more offering of the "dare-to-be-happy" trend or they might buy it, devour it and be quite astonished by it and search for more literature on the subject. It would probably depend on which book they stumbled across and what they are searching for. The same is true of websites.

The paths that lead to the Enneagram are diverse. Mine was one that cannot fail: through someone whom I trusted greatly. It was 1971, I had just started studying a second degree at the National Autonomous University of Mexico (UNAM, according to the Spanish acronym). In that first year I coincided with a classmate who, like me, wanted to study in order to contribute to the creation of a fairer society. The environment was combative, the protest groups and various collectives that formed around the student movement of 1968 were in full swing and historical materialism prevailed over any other approach to understanding reality. Surviving intellectually meant learning to think for yourself and being sure of what and who you trusted.

The day after the bloodletting on the Thursday of Corpus Christi,[1] we had a political science lecture at 7am on the university campus. Obviously no-one could talk of anything else, the fury and bewilderment about what had happened the night before permeated everything. In the Faculty of Medicine, a few steps away from us, in Political Sciences, a murdered student lay stretched out on a black board. Our anger and unease, the tragedy itself, united us all and we sought explanations and consolation amongst our closest friends. I found that friendship, that day and thereafter, in a classmate called Rafael Landerreche. His intellectual inheritance was solid, his search for sense extraordinary. Brave in the face of adversaries, he dispelled my doubts with texts that opened my eyes and my mind. Years later he would be the one to tell me about the Enneagram. One day he gave me an audio tape with a fragment of a seminar by

---

[1] On 10th June, 1971, on the day of the Catholic festivity of Corpus Christi, a student demonstration in Mexico City was violently repressed by paramilitaries working for the government. Many students were killed but to date no-one knows exactly how many.

Richard Rohr[2] in New Mexico and said something like, "This is you". The tape contained one personality type from the Enneagram. I listened to it several times with more and more attention and it impressed me. Where did this long, detailed and accurate description of my strengths and weaknesses come from? It took me years, many years, to answer that question.

I stayed and worked at UNAM. There, I studied a masters and completed my PhD. I became director of university TV; I have taught here for the last 4 decades, here I learnt to do interdisciplinary research; this is where I would choose to die. Although I have tried my hand at journalism and public administration, academia is my thing and certain rules apply in academia. One rule is to do science in the most rigorous way possible and to submit to various periodic academic evaluations.

I am taking the time to spell this out to explain that it was impossible for me to be satisfied with the few background paragraphs or pages that tend to preface books about the Enneagram. I needed to know who the author was, what were his/her sources? What documents back up the claims? What is the epistemological validity of such-and-such knowledge? And so on. Something similar has happened to several people in various countries around the same time. Perhaps that is why so many books have appeared recently, like mushrooms in the rainy season. There is a great need to verify whether we are dealing with an understanding that is based in comprehensible and searchable sources.

This book contains not only the answers I found in each document I read to discover more about the nature of the sources of the Enneagram. It is also informed by my almost daily exercise of

---

[2] Richard Rohr is a scholar and contemporary practitioner of the Enneagram. He was born in 1943 in Topeka, Kansas, and is now a speaker and author of many books, including *The Enneagram: A Christian Perspective*, with Andreas Ebert (2001). He was a founder-member and, since 1986, has been Dean of the Center for Action and Contemplation in Albuquerque, New Mexico.

putting into practice what the Enneagram has taught me so far. When we have the privilege of sharing our lives with someone who is determined to make the most of their talents, who admits their mistakes and pours the best of their energy into making their strengths emerge, the Enneagram becomes a very valuable instrument, an endless key to deciphering the difficult areas of existence and also the places of clarity and innate strength. I will never be able to sufficiently express my gratitude to Life for having placed me face to face and side by side with Óscar Moreno Arózqueta.

One additional fact: I have turned 60 already, that is to say that I am in a phase in which I prefer to write about what has seemed to me to be truly valuable, academically or personally. I have said it many times, here it is once more: I would not like to arrive at the final phase of old age without having written at least a few pages about the subjects to which I have dedicated years just for the pleasure of it, or from mere conviction and without any work-related purpose. The Enneagram, its origins and its reach, is one of those subjects. This book was drafted as part of a search that will not cease while I live. Although I have advanced a good deal in the quest for texts and practice, and although I may understand how it works at higher levels, there will always be too many unresolved mysteries about how we are constructed beyond the tangible body and how it is that we are connected to everything that exists. The anatomy of our subtle nature has been sadly lacking in the paradigm of contemporary science in the West.

This book is intended mainly for those who have at some point wondered where the Enneagram came from. For those who have never heard of it, here are some brief accounts.

More has been written about the Enneagram in the last three decades than in the many centuries it had been around before. It is something very ancient, although for a long time it was not called this way. Some of the very earliest civilizations on the planet have left tangible testimonies of their quest to harmonize human relations, to transcend the limitations of the mind and to discover the links between the human mind and the universe. Recently several authors have located the Enneagram in one or other period or culture, but the full map is not finished. We need more in-depth and sustained research, that can bring together all the clues in a coherent whole that spans at least 4000 years of history.

The Greek etymology, as written in any text about the Enneagram is "ennea", 9, and "gram", text, drawing or line. "The number nine, Εννεας, was a Greek term which was used to designate the plural of plurals, that is to say the infinite, everything" according to a preface to a text by Plotinus.[3] The number 9 in several cultures had a deeper meaning, associated with unity; it was not merely an indication of nine units, but rather a mathematical convergence related to everything that exists.

The word Enneagram also makes reference to a symbol or diagram that is illustrated in the hundreds of essays on the subject and which appears on the cover of this book. Where does it come from? Has it evolved or has it always been drawn as we know it today? Who drew it? When? Where? Perhaps one day a team of philologists, historians, or people passionate about this subject, may dedicate a few years to immerse themselves in ancient texts and then be able to answer these questions precisely. There will also be a day when it will be possible to verify the existence of a symbol traced in rubies on Afghan marble at a monastery in the Hindu Kush. But for now, in this book, I present to you what I have found so far. I feel better for finding them, and at the same time enthusiastic about future findings.

The background to this Enneagram symbol, its uses, interpretation and meaning is dispersed in history. I took my search as far back as possible and this journey is the main part of this book. The more I

---

[3] Taken from a Spanish translation of Plotinus (2009 [3rd century CE]), page 13.

made advances towards a construction of a hypothesis about the origin and development of this knowledge, the more doors opened and more potential research questions arose. Each time this happened, I formulated a pending area of study. This book then is full of clues and questions.

Let us continue with a definition of the Enneagram. Those who believe that it is just a game of 9 personalities are stuck at the mere beginning of the subject. This is just the first step that anyone would have to take that wanted to make their life more entertaining and to have fewer conflicts with those around them. Beyond the Enneagram there is a groundswell of knowledge that goes as far as the origin and function of the universe.

Lets begin with the definition of an American scholar. Sixteen years after publishing her first book on the Enneagram, that is to say having reflected further and had more contact with the concrete functioning of this knowledge, Helen Palmer wrote in the prologue to a book by a colleague, "The Enneagram is arguably the oldest human development system on the planet, and like all authentic maps of consciousness, it finds new life in the conceptual world view of each succeeding generation" (Lapid-Bogda [Palmer], 2004: xi). There is another definition which is also the product of long experience, working daily with the Enneagram: "It is a vital matrix that reveals the energy stamp of an individual, an essential characteristic of each person, and also the root and sources of all the relational processes of a personality" (Pérez, 2015: 11).

Another well known definition of the Enneagram, that seems relevant to me because it implies a history and teleology, comes from a gem of a text, written by John G. Bennett a little before his death in 1974. In just a few paragraphs this charming man[4] first

---

[4] Reading the autobiography of this English traveller, diplomat and scholar is to discover that there are human beings who manage to combine the thirst for scientific knowledge with intuition, perseverance, and the humility of self-criticism. *Witness* was published in 1974, edited by Omen Press of Tucson, Arizona.

synthesizes that faction of humanity that has always sought self-renovation, and then goes on to explain, in the terms of some ancient mathematicians, how it is that one can be an "endless recurrence of the number *nine*" (Bennett 1983: 2). After a few calculations he concludes, "These properties were combined in a symbol that proved to have amazing significance. It could be used to represent every process that maintains itself by self-renewal, including of course, life itself. The symbol consists of nine lines and is therefore called the Enneagram" (Bennett, 1983: 3). To this he adds something equally important: "[The Enneagram] is an instrument that enables us to see when and how events conform to cosmic laws and so recognize what is possible and what is impossible in human undertakings" (Bennett, 1983: 6). This requires us to leave our prejudices aside for a moment. If the idea of "cosmic laws" already seems like hackneyed esoteric nonsense, try to carry on reading. You can choose not to accept any law, retain your own explanation of how life works and just hold on to the idea of a historical precedent of an effective typology of personality. Although I have to warn you that it is not just a question of putting prejudice aside, but rather of accepting that the roots and development of the Enneagram are based on an organicistic concept of life and evolution instead of a mechanistic vision based on lineal causality. Otherwise it is not possible to grasp what Bennett or his master, Gurdjieff, intend.

According Laleh Bakhtiar (2013b), in the Arabic etymology, the Sufi Enneagram is known as *Wajhullah*, meaning "Sign of the presence of God". The author of the introduction to one of her books asserts that "The quest for the Enneagram is to become a "Zero," and this occurs when the empirical ego or false personality dissolves into the Supreme Identity".[5] As we can begin to perceive, the topic that we are working on has a much greater complexity that is commonly thought.

---

[5] Introduction by Samuel Bendeck Sotillos to *The Sufi Enneagramm: The Secrets of the Symbol Unveiled* (Bakhtair 2013b: xxxiv).

A disciple of Gurdjieff reported his explanation, "The enneagram is the fundamental hieroglyph of a universal language which has as many different meanings as there are levels of men... The enneagram is perpetual motion, the same perpetual motion that men have sought since the remotest antiquity and could never find. And it is clear why they could not find perpetual motion. They sought outside themselves that which was within them; and they attempted to construct perpetual motion as a machine is constructed, whereas real perpetual motion is a part of another perpetual motion and cannot be created apart from it. The enneagram is a schematic diagram of *perpetual motion,* that is, of a machine of eternal movement" (Ouspensky, 2001 [1949]: 292).

There are another couple of definitions that include a key element in the description of the nature of the Enneagram: perennial wisdom. One was written by Jerome Wagner: "The Enneagram is a psychological/spiritual typology with roots that trace back through many traditions of perennial wisdom and tendrils that spread across many schools of modern psychology" (Wagner, 1998:1). Taking up the idea of the perennial philosophy, Richard Riso and Russ Hudson give another definition: "The modern Enneagram of personality type has been synthesized from many different spiritual and religious traditions. Much of it is a condensation of universal wisdom, the perennial philosophy accumulated by Christians, Buddhists, Muslims (especially the Sufis), and Jews (in the Kabbalah) for thousands of years" (Riso and Hudson, 1999:19). It is called perennial because it lasts indefinitely, because it cuts through the scientific and philosophical paradigms that human beings construct to advance our knowledge of the world.

One final definition seems marvelous to me. Anthony G.E. Blake says that the Enneagram is a masterpiece of symbolic art and that it is just the top of an iceberg, whose mass is made up of the unspoken thoughts of all humanity which are sometimes called the noosphere (Blake, 1996). This is, he adds, not an end point, but rather just the beginning. The more we immerse ourselves in it, the more the Enneagram dissolves in an intensity of thought that it is hard to sustain. It is no different, Blake continues, to the Cabalistic Tree of Life or the I Ching. In order to see them we have to be able to create our own ways of seeing. "The essential features of the enneagram are really universal. I have found them in science, business, myth and movies. They are locked up in the ancient liturgies... the enneagram is not just a model for what we do or study, but an *intent*. It is a stubborn human cry of desire for meaning" (Blake, 1996: xviii).

We could look at dozens of other definitions, but for now these are enough, given that they bring up two important elements: the processes of self-renovation and perennial wisdom. I have no doubt that in both of these is the line of continuity that has been missing for a long time.

In the writing of this book, I made many false starts before I found the guiding theme. My conviction about the antiquity of the Enneagram was always a driving force. What held me back for months was that I could not isolate a convincing hypothesis. I had several. After reading in full some of the texts in the bibliography I was inclined to refute the conclusion that John Bennett came to almost at the end of his life: "the knowledge that Gurdjieff afterwards taught as his 'Ideas' came from putting together two halves of a single truth. One half is found in the Western - chiefly Platonic - tradition and the other half is in the Eastern - chiefly Naqshband - tradition" (Bennett, 1975: 60).

Something bothered me about Bennett's conclusion: it felt as though, on the one hand, he had placed the Greece of Plato and Pythagoras as the civilizing head of the West, without decanting its sources and without considering the civilizations that preceded and informed them. On the other hand, I had the impression that in the 1950s he had been dazzled by the Naqshbandi Sufis during a visit to the ancient region of Bokhara, whereas the knowledge that Gurdjieff received came from another source and it needed to be located. That was what I focused on.

If there are four ancient human civilizations - Babylonian, Egyptian, Indian and Chinese - then that was where I had to start, in the understanding that everything else came afterwards, including Classical Greece. With this in mind, I started reading what I could find, but gradually I was drawn towards an implicit order dictated by the dozens of introductory pages I had read about the history of the Enneagram. None of them spoke of China or India. Egypt appeared every now and then, sometimes referring to the two periods in which it was dominated by the Persian Achaemenids, and sometimes referring to the body of knowledge gathered by Egyptians and Greeks between the 3rd and 1st centuries BCE,[6] known as the *Corpus Hermeticum*, in which it would be easy to lose my way in the search for the origins of the Enneagram. I did not wish to get lost in that labyrinth. It was then that I remembered an idea by Norbert Elias, a scholar of civilizing processes: "The European tradition, as a continuous development, goes back to Near-Eastern and Greco-Roman Antiquity. One can travel it from there via the Middle Ages to modern times" (Elias, 1998: 190). If the Greco-Roman influence was later, I had to begin with the Near East.

Where to begin was clear: the region between the Tigris and the Euphrates rivers would be the entry point; as it turned out it would be an axis of my research taking me from 2000BCE to the 20th century. Then came the hypothesis: the Enneagram is not made up of two halves. If we start with Babylonian civilization, we can discover only one common thread that includes cultural exchange with Egypt, migrations towards Persia and sources in Classical Greece, without overlooking primitive and Eastern Christianity, up to the 13th century, a time of exchanges with the Muslim world. Seven centuries later, having endured inquisitions and secrecy, something of this tradition of learning was handed down to

---

[6] Contemporary historians no longer use the term BC (Before Christ) and AD (Anno Domini), in recognition of the concerns of non-Christian researchers. It is now more common to use BCE (Before the Common Era) and CE (Common Era) to refer to the same two periods.

Gurdjieff as a complex and cryptic knowledge with areas yet to be deciphered.

I had to show, then, that there are not two halves, but rather a wisdom that arose in Mesopotamia and which has been preserved to the present. Not two halves, but a series of fragments waiting to be articulated along a common thread that begins to emerge.

I found reliable evidence of a Chaldean use of the number 9, as well as the use of the circumference and the desire to transcend, and from the human body reach the Absolute. Clear indications emerged of the management of vices and virtues among the Desert Fathers in the 4th century, especially the legacy of Evagrius Ponticus. I was able to verify the use of a symbol very similar to the one in use today, with nine vices and virtues, in the work of Raymund Lull in the 13th century, around the time when the great Sufi masters explain their moral practice. The proto-enneagrams,[7] prepared by Athanasius Kircher in the 17th century, leapt out at me. I was surprised by the environment of the Eastern Orthodox churches in which Gurdjieff had grown up, his interest in the Essenes and his condition as victim in the Armenian genocide in which his father died. I began to understand why so many Jesuit priests had ventured to explore the Enneagram: not because some of them liked the esoteric, nor because the symbol appears to offer a challenge. They are drawn to it because their tradition of more than four centuries invited them towards complex and organicistic visions of the world.

The whole history remains to be written, but it calls for an approach that does not aim to privilege one author, religion, philosophy or tradition over others. There should not be disputes over the origin, it is absurd to say the Enneagram was born among the Sufis and that there is no more to it. It also makes no sense to declare that it only originates from Christian sources. Over the centuries there has been a constant exchange of ideas between the wisdom of the Chaldeans, our Greek inheritance, primitive and medieval Christianity, Arab

---

[7] Proto, used as a prefix, denoting the condition of primitive or incipient.

mathematics, and the vernacular cultures of each era. Our understanding of human self-renovation and its correspondence with all that takes place in the universe brought together elements from several traditions which, in their time, interacted with one another.

The origin of the symbol of the Enneagram escapes us. The circle or unity, the triangle and the three ancestral forces of many traditions, along with the hexad which explains movements and actions, is a challenge in terms of what is symbolized and in terms of where it came from. Our curiosity is constantly rekindled. If we take a moment to observe the Chaldean tablets that have survived (with translations of the cuneiform writings by the archaeologists at the Universities of Yale and Columbia) it seems increasingly possible that amongst those 500 000 pieces of clay there could be one with a symbol of the Enneagram. This is a query that I have not been able to resolve during the writing of this book and it has only increased my interest in the Chaldean Magi, from whence it probably comes. The mystery on this point, I confess, remains.

Everything up to this point refers to what I wished to read one day, articulated into a single account. I did all I could to find the most direct sources, but I am still hoping that other researchers may one day write a definitive version of this story which - for centuries - has been the reserve of lettered elites: guarded knowledge.

I hope that this text might entice someone, not only to know more about the subject, but to live it. Also, of course, to dig with greater philological and historical depth into some of the lines of investigation that come to light in this book. It is a subject of great complexity that taken seriously could lead to a crisis. I had several, very healthy ones. On 4th June 2014 I was about to destroy the 80 pages I had written up to that point. I read the brief preface A.G.E. Blake wrote in 1979 for *Enneagram Studies* by J.G. Bennett (1983 edition). In his last paragraph he made me feel the futility of my endeavour. If the knowledge of the Enneagram comes from a higher source,[8] what was I doing looking for documentary evidence of its origins? At that moment I felt like I was writing an essay in primary school. Why should I look for empirical evidence of something that by its very nature might not have it? I buckled.

For days I came to a standstill until I re-read, more calmly, the following fragment of the same paragraph: "New knowledge has been released to a few people in the West but has to be transmitted in a practical way through real inner work. It is enough to say that all who have a will to understand will find a way to the material they need and what is included in this book may serve as a stepping stone to some".[9] If that is so, I have no intention of leaving the stepping stones. While I am on them, I will continue my rational search through the history of humanity. Other authors, convinced of a superior origin, have continued their quest; we are dealing with a profound and intelligent metaphysics, capable of being followed rationally without any problem. Undoubtedly, we need intuition and to search for a less dense state of consciousness.

As Blake says, "Work with the enneagram proceeds by progressive approximations" (Blake 1996: 200). At this time, in the second half of 2015, I have to wait and hope that other scholars take up the challenge. For my part, I have decided to bring this text to an end.

Just one last comment before I move onto the historiography. In the following chapters I have included all the most important contributions to the study of personality, from their beginnings to the present. I introduced this information for two reasons. The first: I am convinced that a first step to accessing the extraordinary

---

[8] Blake is not the only one to assert this. There are many other authors who agree with him. In the introduction to one of Laleh Bakhtiar's books, Samuel Bedeck Sotillos writes that there are two paths to understanding the Enneagram: the traditional one, associated to divine revelation and the modern one that arose from the first (in Bakhtiar 2013b: xii). The work of Raymund Lull begins with a vision of the symbol of the Enneagram in a cave on the island of Majorca.

[9] Taken from the Preface by A.G.E. Blake to J.G. Bennett's *Enneagram Studies* (1983: x).

understanding of the Enneagram is locating our own personality and that of the people that we interact with on a daily basis. It is an essential step towards self-knowledge, to our understanding of the mechanisms we use to relate to others, and it is a key instrument to avoid or resolve human conflict.

The second reason is that there is an unexplored communicational aspect in the manner in which each personality type interacts with others. I am convinced that if we fully understand how we communicate with others, that is to say, if we can grasp which are the features or characteristics of our way of communicating and that of our interlocutors, it will become easier to build community and also possible to detect areas of irritation before prejudices and labels arise.

I highlight the latter also for biographical reasons: first I studied a degree in Communication at the Universidad Iberoamericana, at a time when the Jesuits still taught some of the classes and media experts the rest. Then I studied Sociology at UNAM, and I continued in this subject area for my masters and PhD. Thus my curiosity about how we communicate with others and how we can build bridges from different perspectives is a constant in my life which appears intermittently in this book.

This journey through the Enneagram has made me think a great deal about the history of the universe: once set in motion we seek its origin. The centuries reveal different hypotheses about how it was formed and how it can still be expanding today. The same has happened with the human body: we still have not finished learning how some glands work and what their influence is on the innate conduct of each individual. We also do no know what our relation is to everything in existence.

In the future I would like to do an in depth study of the indirect heirs of Gurdjieff, some of whom have written wonders I have barely had a chance to skim. His law of creation is marvellous and his Law of Seven allows me to see almost daily how and where my

Enneatype blocks my attempts to evolve, to widen my consciousness, to be a better human being. I think his concept of evolution deserves a debate with contemporary scientists like Eva Jablonka.[10] I also believe that it is a waste that those who follow the orthodoxy of Gurdjieff cannot also capture the value of the many current studies about that first step in human evolution: self-knowledge. Both visions complement one another. And one more wish: that clinical psychologists and therapists also open their minds to this instrument that is not centered on pathology, but rather places the areas of darkness and the natural strengths of each human being on the same level.

I have no doubt that in these times of intolerance, fundamentalism and the oppression of the other and of those who are different, we need a counter balance. 7 200 million human beings permeated by individualistic attitudes and with exhausted political and economic paradigms need models in which they will fit, where all can co-exist, where - in spite of differences - everyone can have equal opportunities of growth and where everyone can see a light at the end of the tunnel. The Enneagram, truly, is one of those models.

---

[10] Genetist born in Poland, now living in Israel. She works at the Cohn Institute for the History of Philosophy of Science and Ideas at the University of Tel Aviv. Author, with Marion Lamb, of *Evolution in Four Dimensions. Genetic, Epigenetic, Behavioral and Symbolic Variation in the History of Life* (2005) MIT Press.

Chapter 1

Babylonia: a great civilizing center
for contemporary humanity

The search for the origin of the Enneagram does not, by any means, need to take us back to Neanderthal man, or to the Paleolithic. What happened 60 to 35 thousand years ago is not important for our current research. This investigation aims to discover the vestiges of civilizations that asked themselves why they had been born.

Perhaps the history we seek begins in Uruk, a settlement on the Eastern bank of the Euphrates, 225km from modern Baghdad. Uruk, which may be the origin of the modern country-name Irak, was at its height in the 3rd millennium BCE and is important to this history because there was a temple there (Cassin et al, 1982: 42), that is to say, a place of meeting for the human community, an incipient vestige of a great civilization: the Chaldean and the Babylonian. This city is described at the beginning of one of the oldest jewels of literature: the epic poem of Gilgamesh, who was at one time King of Uruk. As we will see, this relic of Mesopotamian culture would be mentioned by John Bennett, one of Gurdjieff's disciples.

The ancient world, in which the wisdom of the Enneagram was forged, was not divided into nation states, nor were the frontiers between countries those that we know today. Knowledge flowed, sooner or later, between those truly interested in the fundamental questions of human beings and of the world. In spite of the —for us — precarious modes of transport, in the centuries before the common era there was a great exchange of information and practices between those who sought to further the development of the mind and the potential of men and women.

The categorical division between East and West clouds our perception of reciprocal influences in ancient times. There is evidence of contact, for example, between the Chinese and the area where we are going to focus a great deal of our attention: Turkestan.[11] An outstanding scholar of Taoism, doctor of philosophy and translator of the Tao Te Ching into Spanish, Iñaki Preciado writes "Towards the end of the 3rd Millennium BCE, as a result of the Huaxia[12] expansion, some tribes that had until then lived on the plains of central China, were expelled and had to move to the lands of present day Turkestan... According to another version, a chief of the Zhou tribes sent one of his advisors to the region of the Pamir where he founded a kingdom" (Lao Tsé [Preciado], 2012: 45). Both accounts refer to areas in which Gurdjieff travelled before he founded his school; at the same time they are an example of how relative historical statements can be.

There are also similarities - though not necessarily through direct contact - between Greek and Chinese writings in the 5th century BCE: "... there are no fundamental differences in Eastern and Greek thought during the Pre-socratic period. It is from Plato and Aristoteles onwards, and more specifically from Euclides and Archimedes, that Greek thought takes a new turn which becomes decisive for the Western world" (García, 2000: 188).

In antiquity knowledge had a locatable origin, but as it developed the different authors' tracks become blurred as cultures, learning and behavior blend. Unless defending a specific cause, religion, ethnicity or sect, those who seek the roots of the Enneagram must

---

[11] Turkestan has never been used to refer to a single nation state. It has been used historically to refer to all or parts of the regions occupied by Turkic-speaking peoples in Central Asia, from modern Turkey to western China. Today it is most often used to refer to the Central Asian republics of Turkmenistan, Uzbekistan, Kazakhstan, Kyryzstan and Tajikistan. (Not to be confused with the city of Turkistan, now in Uzbekistan.)

[12] The Huaxia, writes Preciado, are the people from whom the Han descend, formed by the union of two great tribes, one led by the Emperor Yan and the other by the Yellow Emperor.

agree that the confluence of different forms of knowledge has given us all we know today.

The last 25 centuries of humanity present a history of mixtures, fusions and coincidences of discovery in one place or other. It is also a record of hostilities, comparisons of different approaches, of battles to gain leadership for a chief or an author. Those who are genuinely interested in objectively knowing the roots and reach of the Enneagram cannot claim it for their particular line of thought, they cannot plant the flag of their own ideology on whatever they discover. It is a collective work, in which there have been geographically locatable findings, in which there have been and continue to be valuable contributions, but which in the end all form part of a common legacy, a collective inheritance. None the less, it is crucial to immerse ourselves in the history to find precise facts that can confirm or refute hypotheses. I hope that in the next few years researchers will emerge who will want to specify where current information came from and will want to find the original inscription of the Enneagram symbol. It is important that this happen.

For different reasons and with different interests, human beings have always sought evidence of ancient times. Many of us want to know where something that catches our attention began or originated. It has become easier and easier to learn about almost every subject without having to go to a library. The history of humanity is increasingly accesible to anyone who can use the internet. Thanks to this vast resource it is possible, for example, to know that a contemporary mathematician living in Barcelona is interested in the origin and cultural dimension of mathematics and its influence on the history of ideas. Reading his texts online and seeing the photographs of some of the Babylonian tablets, dated to almost 2000 BCE, makes you wonder about the other 500 000 tablets that have been found and whether one of them might contain the symbol of the Enneagram. This mathematician, Pedro Miguel González Urbaneja, born in León, Spain, informs us that archaeologists found half a million Babylonian clay tablets written in cuneiform script, of which 300 contain mathematical information (González Urbaneja, 2008). And the rest? One of them, designated "Yale Y BC 7289", has been studied so that we now know that the cuneiform characters, written in sexagesimal numbering, when translated to the decimal system turn out to be a primitive and empirical application of Pythagoras' Theorem (González Urbaneja, 2008). Why not carry out a similar translation exercise on any other tablets which carry a symbol similar to the modern-day Enneagram? The University of Columbia also has another tablet, known as "Plimpton 322" which the experts claim is the most important mathematical document in Babylon.[13] What if one of these 499 700 odd tablets contained the original symbol whose replica was passed down to Gurdjieff? Or if one of the ones marked with Chaldean numbers is precisely that? I repeat: I hope someone decides to dedicate the time to investigating it!

For now, the first graphic representations of the Enneagram symbol cannot be dated to before the 13th century and have not been made public.[14] Before this date, as far as I am able to ascertain in 2015, no other tablet, stamp, document or any other original material is known that represents it.

There is talk of an Egyptian papyrus that contains the symbol but until it is made public, it is mere conjecture. We know that the Brenner-Rhind papyrus mentions nine manifestations that give rise to the inhabitants of the Earth and that form the *Pesedjet* of Heliopolis,[15] better known by the Greek term of the Ennead. We would have to investigate further whether this nine, or plural of plurals, has any connection to the Chaldean sense of nine.

---

[13] This tablet is dated between 1900 and 1600 BCE. For more information, see González Urbaneja (2008).

[14] Some authors mention that Evagrius Ponticus used the symbol in the 4th century, but the sources and the diagram have not been published as far as I am aware.

[15] In Hart, George (1997) *Egyptian Myths*, University of Texas.

To continue searching in the hope of finding, in some historical relic, a representation of the circle and triangle known as the hexad or hexagram is important, but not absolutely necessary. There is no certainty that the figure first appeared in one of these early civilizations. To date, the empirical evidence suggests that the symbol could have been designed in the Middle Ages when diagrams were used more often to explain the surrounding reality and when mathematical geniuses emerge amongst the descendants of the Chaldeans and the Persians. What *is* evident in the ancient cultures, is the human need to transcend towards something that goes beyond the body. We *are* able to trace a fair part of the contents of the contemporary Enneagram. Meanwhile, however, we must simultaneously maintain the hypothesis that there was a Chaldean stamp which has today, been lost.

The complete Enneagram, which goes beyond the nine personality types, points to something intangible which in different cultures is called by a variety of terms such as spirit, soul, vital energy, qi and essence. This was the focus of interest for those who started talking about the meaning of the nine-pointed symbol; this is where the search has been focused for centuries at different latitudes and in different cultures. The identification of each point with a personality type is a 20th century contribution.

It is not pointless, however, to immerse ourselves in more ancient history in order to find reliable and incontrovertible facts that shed light on the origin of the Enneagram. Below I present some relevant findings in this area. Since the Chaldean world has been repeatedly indicated as a potential beginning, it was necessary to find evidence in the primary sources several centuries before what we know today as the common era.

No ancient culture is 100% pure. Influence or hybridization takes place as a consequence of contacts with others, with those who are recognized as having knowledge or skills that ones own tradition does not have. The fusion of ways of thought and action is normal in peoples that evolve. This is why this historical research is not linear; it is important to detect the enrichment that occurs in cultural encounters.

This amalgam of traditions is whence the knowledge comes that Gurdjieff and his disciples made more widely known in the 20th Century. To discover where these ideas came from we need to look at the earlier centuries.

Among the accounts of the origins of the Enneagram there is one that has been taken up by serious scholars and, while it does not represent hard fact or documentary evidence, it remains difficult to rule out. It is J.G.Bennett's reference to the historical period in which the epic poem Gilgamesh was compiled. Gilgamesh is the most famous Assyrian hero, known for his conquest of immortality in a poem called *He Who Saw The Deep*. The legend, which is based on a historical figure —a king of Uruk in the 3rd millennium — reveals a curiosity to discover an afterworld and the fear of death (Sanders, 1973). Bennett writes that, four thousand five hundred years ago, at the time of the poem, "there arose in Mesopotamia a brotherhood of wise men who discovered the cosmic secret of perpetual self-renewal and passed it down from generation to generation. For a long time it was preserved in Babylon: 2500 years ago it was revealed to Zoroaster, Pythagoras and other great sages who congregated in Babylon at the time of Cambyses (the Persian king who conquered Egypt in 524BC). Then the custodians of the tradition migrated northwards and about a thousand years ago reached Bokhara across the river Oxus" (Bennett, 1983: 2). Bokhara is not only a city, but a region, located to the north of modern Iran and Afghanistan.

This affirmation has been subject to historical verification since then. It is surprising that a man like Bennett, with scientific talent, should use it as a starting point in his writing.

The quotation above brings up several important points:

- First: the search for permanent self-renovation, which is a central element of the Enneagram.

- Second: the appearance of a brotherhood of sages precisely in the birthplace of Babylonian culture, expanding northwards, towards the area of Bukhara and Nishapur.

- Third: the oral transmission of the Enneagram from one generation to the other until the 20th century

- Fourth: the existence of an information exchange between Chaldeans, Persians, Egyptians and Greeks, which will later also include Arabs and Christians.

- Fifth: the emigrations and expansion of knowledge from Babylonia towards the region where Gurdjieff says he received his knowledge. The river Oxus, cited by Bennett, was also called Pamir, and is located precisely in the area of the modern boundaries of Afghanistan, Tajikistan, Turkmenistan and Uzbekistan.

These five derivations of the quotation lead me to propose a hypothesis that some of the founding concepts of the Enneagram come from the region in which the Persians and the Arabs later flourished. To this we should add another crossing of cultures and language: that which takes place in the 13th century between some Sufi lineages, some Persian and Arabic scientists and some medieval Europeans. One derivation of this knowledge is what Gurdjieff receives at the end of the 19th and beginning of the 20th century. Keep this hypothesis in mind while we review empirical evidence of our Chaldean inheritance.

The Chaldeans

In various texts and testimonies we encounter the same assertion: the Enneagram symbol is of Chaldean origin. Authors rarely say more, very few question the statement or ask what it means or whether there are sources. A profesional search through the historiography would be helpful; for now, here are a few elements to move in that direction.

To locate the Chaldeans it is necessary to be aware of the region of Mesopotamia, whose etymology ("between rivers") makes reference to an unmistakable part of Asia: the area between the rivers Euphrates and Tigris. Two millennia before the common era there were two empires settled here: the Assyrians in the north and the Babylonian in the south. The latter had two periods when it flourished, the second between 625-538 BCE. This resurgence occurred with the support of a Semitic people, the Chaldeans, of the Aramaic family,[16] who were settled in the south of the Babylonian empire. The Babylonians had conquered the Acadians who gave rise to the term Chaldean (from *kaldú*); later the Greeks would use the term *Chaldea* for all of Mesopotamia, but with the passage of time, scholars have tended to use *Chaldean* only for those that have great knowledge about the stars and human nature. They were also called Magi and with this meaning it came into Persian, although it later acquired a negative connotation. "This double meaning, 'dignified priestly tribe' from Media and 'quack' was known in Greece from the 5th century BC onwards [...] Greek authors went out of their way to emphasize that the Magi, i.e., the 'clergy' of Persia, did not practice magic in a pejorative sense" (Meier, 1997: 650). It was the Roman Empire which gave it a negative connotation, "although the word 'magos', with its echoes of oriental mysticism could be understood in a positive or negative sense" (Meier, 1997: 649).

In the middle of the 9th century BCE the Chaldeans establish six principalities, and "in these new populations, and in particular at Bit-Yakin, Babylonia will once again gain vitality" (Cassin et al, 1983: 2). This explains why the terms Chaldean and Babylonian are sometimes used as synonyms.

---

[16] Information obtained from the research of a group led by historian Elena Cassin, specialist in law and economy in Ancient Babylon. Consulted in a Spanish translation, first published by Siglo XXI de España in 1971 (12th edition 1983). Original published in German in 1965 by Fischer Bücherei k.g. of Frankfurt.

In his attempt to reconstruct the history of the first civilizations, Hegel points out the connections between the Babylonian cultures with their contemporaries in Asia Minor and North Africa. "The Jewish people succumbed to superior force; the Jews were carried captive to Babylon, and from them we have accurate information respecting the condition of this Empire. According to Daniel's statements there existed in Babylon a carefully appointed organization for government business. He speaks of Magians, and amongst them are the expounders of sacred writings, the soothsayers, astrologers, Wise Men and Chaldeans who interpreted dreams" (Hegel 1974: 338). Hegel's mention of the Magi is relevant because it coincides with opinions that consider the Magi to be a highly learned group, possessing knowledge that they did not share easily.

In the Middle Ages and until the 13th century, the denomination of Chaldean was commonly attributed to astrologers and mathematicians, as a Roman inheritance. The term was not used for the inhabitants of a part of Mesopotamia, but rather for those who possessed certain knowledge.

The reconstruction of the Chaldean world has been carried out using empirical evidence since 1802, when the cuneiform writings of the Persians were first deciphered. Before that, the only sources of Chaldean history were the Bible, oral tradition and a few Greek texts.

During the 19th century, translations were published of many original texts in Ancient Persian, Elamite and Assyrio-Babylonian. European archaeologists and historians[17] applauded the appearance of a series of original documents from ten centuries BCE. "Thanks

---

[17] Among others, three born in the early 20th century: Jean Vercoutter, member of the French Institute for Oriental Archaeology in Cairo and honorary member German Institute for Archaeology in Berlin; Elena Cassin, historian of religion specialized in ancient Babylon and Jean Bottéro, professor of the Ancient East at the École des Hautes Études in France, who deciphered the royal archives of Babylonia.

to a stroke of serendipity, the library in Nineveh of Ashurbanipal (669-627 BCE) was discovered. He was the last Assyrian king, who had collected all the literary and religious works available in his time, of the Babylonians and the Assyrians, as well as of the Ancient Sumerians" (Cassin, 1982: 3).

Some believe that in this library - which, according to Cassin and her team, contained more than 100 000 clay tablets[18] - there could be a tablet that carries the symbol of the Enneagram. It is probable. There is no definitive evidence of a stamp of the time that depicts it. What is certain is that the peoples settled between the Euphrates and the Tigris used stamp and cylindrical seals, carved with a fine reed chisel on soft clay, which were later pressed on to tablets for their identification. The much sought-after symbol may have been drawn on one of these, but it may also be a later creation, after the fusion of Chaldean, Sufi and Christian elements that we will talk of in the following chapters. This remains to be seen in future historical investigations.

The Chaldean wisdom was built upon for centuries through interactions with other cultures in the region with whom they established relations through exchange or war. The men of knowledge of ancient Egypt and some classical Greek philosophers received information from the wise men of the Akkadian Empire, and from their predecessors. It is very probable that the wisdom of the Enneagram, or the remote precursor of what emerges in the 20th century, was known to the Chaldean Magi, who in turn undertook exchanges of knowledge and experience with the wise men of other regions and whose descendants emigrated towards the North East of Mesopotamia, as Bennett suggests. Several scholars concur that the Chaldean Magi are the original source of the Enneagram.

---

[18] Researchers do not coincide on the number of tablets found. Cassin writes of 100,000 while González Urbaneja mentions as many as half a million. The physical location of the tablets is a pending question also, in order to discover whether there really is one with the Enneagram symbol on it.

Where Bennett writes of that distant time, he frequently mentions the Chaldeans. He writes that a central concern of Gurdjieff's teachings was the attempt to transform human energies for the highest purposes and he affirms that the Chaldeans knew this: "I think that this doctrine was held by the Chaldeans up to the time of the destruction of Babylon ..." (Bennett, 1975: 43). He continues: "My own guess is that this is something Gurdjieff learnt through contacts made in those parts of the Middle East that for millennia have been called Iran. Hence also his deep interest in Babylonia. Nobody can read what Gurdjieff writes about Babylon without seeing how deeply it impressed him" (Bennett, 1975: 45).

There are numerous references to Chaldean wisdom in the ancient texts from classical Greece to the Renaissance. Pythagoras, who lived for periods in Babylon, was aware of the Chaldean legacy which began many years before his birth. He, in turn, taught what he had learnt during multiple visits at cultural centres in various regions. There are those who assert that Pythagoras was initiated by the Chaldean Magi: if Gurdjieff "really did find the Masters, the successors of the Magi who initiated Pythagoras, then not only does it make his own work much more interesting for the purposes of objective study but it also has great implications for the rest of us" (Gilbert, 2002: 43).

For 40 years, Pythagoras taught students who went on to disseminate his learning to different latitudes, for century after century, until, in the 15th century, they dazzled Pico della Mirandola to such a degree that he decided to study Assyrian-Babylonian in order to read the legacy of the Chaldean Magi, much-mentioned by the Pythagoreans and later authors, in the original. In his celebrated *Oration on the Dignity of Man*, this Renaissance man explains that the Chaldean Magi have nothing in common with sorcerers, and should instead be associated with the perfect and supreme wisdom: "The term 'magus' in the Persian tongue, according to Porphyry, means the same as 'interpreter' and 'worshipper of the divine' in our language" (Pico della Mirandola, 1486). In another passage of the same text he writes that the Chaldeans are fathers and founders of the ancient wisdom.

The Chaldean Magi, according to Bennett, were members of a caste that existed in Central Asia before Zoroaster. He tells how two of them were entrusted with the task of testing Zoroaster's knowledge and they found that his initiation went further that any wisdom known to them. When this disciple of Gurdjieff expresses his ideas about his master's references, he mentions the Chaldean Magi as the source of his knowledge about the construction of the natural order: "part of it coming to the West - almost certainly through Pythagoras as Plato suggests in the *Timaeus* - and partly remaining in the East among the Chaldean Magi and moving Northward when there was the break up in the Achimenean Empire after Alexander's invasion" (Bennett, 1975: 60).

In his historical reconstruction of the Persian Empire, Hegel writes that "the authenticity of the books of Zoroaster has often been attacked. It is undoubtedly admirable that such a small people has guarded the books of a man whose time we cannot even know. But their authenticity is proven by their contents and by everything we know about the Magi" (Hegel, 1974: 327). The Chaldean Magi thus formed a community of sages before Zoroaster, and one of their areas of expertise was astronomy. On this subject there are some lines of inquiry we have yet to explore, for example the Dead Sea scrolls which constituted the library of the Essenes[19] a few centuries BCE. In this collection there are astronomical texts that would be

---

[19] See the detailed celestial observations in the chapter on astronomical texts in *The Dead Sea Scrolls Translated*, edited by Florentino García Martínez and translated from Spanish by Wilfred G.E. Watson (1996).

worth studying philologically to determine their probable connection with the Chaldean astronomers.[20]

Bennett adds that after the conquests of Cyrus, the Magi spread throughout the Persian Empire and reached Syria and Egypt. "The word *maga* meant the gift or 'grace' of God, by which men have the power to perform great works. This sacred power was the secret of the Magi" (Bennett, 2013).

For Bennet there were three castes of Magi: first the exoteric, made up of priests who carried out the religious ceremonies. The second had the mission of preserving the sacred literature, from which they knew its secrets. The third was the esoteric caste, which had superior skills and their centre in Asia Minor continued to work for more than 300 years after the time of Christ and transmitted their secrets to the Christian Brotherhood of Cappadocia, at the same time as they supported the establishment of the Essene Brotherhood in Judaea, some 200 years BCE (Bennett, 2013). As we shall see, Gurdjieff was in contact with the Essene tradition through a countryman of his, Father Evlissi, who lived in a monastery of the order in Palestine. Some of the Essenes belonged to the third caste of Magi.

Amongst those who have attempted to understand the Chaldean wisdoms, there are some who are directly interested in knowing the origins of the Enneagram. J.G. Bennett is one of these; his account of the period leaves an open line of research about what the management of self-renewal consisted of in Mesopotamia and who the guardians of the tradition were, that emigrated. This author, who had a great interest in the mathematical aspects of the Enneagram symbol, talked at length with Gurdjieff on the subject and then

---

[20] The mention in the New Testament of the Magi who travelled from the Orient towards Bethlehem, guided by a star, could correspond to a popular interpretation of the Chaldean wise men, an account which might well have reached Matthew the Evangelist. The versions by Reina (1569) and Valera (1602) are practically identical to the Catholic edition of the Jerusalem Bible (C.fr. Mt, 2, 1-12). None of them give a geographical place of origin for the Magi.

travelled to the places where Gurdjieff had been and spoke to the same informants, until he formed a more precise idea about the origin of this knowledge which he presents in his books and attempted also to practice.

Bokhara was the centre of the Persian civilization from the 6th century BCE. The Oxus River, cited by Bennett, previously also known as the Pamir and now known as the Amu Darya, has its source in the Pamir mountain range and follows what is today part of the borders between Afghanistan, Tajikistan, Turkmenistan and Uzbekistan, that is to say, some of the places that Gurdjieff visited.

The key phrase in Bennett's quotation is the one in which he mentions "the cosmic secret of perpetual self-renewal" (Bennett, 1983: 2). We can only understand why he calls the Enneagram "an instrument that enables us to see when and how events conform to cosmic laws and so recognize what is possible and what is impossible in human undertakings" (Bennett, 1983: 21) if we undertake a study of his entire oeuvre, as well as that of his disciple A.G.E. Blake.[21]

Blake frequently refers to Bennett's work, but he goes further than his master in the development of the cosmic laws from the perspective of human nature and the possibility of developing them through action, both in the microcosmos and the macrocosmos, forming a quantum whole (in his words) within the framework of the Enneagram.

The intellectual and practical undertaking of Bennett, Blake and various other authors who have explored the ultimate meaning of the Enneagram in depth, consists of the same elements as those proposed by the Chaldean Oracles, but now no longer exclusively interpreted in terms of a divine origin nor through faith, but rather

---

[21] A.G.E. Blake (1939-) studied physics at the University of Bristol, UK, and then History and Philosophy of Science at Cambridge University. He worked with Bennett for 15 years, until his death in 1974. His principal publication on the subject is *The Intelligent Enneagram*, Shambala, Boston, published in 1996.

also in the light of our understanding about the expansion of the universe and the behavior of the smallest particles of matter that have been recorded in the 20th century.

The Mesopotamian inheritance, however, remains current today, as the English physicist and historian Patricia Fara writes: "The Babylonian way of thinking about the Universe still profoundly affects people today" (Fara, 2009:7). She also writes something that comes a little closer to the Enneagram: "Babylonians used their calculations not to map planetary orbits, but to work out how the heavens affected individuals" (Fara, 2009:15).

From the highest levels of contemporary philology there are findings which also cast light on the meaning of the Enneagram, be it unintentionally, because the subject is not of their direct interest. There are several scholars who over the last century have worked on the Chaldean Oracles. One of these is Ignacio Gómez de Liaño, who obtained his doctorate at the Universidad Complutense in Madrid, Spain. In his search for the diagrams of ancient knowledge in several traditions, he collects several interpretations of the term "Chaldean" and, basing his work on Cumont,[22] he suggests that it was first applied to the inhabitants of Lower Mesopotamia and later it was restricted further to apply to the Babylonian priests. This scholar also writes that Quinto Curio[23] tells that in the official processions in Babylonia the Magi or Persian priests went first and then the Chaldeans or local priests. He adds "the term was also used to designate the Greeks who had undertaken astronomical studies in Babylonia" (Gómez de Liaño, 1998:705).

We also have the doctoral thesis in Greek philology of Álvaro Fernández Fernández about the Chaldean Oracles, presented at the University of Granada. His research subject was *The Theurgy of the*

---

[22] Franz Cumont (1868-1947), Belgian scholar who wrote *The Mysteries of Mithra*, *Astrology and Religion Among the Greeks and Romans* (1903).

[23] Roman historian, of the first century CE who wrote about the life and exploits of Alexander the Great.

Chaldean Oracles. Lexicon y historical context (Fernández, 2011) and he makes an exhaustive and thorough search of known sources and perspectives on the Chaldean Oracles. The author has little doubt that the fragments that have survived to the present were written in the 2nd century CE and that, strictly speaking, they do not come exclusively from original Chaldean sources. However, in the 526 pages of this doctoral dissertation, there are elements that contribute to several hypotheses about the Chaldean inheritance among the Greeks, in which we find evidence of a relation to the Enneagram. Here again, is a pending research project that hopefully someone will take up.

Here are just some of the clues on the subject of our interest. It is important to note that this philologist begins the preface of his dissertation with the words, "The title *The Theurgy of the Chaldean Oracles* refers to the existence of an ancient religion called 'theurgy' that had its origin and foundation in a collection of divine revelations known as the Chaldean Oracles, or simply Oracles, that are commonly dated to the end of the 2nd century CE" (Fernández, 2011: IX). After studying the multitude of comments that have been made on the Oracles, he points out that some authors suggest a non-human origin of the fragments: it is considered "a sacred text with a divine origin" (Fernández 2011: 194).

He goes on to say "I don't believe that today anyone would question that the Oracles were the sacred literature that the theurgy was based on: without them, although it might have suffered debatable foreign influences, it should not have existed. As I understand it, any collection of beliefs and the practices linked to them, which is based on a divine text, and which gains consistency by the accumulation of later interpretations that are made during an uninterrupted period, constitutes a religious manifestation: this is the case of the theurgy based on the Oracles" (Fernández, 2011: 281).

Amongst the useful elements that the Chaldean Oracles offer us to build our hypothesis about the elements that constitute the

Enneagram, are some Latin fragments about the Greek originals, commented on by Wilhelm Kroll, a German philologist who made the first modern compilation.[24] Both Kroll and Álvaro Fernández are of the opinion that the fragments of the Oracles are called "Chaldean" because they were initially circulated by the Chaldeans, although the written texts are not exclusively prepared by them. "But we should set limits of what we understand by 'Chaldean contents': if we are dealing with teachings which were original and exclusive to the Oracles, I think we can conclude that the Oracles were labeled 'of the Chaldeans, Chaldeic' in honour of the people responsible for this type of learning: the Chaldeans; if, on the other hand, 'Chaldean contents' refers to doctrines that come from a Chaldean tradition which originated in some part of the Near East, it does not seem possible to identify this supposed tradition for lack of pertinent documents in the Greco-Roman literature. According to Hadot,[25] there is apparently no treatment of strictly 'Chaldean' (or 'oriental') subjects in the Oracles; he is also surprised that they only mention divinities of the Greek tradition" (Fernández, 2011: 106).

The fragments have been studied by numerous researchers whose theses led the philologist from Granada to three hypotheses about the authorship of the Oracles, in addition to the divine origin which is not traceable in the sources:

1) there was a single author, who could have been Julian (without specifying if it is the Chaldean or the Theurgist)

2) there could be double authorship with several interpretations

3) it is anonymous (Fernández, 2011)

---

[24] Published in 1894 by Verlag von Wilhelm Koebner, in Breslau, with the title *De Oraculis Chaldaicis*.

[25] Pierre Hadot (1922-2010), author of *Bilan et perspectives sur les Oracles Chaldaïques* (1978). French philosopher specializing in ancient philosophy. He was director of the École des Hautes Études en Sciences Sociales from 1964 to 1986. Professor of the Collège de France from 1982 to 1991.

Independently of which of these hypotheses is more supported by the empirical evidence, the important thing to mention is the contents of the Chaldean Oracles and why they were taken up again by Pythagoras, by the Neoplatonians and by later scholars right up to the present.

As a starting point we should say they give as much importance to the material nature of which human bodies are made, as they do to the soul or essence. They do not consider them two separate entities, but see them rather as interdependent. One thing that bears a resemblance with authors who go much further than the nine personalities of the Enneagram, is that the Chaldeans sought the way in which material human nature could find its way back to its essence. Later on we will consider the theses of those who contend that the objective of the Enneagram is precisely to transcend the personality to reach the Absolute.

It would appear that there is consensus on the fact that if there was something that interested the diverse cultures that developed between the Tigris and the Euphrates before the common era, it was working with the dense or physical body to reach a subtle level. On this point, another PhD thesis, this time from the Faculty of Philology of the Universidad Complutense in Madrid, proposes the following: "… the concept of science in ancient Babylon was based on the development of the normal potentialities of man; it was taken for granted that one of the obligations of life was the development of second and third centres or bodies… Life in ancient Babylon was organized by this; and art, literature and work were subordinated to it" (Aranda Pescador, 2013: 389).

Over the centuries, the Chaldean Oracles have been analyzed over and over again. The fragments that have survived have been numbered and commentated for study. In order to know which fragment corresponds to a given comment, we have to identify the scholar and his sources. One of the most often cited indices is the one made by the French Jesuit Edouárd des Places (1900-2000) who compiled 227 fragments. Another specialist in the Oracles, Ruth

Majercik, consults him and sometimes disagrees with him. Both are key sources for Álvaro Fernández.

There are many fragments which make direct or indirect reference to the Enneagram and its symbol. For example, referring to the triangle, Des Places labeled τριουχον (−ov) or "containing a triad" as fragment 26 and his comment was "in coherence with the Chaldean doctrine, according to which in every world a triad shines, governed by a monad" (Fernández, 2011: 265). With regard to the centre of a circumference, Majercik takes up the Neoplatonic comment of Proclus to assert, in fragment 167, that "from the centre all things are equidistant to the edge" (Majercik, 1989: 111).

With regard to the central issue of a return to the essence, in fragment 155 of the Chaldean Oracles, it speaks of the obstacles that prevent the soul from ascending: "It looks for the conduit of the soul from where, working every day for the body, the soul has descended in a certain order and how you can raise it again, in order, when you unite action and the sacred word" (Gómez Liaño, 1998: 480).

In fragment 117, there is a mention of how the whole world was created from fire, air, water, earth and the all-nourishing ether. This reference to the basic elements of existence appears in Greek authors before Hippocrates such as Alcmaeon of Croton who, for decades, formed part of the Pythagorean school and he receives the Chaldean teachings about the human body, as science historian Debus puts it: "… in addition to the survival of ancient philosophical concepts, there was also an imposing body of anatomical and physiological information that had come down from antiquity. Both Alcmaeon of Croton (c. 500BC) and Aristotle (384-322 BC) had been interested in the description of the parts of men and animals … " (Debus, 1978: 55). Hippocrates does not, then, start from scratch in his study of the temperaments; before him the Pythagorean school had already begun to work on them and even others: "The theory of the four elements emerges with

Empedocles and the pre-socratic philosophers of Greece" (García, 2000: 162).

The number nine that gives its name to the Enneagram has a significant place in the Chaldean philosophy. In one of the classifications of the Oracles, fragment numbered 186, it is said that the number nine is divine because it is made up of three triads and reaches the pinnacle of theology, according to the Chaldean philosophy, as Porphyry writes.[26] For his part, on the subject of the Enneagram and the number 9, A.G.E. Blake specifies that, "The quantum whole is number 9 on the enneagram. Points 3 and 6 form interfaces dividing and connecting three domains of action" (Blake, 1996: xvi).

These references to the importance of the number nine for the Chaldeans coincide with the conclusions of Gómez de Liaño, who spent 10 years of studying diagrams of learning from different traditions: "From its diagrammatic structure, the system of Chaldean Oracles that we have just sketched is close to Metrodorus' zodiacal mnemonic, to the 'Chaldean methods' of Dionysius of Miletus and to the diagrams of the Gnostics, but while the latter chose the pentad-decad, the Chaldeans prefer the triad-enead" (Gómez de Liaño, 1998: 483).

If we observe the Enneagram symbol, this quotation allows us to think of the triangle and the remaining 6 points around the circle. Equally, the three triads, each with three domains of action that add up to nine, form the triad-enead of the Chaldeans. The central elements of the symbol are already here. Everything points to a Chaldean origin, but we must be aware that in human history it is difficult to find pure traditions.

The last quotation by Gómez de Liaño brings up another element that we should take note of: the system of Chaldean Oracles is close to the Gnostic diagrams, although the Chaldeans focus on the triad-

[26] Porphyry of Tyre (232-304) was a disciple of Plotinus, who synthesized his work and it is to him we owe the sharing of the *Enneads*.

enead, that is to say, the triangle that is inside the symbol and on the 9 points of the star. In the Gnostic tradition there are also lines of inquiry to follow for those studying the origins of the Enneagram. This would not be a pointless or purely theoretical project. It is part of a very long experience lived by innumerable human beings over time; searching for its origins and ingredients is a worthwhile endeavour.

If the knowledge and practices that gave rise to the Enneagram have precedents in Chaldean sources, it is highly probable that all of this came into the hands of the Gnostic sects or secret societies which, as Randal Collins explains, defended the many versions of primitive hermeticism. He writes, "The structure of the Gnostic and occultist groups may be inferred from the proliferation of anonymous and pseudonymous manuscripts claiming to represent the ancient wisdom of Hermes Trismegistus, of Pythagoras, of the Chaldeans (Babylonian priests) or Egyptians. The form and content of the texts imply a series of small secret groups, based on transmission from a revered master to initiates" (Collins, 1998: 121).

These secret and usually small groups appear in the history of humanity when something becomes institutionalized, be it a church, a cult or a philosophical tradition. Tracing them is problematic because historical documents do not exist and we are left proposing hypotheses until more tangible evidence is found. One such evidence is that in the 1st century BCE there are Gnostic groups who recover, as Reitzenstein[27] puts it, elements of Iranian religions which will influence the genesis of primitive Christianity.

The Chaldean Oracles have always been the subject of study, and especially since the 15th century when Pico della Mirandola found the original Chaldean document, which then passed into the hands

---

[27] Richard August Reitzenstein (1861-1931), German protestant philologist and theologist who belonged to the History of Religions School (Religions-Geschichte Schule). In 1910 he wrote a text about the Greco-Roman mysteries and an essay on syncretism in antiquity, published in Leipzig and Berlin in 1926.

of another celebrated Renaissance man, Marsilio Ficino.[28] In the following centuries these documents were analyzed by many other authors[29] who verify the understanding that Plato and the Neoplatonians had of the Chaldean Oracles. This sum of knowledge or these fragments of perennial philosophy certainly share a thesis with the Enneagram.

Hegel established comparisons between what he called the four regions of Asia: China, India, the valley of the Nile[30] and the region we have spoken of in this chapter: the valleys of the Amu Darya (Oxus) and Syr Darya, the Persian plateau and the valleys of the Euphrates and the Tigris. In this comparison, the importance he attributes to the link between the material and the spiritual in these cultures is worthy of note and leads us to make an association with the search for the Enneagram: "Zoroaster's 'Light' is the first that belongs to the World of Consciousness, the Spirit as a reference to something distinct from itself. Here also we see the Unity of the spiritual and the natural; the finite world is contained in one and the natural in the light … we see here a pure and sublime unity which is considered as a substance, which leaves the particular existences that inhere in it, free, such as the Light, which only manifests what bodies are in themselves; we perceive a Unity which governs individuals only to excite them to become powerful for themselves, to develop and assert their individuality" (Hegel, 1974: 324).

---

[28] Ficino founded the Platonic Florentine Academy in 1495, and translated Plato and Plotinus from Greek into Latin.

[29] Among others two pioneering books stand out by two Englishmen: T. Stanley's *The Chaldiaak Philosophy* (1701) and T. Taylor's *The Chaldean Oracles* (1806).

[30] Hegel includes the Nile in Asia. Compare page 217 of *Lectures on the Philosophy of History* (Hegel, 1974 (Spanish translation).

Chapter 2

The Enneagram: a current
piece of the perennial philosophy

Before continuing with the exploration of historical events surrounding the Enneagram, it is important to understand what many contemporary authors have associated with the Enneagram: perennial wisdom.

What is perennial wisdom? Jerome Wagner,[31] one of a number of Enneagram scholars who mention it explicitly, writes that it comes from several traditions of perennial philosophy. Two other authors identify the traditions: Richard Riso and Russ Hudson write: "The modern Enneagram of personality type has been synthesized from many different spiritual and religious traditions. Much of it is a condensation of universal wisdom, the perennial philosophy accumulated by Christians, Buddhists, Muslims (especially the Sufis), and Jews (in the Kabbalah) for thousands of years" (Riso and Hudson 1999).

Although this accumulated wisdom that brings together common principles and values from diverse traditions is very ancient, the term perennial philosophy was first used in the 16th century to refer to Marsilio Ficino's synthesis of Neoplatonism and the Christian traditions. Ficino was a Renaissance scholar who coined the term *Prisca Theologia* for the inheritance of the Chaldean Oracles, Hermeticism and the Greeks who sought a return to divine nature,

---

[31] Jerome Wagner was already writing about the Enneagram in the early 1980s. In 1983 he published, with Ronald Walker, a paper: Reliability and Validity. Study of a Sufi Personality Typology: The Enneagram, *Journal of Clinical Psychology*, Volume 39 (5). One of his more recent books is *Nine Lenses on the World. The Enneagram Perspective* (2010).

in the same way as some sectors of Christianity, both in Eastern and Western Churches. It includes also the work of Raymund Lull which began to be known with increasing force in the second half of the 14th century.

Towards the end of the 17th century, Leibniz sought to find harmony, continuity and universality in the ideas of various erudite and scientific societies, distinguishing substances and relations; for this work he was considered a perennial philosopher, dedicated to the conciliation of conflicting ideas. For Leibniz, the term perennial philosophy includes his proposal of the monads or only real substances, versus the material things which are only temporary phenomena. Leibniz has a dominant place in the history of ideas not only at the end of the 17th century, when he was writing, but also in terms of his influence on later scientific writers. Rolando García, a historian of science tells us: "The concomitance of Western thinkers and the organicism of Taoism is no coincidence. The science that emerged from the scientific revolution in Europe was exported to China but the Jesuits[32] who took Galileo and Newton to the lands of Confucius and the Tao, brought their doctrines back. Three among them, Mateo Ricci, Grimaldi y Bouvert, had a strong influence on Leibniz and this influence probably had to do with the fact the Leibniz was the first Western philosopher to have an organicistic concept of the world" (García, 2000: 166). This fact is interesting because it shows that those who are considered perennial philosophers did not have one single vision of the world, but rather amalgamated several cosmovisions with a very precise central idea: a determined quest for the absolute in human beings.

In the writings of Ficino we also find this interest in giving meaning to the relationship between human nature and the cosmos, in light of the traditions known to him at that time. His is the phrase, "we are not slaves of nature, but emulate her" (Berlin, 2000: 45). The idea

---

[32] The author generalizes in this reference to the Jesuits. Each one deserves to be studied separately. Ricci could not have carried the news of Newton's findings to China because he died before Newton was born. Grimaldi was a significant influence on Leibniz but he did not travel to China.

that humans behave according to unspoken laws that govern the universe, is not only shared in the 15th century by scholars of diverse traditions, but also comes down to the Gurdjieff school, as we will see later.

Agostino Steuco was a 16th century monk with knowledge of Greek and Hebrew who was sent by Pope Paul III to the Council of Trent, which began in 1545 as an attempt to reconcile the Catholics and Reformists. Five years before his mission against Luther's theses, he wrote a book entitled *De Perenni Philosophia* in which he echoes the Renaissance eagerness to find a doctrinal unity for all human beings. Steuco, refers and cites Marsilio Ficino on the subject of the link between *Prisca Theología* and Christianity, but his efforts are focused on giving priority to the data he finds on the Biblical tradition. A contemporary Spanish scholar of his writings points out that Steuco insists that, in spite of deformations that the histories of Biblical figures have undergone, "the literary remains conserved of the oldest peoples - the Chaldeans, Egyptians and Phoenicians - contain and transmit, in a somewhat hidden or obscure way, the fundamental truths ... which thus become world heritage knowledge of all humanity: the *perennis philosophia* -the name with which Steuco designates what Ficino called '*priscae theologiae sibi consona secta*'- which was transmitted from those ancient peoples to more recent times" (Granada, 1994: 24). Steuco openly mentions the Chaldean Oracles but always gives priority to Hebrew elements over inheritances from other cultures: "Moses is the first writer and therefore Hermes Trismesgistus and Zoroaster, the first theologists and writers of Egypt and Chaldea, must be later" (Granada, 1994: 25).

In the 20th century it would be Aldous Huxley who, in 1944, began to popularize the concept of perennial philosophy in his commented anthology which begins with the statement "*Philosophia perennis* ... [is] the metaphysic that recognizes a divine Reality substantial to the world of things and lives and minds" (Huxley 1947:1). To illustrate his concept the English author eliminates those who speak of the perennial philosophy second hand and presents a selection of men and women who, he believes, directly experienced Reality, with a capital letter. Isaiah Berlin,[33] his contemporary and acquaintance, writes that Huxley "bore the frequent accusations of betraying his original rationalism in favour of a confused mysticism" because he was conscious of what he was saying and "He persisted not because of some softening of a once gem-like intellect, but because he was convinced that his chosen field was the region in which the greatest and most transforming advance would be made by mankind" (Berlin, 1998).

Huxley does not seem to have had a predetermined quest, he was curious about all the traditions or writers who could offer him something. He read very different authors and sought to meet people who caught his attention. Bennett makes reference to this, writing that Huxley came to some presentations given by an Indonesian guru called Pak Subuh and before that, in the 1930s, "he used to come regularly to Ouspensky's meeting in Colet Gardens, say nothing and go away" (Bennett, 1974: 342).

The most appropriate definition today of perennial philosophy, to account for the Enneagram, is given to us by Raimon Panikkar, who died recently. He asserts that we are not dealing with something that belongs to a church or a particular group of humans, but rather something that is part of the primordial tradition of all humanity, whose origin can be found beyond everything else. He sheds light on how the Enneagram fits into the idea of perennial wisdom with his declaration about the weak side of the *Philosophia Perennis*, which he defines as "a possible immobility and absolutism of tradition that does not take into account the wisdom of the very

---

[33] Isaiah Berlin (1909-1997) was historian of ideas and a great liberal thinker of the 20th century with a vast output. Jesús Silva-Herzog Márquez writes of Berlin that: "…he was persecuted by two totalitarian states, the Soviet and the Nazi… In the works of this formidable essayist we can perceive the enormous distance that exists between vivacity in erudition and the dry plaster of academicism…
Nobody has delineated so pleasingly the profile of the great political thinkers and disentangled the threads of their reflection" (Periódico Reforma, p.22-A, 10 November 1997).

words it uses: *perennis* does not indicate immobility, but rather a regular appearance *per annos* and a *tradition* is not a tradition if it is not 'transmitted' from one generation to another and if it is not incarnated in time and space" (Pannikar, 2006: 41).

The Enneagram is still valid today, precisely because, although it brings together ancient and diverse wisdoms, it does not limit itself to that ancient wisdom and, in the case of the nine personality types, it takes into account very varied contributions including several that correspond to 20th century schools of psychology. This at the same time as reconsidering elements like the essence, which have been touched upon by many thinkers at different times with some conspicuous representatives in the present day. There is something in the perennial philosophy that remains alive, in hostile environments, even after the Age of Enlightenment. It has overcome attacks from so-called Post Cartesians but who had not read Descartes[34] and has found respect even among some of the most hardline positivists. We are dealing, then, with a remote and at once modern knowledge, which is not the product of any single period or culture. It is patrimony of all humanity, even the present humanity that lives in the Digital Age.

Oriental cultures have also made enormously valuable contributions to the perennial philosophy with one additional advantage: through the centuries they have managed to maintain —without modifications— some of the practices that lead to an opening of the mind. Chinese culture is paradigmatic in this sense. Having overcome the rivalries between Buddhism, Confucianism and Taoism, we can say that the latter, with the three texts best known in the West (Tao Te Ching, Zhuang Zi and Lie Zi) has been considered as a relevant part of the perennial philosophy. In one of the best

---

[34] In works like *Passions of the Soul* or the *Treatise on Light*, Descartes painstakingly sought explanations about the function of the pineal gland, "a little gland in the brain in which the soul exercises its functions" (Descartes (1995 [1649]): 122).

translations of the Tao Te Ching[35] we learn: "Taoism —ancient, fascinating, mysterious and poetic— emerges from the dense darkness that surrounds the most ancient roots of civilization, it is a testament to a way of life which has been lost in the deep ocean of time and which now forms part of the cultural legacy of China. We can refer to Taoism as a combination of folklore, esoterism, literature, myth, legend, poetry, art, philosophy, mysticism, yoga, meditation, and as one of the great pillars on which the Perennial Wisdom is founded" (Lao Tsé [Román], 2012: 11).[36]

Joseph Needham (1900-1995), a British biochemist considered one of the most profound scholars of Chinese history in the West, offers a hypothesis which brings us, once again, to Mesopotamia and thus the Chaldeans and Babylonians as the origin of the perennial philosophy, which —according to Needham— includes the wisdom of the Far East. "In view of the duodecimally based mathematics and world outlook of the Babylonians, one cannot but suspect an influence from ancient Mesopotamia on early China in this respect...so far as the cuneiform texts have unravelled it, Babylonian medicine has been largely magico-religious in character, but one cannot help feeling that there must have been some schools of proto-scientific medicine in Mesopotamia which bequeathed their ideas about the subtle breaths..." (Needham, 2000: 44). Add to this that there must have been a civilization more ancient than those of Greece, India or China which generated these ideas and sent them out in all directions. He concludes with "... Mesopotamia must have been their home." This would be the end of the enduring idea that there is a categorical separation between East and West, at least in all that pertains to ancient civilizations.

---

[35] Introduction and translation to Spanish by Iñaki Preciado Idoeta, published by Editorial Trotta, first edition 2006.

[36] The quotation is taken from the Presentation, by María Teresa Román (PhD at Universidad Nacional de Educación a Distancia, Madrid) to the translation by Preciado of the *Tao Te Ching* (Lao Tsé, 2012).

Let us return to the perennial philosophy. This wisdom derives its name from the Latin *perennis*, which comes from *annus*, because it lasts all the years, perpetually, continuously, without stopping or dying or running out after a time as other things of its kind do, in this case other philosophies. One of the characteristics for a philosophy to be perennial is for it to maintain its essence even if the form varies. This is the case of the Enneagram and also some oriental practices which have preserved their inherent nature in spite of the adjustments that have been made to them over the years.[37]

If one thing emerges with clarity from this search for the roots of the Enneagram, it is that those who only perceive it as a system of nine personality types are missing the original meaning and most important purpose: the practical exploration of human transcendence, the recovery of lost potentialities, the interaction between people who see the world in different ways.

The classification of the personalities goes back to the 5th century BCE and no-one doubts its relevance, but to focus exclusively on this aspect of the Enneagram, without using it as a bridge to understand and to relate to others, is to see just one of its many facets and miss that which gives it coherence and reason to exist.

The books about the Enneagram that go further than the ego-game of the nine enneatypes necessarily propose a dichotomy of personality/essence which must be resolved. Some go further than others but those who touch upon it have embarked on a well travelled road with many of the most tenacious seekers of humanity. Claudio Naranjo, for example, in the theoretical framework he describes in his introduction points out that the central distinction is "between 'essence' and 'personality', between the real being and the conditioned being with which we normally identify... the 'map of the psyche' ... is only complete if we claim that it also maps the space in which the centres of personality and essence exist —a

---

[37] This is the case, for example, of Zhineng Qigong, one of whose roots is Taoism. It comes from the qigong thousands of years ago but its current forms were given by Dr. Pang He Ming, in the second half of the 20th century.

space that may be taken as an apt symbol of consciousness itself" (Naranjo, 1994:10). Riso and Hudson dedicate a chapter to this problem in which they tell us, "Our personalities are no more than the familiar, conditioned parts of a much wider range of potentials that we all possess. Beyond the limitations of our personalities, each of us exists as a vast, largely unrecognized quality of Being or Presence - what is called our Essence" (Riso and Hudson, 1999: 21). Other authors do not use the concepts of personality and essence but they refer to the same thing, each from the perspective of their own cosmogony and experience.

A.H. Almaas is one author who, throughout his studies, shows great interest in this central aspect of the Enneagram. This path brought him to the Enneagram, but before we speak of Almaas we must return to our trail through the distant past.

Chapter 3

Derivations from original civilizing nuclei

Of the four ancient civilizations that predate the splendour of Greece and Rome, two - India and China - do not appear in the panorama of roots of the Enneagram, but Egypt, and especially Babylon, do. We can locate contributions from both of these in the history that we are studying and there are recorded cultural exchanges between them at different times. This is why the Hebrew and Greek origins are not treated here as separate influences, but rather linked to the Egyptian and Babylonian sources.

In this reconstruction of the roots and influences of the Enneagram we must keep in mind that the history of the Hebrew people cannot be dissociated from what happened between the Tigris and Euphrates and also in Egypt before the common era: "Israel emerged at the crossroads of Asia and Africa, separate from the advanced civilizations of Chaldea and Egypt... The cuneiform sources called them *habiru*, the emigrants, peasants, slaves or mercenaries who appear in Babylonia, in Assyria, in Asia Minor, in Egypt and in the Holy Land and who claim descent from Abraham" (Chouraqui, 1991: 9). It is said that the patriarch of the Jewish people, Abraham, was born in Ur in Chaldea and that he lived there at the time of the Sumerian Akkadian Empire of Ur-Nammu, founder of the dynasty that governed Ur in the period 2070-1960 BCE. From there Abraham went to Haran, ancient city of Mesopotamia, where he stayed until his father's death. Then he travelled to Canaan and to Egypt, eventually to settle in the oak forest of Mamre, near Hebron, where he would die.[38] According to the Jewish tradition, superior worlds were revealed to Abraham, and this is recorded in the Torah. Around 1500 BCE Moses received the Commandments and then, from Jethro, the father of his wife Zipporah, he also received the teachings of ancient Egypt, which would enable him to overcome the trials of the Jewish exodus to Palestine. The confluence of knowledge and belief between the different peoples of the ancient world is a constant which sometimes makes it difficult to draw clear lines between the different cultures; there was a combination of learning, in the same way as we find with the Enneagram.

In one of Gurdjieff's texts[39] there is a direct reference to the early Hebrews that is important to highlight because it contributes to the hypothesis that the knowledge this man found is much more associated with the Hebrew-Babylonian nucleus than with any other tradition. Gurdjieff writes: "What struck us most was the word Sarmoung, which we had come across several times in the book called Merkhavat" (Gurdjieff, 2011 [1963]: 62). What is Merkhavat? It is the vision of a carriage as the throne of God that appears in Jewish mysticism before the Kabbalah. In his second conference, entitled *Merkabah Mysticism and Jewish Gnosticism,*[40] Gershom Scholem locates some vestiges of literary production before the common era and mentions - without development - a syncretism with the East, which could refer to the Chaldean Oracles. He adds something else that also seems to link him with Gurdjieff: "Be that as it may - and even granted that it may be

---

[38] Abraham is the great pilar of the Jewish religion and is also an important figure in Islam and Christianity. His tomb, in Hebron, is currently the object of a dispute between Palestinians and Israelis. His and his wife Sarah's tombs, along with those of his son Jacob and his wife Leah, are inside the synagog, while those of his other son Isaac and his wife Rebecca lie a few meters away in the Arab mosque, guarded by armed militia.

[39] Gurdjieff GI (1963) *Meetings with Remarkable Men*

[40] Published in *Major Trends in Jewish Mysticism* in 1946, republished by Schocken Books in 1995.

possible to trace the influence of the Essenes in some of these writings - one fact remains certain: the main subjects of the later Merkabah mysticism already occupy a central position in this oldest esoteric literature, best represented by the Book of Enoch" (Scholem, 1995 [1946]: 43). Why is this a link to Gurdjieff? Because when he writes about one of *his* friends, he says he "is still alive and well, and has the good fortune to be an assistant to the abbot of the chief monastery of the Essene Brotherhood, situated not far from the shores of the Dead Sea" (Gurdjieff, 2011 [1963]: 42). The Essenes, better known after the discovery of the Dead Sea Scrolls, also appear in the testimonies of Gurdjieff and his disciples.

Returning to the quotation about Merkhavah, it is important to remember the precisions and complements formulated by another contemporary scholar[41] about the "Merkhavah mysticism. The type of literature in which we find this mysticism is called Hekhalot literature; that is, the literature that deals with the *hekhalot*, the heavenly "palaces" or "halls" through which the mystic passes to reach the divine throne ... Whoever undertakes the dangerous ascent to the divine throne is called the *yored merkavah*, literally one who "descends" to the chariot" (Schäfer, 1992: 2). This ascension made sense to Gurdjieff because the traditions in which he had grown up, as we will see in due course, had the same objective: a return to the absolute.

One of the reasons that it has not been possible to establish a permanent thread through the history of the Enneagram is that it forms part of longstanding traditions that reserve certain kinds of knowledge only for the initiated. The same scholar of ancient Jewish mysticism writes, "The circle of initiates is thus intentionally and artificially circumscribed. The secret knowledge is not for everyone, it requires particular ethical qualities, a specific age or also a limited number of adepts. It is already stipulated in the Mishnah that the central content of the secret teaching, in rabbinic

---

[41] Peter Schäfer, professor of Jewish Studies at the Frei Universität in Berlin and researcher at the Institute for Advanced Study at Princeton.

terminology *ma'aseh merkavah* ("working of the chariot") and *ma'aseh bereshit* ("working of creation"), is subject to certain restrictions …" (Schäfer, 1992: 5).

There is also evidence of the Chaldeans in the Talmud, which records rabbinical discussions about laws, legends and customs; there was a Hebrew version and another Babylonian one, since there were rabbinical academies in Babylon where the scholars discussed the Mishnah, or compilation of opinions and debates. Many Jews return to Jerusalem from Babylonian exile around 538BCE and a century later the great Kabbalists begin to appear in Judea, although the word *kabbalah* seems to come into use in the 11th century BCE to refer to secret Hebrew knowledge. This knowledge, which is being explored more and more by non-Jews, explains each state of creation with its laws, thus sharing an objective with other spiritual traditions. In its practice it attempts to penetrate the divine aspect of human beings to return to the divine origin (*teshuva*).

One man is like a hinge between the Hebrew inheritance and the Hellenistic world: Philo of Alexandria. Scholars place his birth around 30 BCE and write that he was a practicing Jew who lived in "a place of enormous importance both for its excellent cultural and economic situation … but also for the coexistence of people of diverse languages and cultures that occurred there, among whom we can include preeminently the Greeks, at least in linguistic terms, Jews and hellenized Egyptians" (López Férez, 2009: 14). One author with an important body of work on the Enneagram, and a disciple of Ouspensky, insists that Philo achieved the union of Platonism with the Jewish Kabbalah (Collin, 1997 [1954]: appendix XIII).

Philo knew the theses of Pythagoras and Plato, he studied the works of Theophrastus who, like Hippocrates, worked on temperaments and character. In his writings he cites the Essenes, a Jewish movement from before the birth of Christ which will also come up in the history of Gurdjieff. His opus is vast and much of it has been conserved.[42] He was influential in several Jewish communities, though more so in non-orthodox and emigrant groups. Gershom Scholem, scholar of Jewish mysticism, says of Philo: "Although not many traces of it are to be found in Talmudic and early rabbinic literature, there can be no doubt, since Poznanski's[43] researches on the subject, that the ideas of the Alexandrian theosophist somehow spread even to the Jewish sectarians in Persia and Babylonia, who as late as the tenth century were in a position to quote from some of his writings" (Scholem, 1995 [1946]: 114). This information is important; if this researcher is left in no doubt that Philo's ideas reached Persia, it is highly likely that they were part of the transfer of knowledge that was preserved, century after century, and perhaps passed on to the Sufi brotherhoods that Raymund Lull encountered in the 13th century and, later, to those who lived in the spiritual communities in the areas that Gurdjieff and Ichazo would visit. Let us underline the hypothetical perhaps, because we would have to verify it with traceable documents. What we can state as fact is that the Jewish Kabbalah was a force in medieval Europe and today there are many who perceive points of concordance between the Kabbalah and the Enneagram. For example, Rabbi Addison writes that "Like the Tree of Life, the Enneagram is considered to depict not only the structure of ultimate reality, but also different core aspects of personality" (Addison, 2006: 5). The Tree of Life or *Etz Chayim* is a model made up of 10 spheres which together are known as *Sefirot*; about these and their similarities with the Enneagram, the Rabbi continues, "In the realm of personality, both the Enneagram and the Kabbalah claim that although all psyches potentially embody all the potencies, each manifests a predominant type or derives from a particular *sefirah*" (Addison, 2006: 35).

---

[42] The Loeb Classical Library of Harvard University Press has re-edited English translations of Theophrastus' *Characters* and *Inquiry into Plants*.

[43] Scholem refers to Samuel A. Poznanski (1864-1921), a Polish academic and rabbi whose published works in German cover historical and religious subjects.

A 17th century German Jesuit called Athanasius Kircher (who we will come back to later on), wrote a book entitled *Arithmologia* and on the frontispiece we find the elements of the symbol of the Enneagram. Gómez de Liaño, an author who has written a detailed study of Kircher and his works, believes that the Kabbalah was a key element in his studies. In his description of the frontispiece he specifies, "In the placid landscape we perceive the seated figures of a Hebrew sage whose books shows the stars of Solomon and David, and Pythagoras with his theorem. Kircher respected the Hebrew Kabbalah and Pythagorism with regard to the mystical properties of the numbers, but he rejected their magical applications" (Gómez de Liaño, 2001: 19). See Figure 1.

Of all Gurdjieff's disciples, the one that made the greatest efforts to record his teachings was Ouspensky and in one of his books he includes the following note about the number nine in the Jewish tradition: "In the book *Etude sur les origines de la nature du Zohar* by S. Karppe, Paris, 1910, pp200-201, there is a drawing of circle divided into nine parts with the following description of this circle. [There is a diagram of a circumference divided into 9 equal and numbered sections.] 'If we multiply 9x9 the result is shown in the number 8 on the left side and the number 1 on the right side; in the same way 9x8 gives the product shown in the number 7 on the left and in the number 2 on the right; exactly in the same way with 9x6. Beginning with 9x5 the order becomes reversed, that is, the number representing the units takes the left side and number representing the tens takes the right" (Ouspensky, 2001 [1949]: 287). This author, of whom we will also speak more later, points out that the Hebrew tradition uses the symbolic method to transmit learning.

A.G.E. Blake points out the similarities between the Kabbalistic Tree of Life and the Enneagram, as we mentioned in the introduction. Certainly they are similar paths which may share elements in their most ancient roots. In the same way there are forms of knowledge that are popularly held to come from Greece which in fact have a Babylonian origin. This is the case of Pythagoras' Theorem, which was also understood in ancient Egypt.

González Urbaneja, in his excellent research project into the history of mathematics, entitled *The So-called Theorem of Pythagoras. A 4000-year old Geometrical History*, assures us that a thousand years before Pythagoras, the ancient Babylonians already knew aspects of the Theorem (González Urbaneja, 2008).

When Pythagoras comes up in non-specialist contexts, his name is associated with the theorem and with some of his mathematical knowledge and it is always considered a part of mathematical history. If we delve a little deeper into the philosophy of the Pythagoreans we discover that there are arithmetical numbers, geometrical numbers and those that interest us which are the numbers that can be found in the essence of phenomena in order to symbolize them.

Scholars tend to begin their treaties about Pythagoras with the proviso that he left nothing in writing and that all that is attributed to him might in fact be the contribution of many, from the Egyptians and Chaldeans, to the direct disciples of the famous Greek from the island of Samos, men such as Philolaus.

Figure 1: Frontispiece of *Arithmologia* by Athanasius Kircher (1665) showing a Hebrew sage with a book containing the stars of Solomon and David, and Pythagoras with his theorem, under a sign very close to the modern Enneagram. (Zentralbibliothek Zürich, NE 898)

For all of them, mathematics was not only a clever abstract game, but rather the door to explanations of the universe and the reality around them, including the human being itself. There was not a terrestrial, divine or cosmic activity that they were indifferent to, they were looking for the common thread and the reason of existence of everything. Alfonso Reyes, a Mexican Hellenist and great enthusiast for ancient Greece, describes the mathematician-philosopher as follows: "Pythagoras feels that the world was born from music and that the lyre is a mortal imitation of the planetary system. The structure between opposites was the harmony, and it seemed to him the celestial spheres were singing" (Reyes, 1983: 477). Obviously Reyes is not the only one who associates Pythagoras with music, his biographers have often made the link and many scholars make a connection between the musical scale and mathematics as well.

In the 21st century it is somewhat surprising to find that someone with a degree in contemporary Physics and a PhD in History of Science, should digress to mention that "Pythagoras had been seduced by the seven intervals of the musical scale" (Fara, 2009: 5). We mention Patricia Fara's comment[44] because it leads us to make an implicit connection with the Enneagram. "Pythagoras imposed regular sevenfold patterns onto the Universe, maintaining that the orbits of the planets are governed by the same arithmetical rules as musical instruments" (Fara, 2009: 5).   J.G. Bennett makes an explicit link between the musical sale and the Enneagram. "We have here to recall Gurdjieff's use of the seven-toned musical scale as a symbol of the process of transformation... Pythagoras and others established what we now call the seven-toned scale, the notes of which were named by Guido D'Arezzo five hundred years ago (*do - si - la - sol - fa - mi - re)* " (Bennett, 1983:4).

---

[44] Patricia Fara studied Physics at Oxford and did her PhD in History of Science at the University of London. She is currently a researcher in the Department of History and Philosophy of Science at Cambridge University, where she is also Senior Tutor at Clare College. Her principal area of study is 18th century England, but she has published several books on diverse scientific subjects.

Two elements are fundamental to understand the transcendence of the Pythagorean school: first, the accumulation of knowledge that took place in the principal cultural centers of the 6th century BCE and second, the synthesis they carried out was both theoretical and practical and disseminated to numerous students at the school of Croton, in what was then part of Magna Graecia and is today the coast of the Gulf of Taranto in southern Italy.

Pythagoras knew the teachings of the Chaldean Magi, but he also learned geometry and rituals in Egypt and he approached many masters and people of knowledge in Palestine, Hindustan and Crete.[45] What Pythagoras taught was a whole cosmogony, in which mathematics played a central role to demonstrate, among other things, that the constitution and action of people were determined by laws similar to those of the universe. The *matematikoi* or advanced students, who lived in a community, received greater information according to their assimilation and practice, they sought the purification of the body for the immortality of the soul. If one looks further into the methods of study of the schools where the Enneagram was applied and taught it is possible to see certain parallels with the Pythagorean academy, in spite of the brutal difference in time. The Law of Seven and the Law of Three, that Gurdjieff taught, certainly inherited much from the Pythagorean teachings. Tracing this legacy over 25 centuries is a pending task for contemporary historiography.

For now, it seems evident when reading Gurdjieff's disciples, that they were working with ancient numerical representations. On the various occasions when Ouspensky develops some aspect of the Law of Seven, his grasp of numbers is evident, as is the explicit mention of its ancient origins. For example, when he considers the musical scale he speaks of the vibrating frequency and the periods of retardation and mentions the idea of the octave; he writes that the

---

[45] Diogenes Laërtius, Porphyry of Tyre and Iamblichus begin to write about Pythagoras in the 3rd century CE. It is centuries later, when his influence on Plato, Plotinus and the Neoplatonians is verified, that several studies emerge that give account of Pythagoras' life and teaching.

seven tone musical scale is a formula of the cosmic law that was elaborated by ancient schools and applied to music: "The laws which govern the retardation or the deflection of vibrations from their primary direction were known to ancient science. These laws were duly incorporated into a particular formula or diagram which has been preserved up to our times" (Ouspensky, 2001 [1949]: 124).

What is beyond question is the influence of Pythagoras on later Greek schools. Alfonso Reyes writes, "The doctrine of the transmigration of souls, later known - inadequately - as metempsychosis, is passed down to Plato. But it has not been demonstrated that he receives it from India, or even via Egypt, but rather from Pythagoras, who in turn may have inherited it from those Northern mysteries, common source for the Greeks and the Indians, before the Aryan dispersal" (Reyes, 1983: 31).

Derivations from original civilizing nuclei

Chapter 4

The Desert Fathers and the Christian Churches of the East

There are two facts, directly related to the Enneagram, which require a brief review of events in the early centuries of Christianity. One is the cultural and religious environment surrounding Gurdjieff and the other is the trajectory of the church precepts lived by Evagrius Ponticus in the 4th century CE, and in the 13th century by Raymund Lull who, as we shall see, designed several proto-Enneagrams.

Let's begin with the trajectory of Jesus' teachings from 70 CE, when the Roman Empire destroyed the temple in Jerusalem. Many of his followers had already been executed, like Peter in 62 CE and Paul, the apostle of the gentiles, in 64 CE. Once the temple was destroyed, the diaspora was imminent. Jews and Christians alike were persecuted. They fled towards Antioch and the communities in Anatolia that the preachers had reached. Little by little they began to become more institutionalized. At the beginning of the 2nd century the Romans subjugated the Jewish communities and vulgar Greek replaced Aramaic. The Christian communities had named their bishops. In the middle of the 3rd century, the early Christian theologian, Origen, successfully systematized the theology of the day and his ideas spread widely. The Alexandrine theologian would be followed by Evagrius who can be considered part of the history of the Enneagram, not only because he worked on the vices and virtues of the enneatypes, but also as the leader of the Hesychasm, or the ascetic practice that so interested Gurdjieff, according to one of his biographers.[46]

By then the persecutions were intermittent and local. Between the first century and the year 313, when the Emperor Constantine issued the Edict of Milan that allowed freedom of religion, many new communities had been created in the deserts of Palestine, Syria, Anatolia and Egypt. Thus a kind of monastic lifestyle emerged that preferred remote places for a life of study and contemplation. The knowledge of the Chaldean Magi, the Pythagoreans, Hippocrates, Plato, Galen and even ancient Egypt had come this far. In some of these emigrant communities, they strove to increase literacy. New texts, apothegms and community rules emerged.

It is in the 4th century that the Desert Fathers appear; so named when, after Constantine establishes the peace, they leave the cities for a more contemplative life. The movement expands towards Egypt and Asia Minor. They develop the earliest Christian theology. Among them are the so called Cappadocian Fathers or Philosophers. One of them, Basil of Caesarea or Basil the Great, chose as his lector a young ascetic monk called Evagrius Ponticus (so called, because he came from the Roman province of Ponto, now northern Turkey, south of the Black Sea).

Evagrius, a Christian monk born around 345 in Ibora, now in Turkey and known as İverönü,[47] is a character who has gained in depth and transcendence in the 20th century with the translation of his original texts from Armenian, Syriac, Greek and Latin. John Eudes Bamberger, author of the introduction to the English translation, writes "Perhaps the most important problem to be solved at the present is the nature of the relationship between the more speculative and Hellenistic side of his thought on the one hand and the more practical aspect which derives from his own

---

[46] See Moore (1993) *Gurdjieff, a biography*, page 76.

[47] Some historians maintain that he was born in Iveria, a small town in Georgia, East of the Black Sea.

experience and from his having entered so deeply into the Coptic desert tradition" (Evagrius Ponticus, 1972: xxxiv).[48] In effect, Evagrius immersed himself in the traditions of the Egyptian Copts of the first century CE and also in the Pythagorean legacy and the so-called Christian Platonism. He elaborated his own synthesis which he called *hesychasm* or *hesychasmos*, which consisted in bringing together ascetic doctrine and practice, which were widely disseminated amongst the monks of the Christian Orthodox Churches. Evagrius determined to take elements from varied sources and apply them in the control of his own passions. The control of his own vices and the strengthening of his personal virtues is what gives substance and experiential support to his writing on the eight types of sinful thought and in particular his quest for an antidote or remedy.

Evagrius was ordained Deacon by Gregory of Nazianzus, in the year 379. Shortly thereafter he fell in love with the wife of a prominent member of Constantinople society, but he decided to put a drastic end to this troubling situation. He left Jerusalem, studied Origen and, in 383, departed for Nitria, in Egypt, where he would, in solitude, dedicate himself to the analysis of his dominant passions and how to combat them. Thus arose, with full awareness, his powerful conviction to practice and reflect in writing on what he knew of human vices and virtues. We do not know if he knew the work of Cipriano, Bishop of Carthage from 249-258, about the eight capital sins, but in any case his exposition of the eight types of sinful thoughts is eloquent, vivid and comprehensive. As he begins to elaborate them he tells us: "There are eight general and basic categories of thoughts in which are included every thought" (Evagrius Ponticus, 1972: 16) and then he goes on to describe them: gluttony, impurity (lust), avarice, sadness, anger,

---

[48] The genesis of the discovery and translation of his complete works can be read in the introduction by John Eudes Bamberger to the publication of Evagrius's texts: *Praktikos and Chapters on Prayer*, Cistercian Publications, Trappist Kentucky, 1972.

acedia (sloth), vainglory and pride. As he completes the details of each one, he presents a careful appraisal of how to combat it.[49]

Several Enneagram scholars and practitioners have found a link between the work of Evagrius and the contemporary instrument. Andreas Ebert, a Lutheran Minister who has translated the books of Richard Rohr into German, explains his own experience in 1995: "I stumbled on a text by the old Christian Desert Father Evagrius Ponticus that nonplussed me. Even though I didn't understand all of it, I immediately had the sense that this text must have something to do with the Enneagram" (Rohr and Ebert, 2001: 8). Ebert writes that he published his discovery[50] and in May of the same year (1996), Lynn Quirolo came to the same conclusion independently.[51] Fifteen years later Helen Palmer and Ginny Wiltse argue that there is a parallel with the nine Enneatypes: "In his treatise *On the Vices Opposed to the Virtues* Evagrius lists nine pairs: gluttony and abstinence (Type Seven), fornication and chastity (Type Eight), avarice and freedom from possessions (Type Five), sadness and joy (Type Four), anger and patience (Type One), acedia and perseverance (Type Nine), vainglory and freedom from vainglory (Type Three), jealousy and freedom from jealousy (Type Six), pride and humility (Type Two)... Despite the lack of a consistent presentation of a ninth vice, the parallels between the eight *logismoi* of Evagrius and the passions of eight of the nine Enneagram types are unmistakable" (Wiltse and Palmer, 2011: 7). Ebert mentions two more people who associated Evagrius with the Enneagram early on: the German Benedictine Anselm Grün and the North American Jesuit Robert Ochs. As we can appreciate, research on the sources of the Enneagram continues to this day and we can only hope that it will prosper and gradually reduce the gaps and questions that arise.

---

[49] See "Against the eight passionate thoughts", pages 20-42 of Evagrius (1972).

[50] Are the Origins of the Enneagram Christian after all? *Enneagram Monthly*, No. 11, January 1996

[51] Published with the title "Pythagoras, Gurdjieff and the Enneagram" in the April and May 1996 editions of *Enneagram Monthly*.

For their part, Richard Rohr and Andreas Ebert assure us that "the work of Evagrius closely coincides at two points with the Enneagram: in his *Teaching on the Passions* and in the description of a figure that is based on Pythagorean numerological speculation, which displays the essential features of the Enneagram symbol" (Rohr and Ebert 2001:10).

Evagrius also points out that each of the vices and virtues corresponds to a type of body, according to each person's fall because of inattention to God. Each body, according to its vice, requires a different type of contemplation in order to reach the essential knowledge again.[52] This movement towards human perfection is a relevant precedent to understand the enthusiasm of numerous authors and groups, over the centuries, for the methods to gain knowledge and the evolution of each personality type. Evagrius Ponticus is one of the most distant references in terms of this ascendent movement of each type of human being towards his or her perfection.

The writings of Evagrius have been preserved from the 4th century CE to the present thanks to a series of circumstances. In the first place, many of his texts were attributed to others who we not considered polemic, as was the case of Nilo, a courtier in Constantinople, who for years was thought to be the author of the Chapters on Prayer. Secondly, the works were adopted as their own inheritance by several Christian churches, in different parts of Asia and Europe with different ecclesiastical leaders. And thirdly, at times of conflict or persecution, the manuscripts were hidden in monasteries and caves, which permitted the conservation of the documents. Cappadocia was a favorable place for the preservation of these texts, a place that Gurdjieff visited in the 20th century in

---

[52] All this can be found in the series of judgements, numbered 1-100 in the *Praktikos*. These texts went on to form part of the *Philokalia*, an anthology of Eastern Orthodox Christian texts compiled by the ascetic monk Nicodemus the Hagiorite (1749-1809) and Bishop Macarius of Corinth (1731-1805) which include a wide range of texts from the Desert Fathers and the Patristics of the 4th century CE, to the Byzantines of the 14th century.

search of the origins of the Christian liturgy, according to his English biographer.[53]

Ancient Anatolia, now Turkey, received the Palestinian emigrés after the death of Jesus. Studies claim that Mary, his mother, left Jerusalem to live on a hill in modern Ephesus.[54] Many other Christians also settled in modern Turkey in the 1st and 2nd centuries of the common era. The region of Cappadocia, visited by Paul the Apostle (also known as Saul of Tarsus or St. Paul), was an *ad hoc* place for the settlement of emigrants because of its geographical configuration. Millions of years earlier, two volcanoes, Mount Erciyes and Mount Hasan, produced, after their eruptions, a limestone with the ideal properties for building houses excavated in the natural formations without altering the surface relief. Some houses had as many as eight levels underground.[55] In the present day valley of Göreme it is still possible to visit some of these dwellings which, thanks to the absence of light, have preserved frescos from the 2nd to 12th centuries depicting scenes from the New Testament, then in the recent past, and some passages of the Pentateuch. As a hypothesis we could suppose that some Essenes had retired to the caves of Cappadocia, as others of the order did around the Dead Sea. The Essenes would have a powerful influence on Gurdjieff.

Why bring up these geographical characteristics of modern Turkey? Because only in a place like this was it possible to conserve the hidden churches of primitive Christianity and inside the churches, their ancient documents. It is in these churches that the communities would meet that were presided over by the Cappadocian Fathers,

---

[53] See Moore (1993) *Gurdjieff, a Biography*, page 76.

[54] Reference to the carbon-14 tests and other methods used to verify the facts can be found in *Eteria*, Modena, Italy, Year XI, No.41, Jan-March 2007.

[55] So far, 36 underground cities have been identified in Cappadocia: Derinkuyu, Kaymakli, Özkonak, Mucur, Örentepe, Gümüskent, Gelveri, Tatlarin and Acigöl. See details in: Tuna, Turgay and Demirdurak, Bülent, (2010) *Cappadocia*, BKG Publicaciones, Istambul, Turkey.

men like Basil the Great (330-379), Gregory of Nyssa (335-394) and Gregory of Nazianzus (329-389). These three were contemporaries of Evagrius (345-399) and they promoted the First Council of Constantinople, celebrated in 381. The communities they organized in Cappadocia perpetuated primitive Christianity "faithfully transmitting from generation to generation their manners, usages, and modes of worship".[56] Among the knowledge and understanding that remains current in these communities, are the writings of Clement of Alexandria, who lived between the 2nd and 3rd century, and those of his disciple Origen, a scholar and exegete who was preaching in the second half of the 3rd century CE, and of whom Evagrius was a loyal follower.

In addition, Cappadocia is an example of those areas that, like Alexandria which was a Greek cultural metropolis, experienced the meeting of civilizations in their territories; at the same time it was an adequate place for the preservation of ancestral knowledge. In one of his books John G. Bennett, disciple and friend of Gurdjieff, makes a reference to Cappadocia that confirms this: he tells us that before the appearance of Christianity, Cappadocia was the centre of a cult to the Persian goddess Anahita and "with her priests, there came a great body of knowledge, and some of that knowledge, perhaps more than people can readily appreciate, has been brought into the construction of the Christian liturgy" (Bennett 1975: 21). The mystery of the knowledge hidden in the liturgy much impressed Gurdjieff, as Bennett writes, so that he travelled to the Western world "to understand what was being preserved for mankind behind the ritual of the Church... At that time, there were still monasteries in Cappadocia. They remained from about the third century right on and on and on, through the Byzantine Empire, remaining after the Turkish conquest, right through until our day. For sixteen centuries there was a monastic tradition here in Cappadocia" (Bennett, 1975:

---

[56] Cumont Franz, *The mysteries of Mithra*, Dover, N.Y. 1903, 1956, cited by Wiltse and Palmer: "Hidden in Plain Sight: Observations on the Origins of Enneagram", in *Enneagram Journal*, Vol. IV, Issue 1, July 2011. Note 14, Page 28.

21). The religious centres endured the Middle Ages, when opposition developed between Roman Christianity and what was perceived by the Catholic leaders as the heresy not only of the Muslims, but also of Greek Eastern Christianity. The history of the so called Eastern Christian Churches is essential in order to understand the traces of the teachings of Gurdjieff's Armenian mother, as well as of the Nestorian and Armenian Churches. His basic education was Christian, but not Catholic, nor Roman.

Visiting the underground houses of Cappadocia, or the caves that were home to smaller communities, we are obliged to imagine that there must have been unusual rules to encourage harmonious coexistence, because the smallness of the spaces seems unlikely to allow for social life to continue there for many centuries. We can hypothesize that Evagrius' proposals to overcome the eight *logismoi* or *spiritibus malitiae,* translated as mental habits, could be applied to co-existence in these places, and also in Nitria and Kellia,[57] the desert communities in Egypt, near Alexandria, where he lived. This could have been the starting point or one of the seeds of what, centuries later and with the use of the now-familiar symbol and others like it,[58] we know as the Enneagram. Evagrius integrated into his method the influences he had received from the Pythagoreans, the Neoplatonians, Jews and Copts, elements which came to him ready to be enriched and practiced.

Nearly two centuries after Evagrius, in the 6th century, Pope Gregory I (also known as St. Gregory the Great), having consolidated the European Church (but not so the Eastern Church), defined the capital sins as being seven, eliminating vanity from the

---

[57] In Kellia we can see the remains of a Christian Monastery, excavated in a limestone cliff, similar to that of the primitive churches of Cappadocia. See text and photos in: Dunn, Jimmy, *Christian Nitria, Kellia and the life of their ancient monks*. En: www.touregypt.net/featurestories/Kellia.htm Consulted 14 October 2011.

[58] In Athanasius Kircher's book *Arithmologia, sive de abditis numerorum mysteriis*, published in Rome in 1665, we find the circle but it is separate from the triangle and the hexad.

earlier list and giving each sin an opposite virtue, as we know them today. Pride/humility; avarice/generosity; lust/chastity; anger/patience; gluttony/restraint or moderation; envy/charity; sloth/diligence. However, it was not always thus. It is worth noting, skipping ahead to the 13th century, that Raymund Lull mentions nine virtues and vices and places them in a circle with a star, in a proto-Enneagram which, in his own time, will be passed to Oscar Ichazo; but that is contemporary history. Before we get to that, we must say a few more words about the divisions in Christianity in order to propose a hypothesis about how the wisdoms of the Chaldean Magi reached the regions in which Gurdjieff was active as a young man. And I repeat, these approximations require further investigation to establish more precisely how much of the knowledge of the Chaldean Magi was preserved by the Greek, Armenian, Georgian and Nestorian Orthodox Churches.

The cultural inheritance of the 4th century goes beyond the study of temperaments and characters, and seeks a return to the absolute via an encounter with our own essence.[59] The 5th century is important for the history of the Enneagram because at this time there is a major break within Christianity. The Council of Chalcedon in 451 is quite clear about which churches did not participate: "…his delay of two years in recognizing the council helped only its opponents in Palestine and Egypt, from among whom the non-Chalcedonian churches emerged: the monophysite Coptic Church in Egypt, the Nestorian Church in Syria and the Armenian and Georgian Church. They still exist today" (Küng, 2011). This Armenian Church, founded in 326 CE, and the Apostolic Assyrian Church, which is also known as Nestorian and by other names, form part of the Churches that have called themselves Orthodox because they consider themselves faithful to primitive Christianity. The definitive

---

[59] This interest arises in modernity also, in certain intellectual circles in Europe, when people start to look at what rationalism left out. Several contemporary scholars and practitioners follow this line of inquiry. Besides Richard Rohr, Don Riso and Russ Hudson, we can mention A.G.E. Blake, *The Intelligent Enneagram*, and A.H. Almaas with his *Facets of Unity. The Enneagram of Holy Ideas.*

break takes place in 1054 with the mutual excommunication by the Patriarch of Constantinople Michael I Cerularius and Pope Leo IX, which continued until Pope Paul VI embraced the Patriarch Athenagoras I in 1965. However, the Christians in the East are still known as Orthodox and the ones in the West, Catholic. Gurdjieff's maternal family were Orthodox Christians, as we shall see.

The other major schism in Christianity is the Reformation, in the 16th century. We mention it here, briefly, simply to highlight Martin Luther's insistence —among other areas in which he considered the Catholic Church to have erred— on a return to the primacy of the scriptures and a direct communication with God without official mediators. The concern behind this point is that this schism, in addition to the break with the Orthodox Churches, seems to show that something was lost with the passage of time. It suggests that the Catholic Church forgot the teachings of early Christianity and, as Hans Küng would say, held on to the authentic foundations of the church of the Roman Empire.

Chapter 5

The Sufi theses

Identifying the Sufi elements in the Enneagram is a task that requires an in-depth philological investigation, starting with the possible Chaldean inheritance of the Malamati movement at the beginning of Sufism.

In order to undertake a coherent historical review, we would have to avoid two basic paradigms: that of Western orientalists who look on Islam and Sufis as "the other" and that of islamic fundamentalism. We need to find historians whose work is beyond ideological posturing and religious doctrine.

One of the most widespread theses in the West is that Islam and Sufism have co-existed, with the latter, in some cases, considered earlier. Idries Shah[60] is one author who asserts this, writing that "in Sufi tradition, the 'Chain of Transmission' of Sufi schools may reach back to the Prophet by one line, and to Elijah by another" (Shah, 1999: 32) and he adds that the term "sufi" was already in use before Mohammed, with evidence of the pre-islamic use of Sufi concepts. The word Sufi comes, according to the same author, from the nickname for Jabir Ibn el-Hayyan or Jabir Ibn al-Sufi (721-815 CE), known in the West as Geber. Shah also points out that in the Middle Ages, alchemy was called a sophic art. However, in recent years, more complex theories have emerged,

---

[60] Shah is considered by many scholars of the Sufi phenomenon to be a popular writer, rather than an academic. It would be a good idea to contrast his thesis with more specialist and up to date studies.

with greater historiographic precision.[61] Sara Sviri, researcher at the Department of Arabic Language and Literature at the Hebrew University in Jerusalem, suggests that the history of the first years of Sufism has yet to be written, because since the 10th century the compilers of primary sources have wanted to present a uniform spiritual tradition. To this end they deliberately suppressed the dynamic and multifaceted dialogue which had taken place between the numerous centres and masters in the first generations. As a hypothesis we could propose the possibility that before the 7th century some movements involved in this dialogue may have been based on the Chaldean teachings.

Sviri's research allows us to see some interesting parallels between the contemporary Enneagram and early Sufism, "One of the most fascinating and illuminating chapters in the history of these formative years is that of the Nishâpûrî 'Path of Blame', the *Malâmatiyya*. In any attempt to draft the early history of Islamic mysticism, the *Malâmatiyya* movement is indispensable. Yet it is also, and to a no lesser degree, an invaluable phenomenon in the History of Religion at large, especially for its attentiveness, its insights and its formulations pertaining to the psychological obstacles which confront any sincere seeker on the path of the spiritual quest" (Sviri 1993). She refers to the dialectic between the *nafs* (the lower self, centre of ego-consciousness and the lower nature) and the *sirr* (the innermost recesses of one's being). This issue also arises in the Enneagram and transcends the game of the nine personalities and it seems to appear, with other terms, in the Chaldean Oracles. Sviri continues, that it would appear that the *Malâmatî* masters proposed a system in "which sincere self-scrutiny and self-criticism were interwoven into a highly acclaimed social code based on chivalry and altruism and ... spiritual

---

[61] Two studies recommended by Alejandro Volpi are: 1) De Martin Nguyen (2012) *Sufi Master and Qur'an Scholar: Ab ul-Qasim al-Qushayr i and the Lata'if al-Ish ar at*, OUP/Institute of Ismaili Studies. 2) De Yannis Toussulis (2010) *Sufism and the Way of Blame: Hidden Sources of a Sacred Psychology*, Wheaton, IL: Theosophical Publishing House.

superiority" (Sviri 1993). Further study in this area is required to get to the bottom of this aspect of the history of the Enneagram.

On the other hand, it is also important to keep in mind that originally medieval alchemy was a quest for the regeneration of human beings in order to achieve the highest spirituality and this was also the intention of some Sufi brotherhoods. Alchemy, writes Shah, was a terminology adopted by the Sufis for the projection of an allegorical message which had nothing to do with metals: "The regeneration of an essential part of humanity, according to the Sufis, is the goal of mankind. The separation of man from his essence is the cause of his disharmony and unfulfillment" (Shah, 1999: 194). This was the purpose of the original Enneagram also, that is to say the Enneagram that knows that the nine personalities is one more step towards the fading of the ego.

What Laleh Bakhtiar calls the "Sufi Enneagram" is a symbolic manifestation of practical philosophy whose application in relation to human beings takes, as its guiding thread, the notion of the inner battle between passions and noetic faculties[62] in order to restore their transpersonal identity, which shows a close similarity with Gurdjieff's Enneagram.

An academic at the University of Maryland[63] makes another contribution to Sufi genealogy: he writes that the beginnings are rather obscure for researchers because of scarce documentation, but - with evidence - he places the Sufis of Baghdad between the 8th and 10th centuries CE and he also has some advice which is relevant for our research: "In the same time period, other mystical movements took shape elsewhere, notably in lower Iraq, north-eastern Iran, and Central Asia. Mystics who belonged to these latter movements were not initially known as Sufis, and in their thought

---

[62] From the Greek *noetikós*, relating to the faculty of intellection. From *noésis*, the act of perceiving intellectually.

[63] Ahmet T. Karamustafa, Professor of History at the School of Languages, Literatures and Cultures of the University of Maryland.

and practice, they differed from Baghdad Sufis and from each other in many ways, but they gradually blended with the Baghdad mystics, and in time, like them, they too came to be identified as Sufis" (Karamustafa, 2007: 1). He also accepts the existence of other groups, presumably of Chaldean influence, which shared cosmogonies.

The Arabian Peninsula was almost entirely desert, populated by bedouins when the principal cultures of the ancient world had taken shape. It was only in the 7th century CE that one people organized around a religion that Mohammed preached. He began in Mecca, his birthplace, by borrowing some characters and elements from the Christian and Jewish traditions; in 622 he went to Medina, a migration known as Hegira. In uniting a people under his command, he created a state or caliphate which, in time, undertook a "holy war" or *jihad* to fight the non-believers. On his death, there was a rupture over the leadership of the caliphate which endures to the present. In the words of a contemporary scholar: "A line divided supporters of the winners and of the losers in the civil wars of the succession: roughly, the position eventually known as Sunnites, who accepted the political status quo and the victorious lineage, and the Shi'ites, intransigents who held out loyally for the family line of the losing faction. On each side in turn there was further fractionation. The victorious majority developed a pragmatic group who offered compromise with the losers, in effect declaring its willingness not to pursue the old issues of legitimacy and illegitimacy of various claims. On the Shi'ite side, the more vehement rebels were eventually displaced by a faction which held that the Imam, the true successor to the Prophet, was in hiding" (Collins, 1998: 392). This is the political context within which we must understand the Sufis.

Those who have studied the roots of Sufism argue that "more than in any other area, the Hellenistic, Christian, Jewish and Maniquean substrate emerges in a mystic whose genesis, in terms of geography, history and society, is outside the cradle of Islam" (Puech, 1982: 100). Its development, however, continued in the shadow of Islam.

With regard to its identity, Idries Shah writes, "Sufism is believed by its followers to be the inner, 'secret' teaching that is concealed within every religion" (Shah, 1999: 25). The same author points out that Sufis respect the rites of any creed as long as they contribute to promoting social harmony, but also that they widen the doctrinal bases of all religions whenever possible defining their myths with a superior angle. Thus, in recent times, there have been Sufis who have taken advantage of social situations to give out messages and practices appropriate to the moment. Such is the case of a Persian Sufi called Mírzá Ḥusayn-'Alí Núrí (1817-1892)[64] who, in the second half of the 19th century, took the name Bahá' u' alláh and wrote several texts, compiled under the title *The Seven Valleys*, in which he talked about how to achieve an experience of the divine through everyday events. The symbol of the Baha'i faith is a nine-pointed star and it derives from the Arab word Bahá (splendor) and which is identified with the number nine. It would be worth investigating whether this inclusion of the nine has a shared origin with the symbol of the Enneagram. This same quest for the transcendent in daily life has motivated several Sufi communities over the centuries.

Sufism had a first phase of individual asceticism or Anchoritism that ended when Mohammed declared himself against the impositions of ascetic life in Islam, an issue that was then expressed in certain verses of the Koran and whose interpretation gave rise to anti-Sufi feeling, mainly on the part of the Sunnis. By 622, when the Prophet left Mecca on the *Hegira* or migration which marks the beginning of the Muslim calendar, there was already a conflict between traditional Islam and Sufism. Yet this did not impede the proliferation of certain treaties between them.

---

[64] He was born in Teheran to a rich family of imperial lineage, with a good education. He determined to publicly highlight the ways in which a more just social order could be established, with awareness of catastrophes to come. He established relations with the leaders of several nations, was imprisoned by the Ottoman Empire in what was then Palestine and is now Akko, a city in northern Israel, where he was later buried.

In the 9th century the philosophy of Islam became more systematized and there were major debates at the time of the crucifixion of Hussein Ibn Mansur Al-Hallaj, a Sufi martyr and conspicuous representative of the doctrine of Mystical Union or the oneness of being. At this time, Sufism flourished with texts and teachings by numerous mystics throughout the 10th century, who debated with Koran in hand and offered interpretations that moved people to reflect and also to the hardening of beliefs. Different opinions or perspectives gave rise to clearly identifiable groups. There are several mystics who initiated their own Sufi orders, brotherhoods or schools.

The Abbasid Caliphate consolidated its power from Baghdad between 750 and 830 CE, when it lost importance to regional administrators. "… full-fledged independent states divided the region between 950 and 1200", according to Collins (1998: 394). Later there were several waves of conquests by the Turkish Seljuk empire, the Mongols and finally the Ottoman Turks who controlled the peninsula of Anatolia, modern Turkey, from the 14th century until the beginning of the 20th century. All this means that the Muslim religion could not have a centralized ecclesiastical organization and some Sufi orders were able to secretly conserve and intensify their Chaldean, Hellenistic and Neoplatonic inheritance.

Non religious and non orthodox philosophers were protected for centuries by the Caliphate of Baghdad and, from 950CE, when they lose that protection, a new element emerges for survival: the secret societies. Collins illustrates the environment in which these arose: "Although these were predominantly political and religious in their concerns, the secret societies were always in opposition to at least some part of the status quo around the islamic world; and they sometimes looked for allies among unorthodox factions on the intellectual front. Thus one could find unholy alliances between Ismaili or Imamite conspirators and hard-pressed rationalist theologians and philosophers" (Collins, 1998: 394-5). Some Sufi brotherhoods had to keep their knowledge secret in the face of Sunni and Shi'ite orthodoxy.

Distinguishing the chemists from the spiritualists is "one of the tools which unlocks the story of medieval alchemy" (Shah, 1999: 193), which begins in the 8th century with Jabir Ibn el-Hayyan. He was known as "the Mystic", Al-Sufi or Geber in medieval Europe and he belonged to a mystic sect who called themselves the "Brethren of Purity". The connections between mysticism and alchemy occurred more often in Islam than in other cultures. Works on these subjects were declared heretical by orthodox Sunnis and in the 11th century there were persecutions organized against the Sufis, after which the latter kept quiet about the knowledge they held that was not shared by the rest of Islam.

The Brethren of Purity "were indeed the first to work out in detail the consequences of the idea that man is a microcosm or an epitome of the whole universe, finding analogies and correspondences between all aspects of the anatomy and physiology of man and the structure and workings of the world which were then known. In the specific field of chemistry they divided natural substances into two main classes, 'bodies' and 'spirits', by analogy with the view that man was made up of a body and soul" (Mason, 1962: 98). The Sufi Enneagram, as we shall see later on, in the studies by Laleh Bakhtiar, has its roots in the *Epistles of the Brethren of Purity* (*Rasa'il ijwan al-safá*), a text which disseminated Neoplatonic ideas and was compiled in the 10th century. These writings, along with others by the Sufi Avicenna (Ibn Sina) were burnt in 1150 by order of the Calipha Al-Mustanyid.

The history of the Sufis of the 13th century is relevant for the Enneagram because there are figures here who may have had a direct relation to the symbol and the wisdom it represents. Two rival brotherhoods emerge in this century and the next: the *Bektasiyya*, with some Suni and Christian elements, and the *Mawlawiyya* to which the descendants and followers of Jalal ad-Din Muhammad Rumi belong. He was born in Balkh (now Afghanistan) in 1207 and died in 1273 in Konya (now Turkey). Known as Rumi, he was taught by his father and other poets and Sufi practitioners, and it is said that he was given the *Asrar Nameh*, or the Sufi book of secrets, by Farid ud-Din Attar. It is with Rumi that the order of the dancing or whirling dervishes begins, the ones who meditate in movement. Rumi wrote two poetic works: the *Masnavi* and *Diwan-e Shams-e Tabrizi*.[65] The first contains moral and mystic stories and, according to Laleh Bakhtiar, a verse that contains the Sufi Enneagram. The second is made up of six books, the last of which is unfinished, and speaks of the spiritualization of Sufism.

Rumi and a possible Enneagram that underlies the 13th century verses

One Iranian-American woman brought together several factors that shed light on the Sufi Enneagram. She was born in New York in 1938 to an American mother (Helen Jeffreys) and an Iranian father (Abol Ghassem Bakhtiar). She studied history and married an Iranian architect, with whom she had three children. She lived in Iran for 20 years, published books on Sufism and returned to the United States to study philosophy with a specialization in Religious Studies. In order to have an income, she also studied psychology. One day, at the end of a Group Counseling class, as she was preparing to leave, the lecturer added, "Oh, there is one more method of group counseling you may be interested in. It is called the Enneagram and it has Sufi origins" (in Bakhtiar 2013a: 116).[66] That was her "wake-up call", she felt that she had found an area where she could combine her Iranian background with her

---

[65] Information from *Rumi: a monarch of divine love*, a pamphlet written by Sheija Amina Teslima al-Yerráhi, published by the Sufi Order Nur Ashki Yerráhi of Mexico, with offices at Calle de Sinaloa 213, Mexico City.

[66] Interview with Laleh Bakhtiar PhD by Jim Gomez first published in *Stopinder* en April 2003. Reprinted in *Rumi's Original Sufi Enneagram* by Laleh Bakhtiar (2013a).

knowledge of Sufism and her new studies, and she began to do research into the Enneagram. Her name was Laleh Bakhtiar.

Since she spoke Arabic, Persian and English, Bakhtiar could delve into the familiar territory (for her) of the Sufi tradition in order to contribute an explanation in the West about the location of what she calls the Sufi Enneagram. She begins defining it as "a symbolic manifestation of practical philosophy" (Bakhtiar, 2013a: 41), which requires spiritual hermeneutics in order to be understood and applied. The epistemological framework is given by the mystical and moral dimensions of Islam, understood as spiritual warfare (*jihad al-akbar*)   between reason, or noetic capacity, and the passions.

The battle or struggle that humans are engaged in to balance reason and passion is the backdrop to the Sufi Enneagram. Reason and cognition, writes Laleh Bakhtiar, guide the spiritual heart towards conscience, while the passions distance one from it and serve the ego. Anger and lust are two characteristics of the animal soul that we humans share, but are not necessarily negative traits since they also preserve us as a species. The division between avoiding harm (anger) and seeking pleasure (lust) is artificial, but it allows us to observe the natural state of human beings. Disciplining our passions and nurturing our reasoning abilities leads us towards the necessary inner balance, according to the original Sufi Enneagram. Achieving these aims means we have attained the cardinal virtues of wisdom, temperance (or self-esteem) and courage (Bakhtiar 2013a: 42).

In the preface to her book *Rumi's Original Sufi Enneagram*, after mentioning the contents of each chapter, Bakhtiar goes on to explain that the known Enneagrams differ from Rumi's original Sufi Enneagram and she gives two cases as examples: she says of Gurdjieff that perhaps he was not given a clear explanation or the explanation was given in a language he was not well versed in, because it turns out that he makes the first major change compared to the original in that he places the main segment on the left instead of at the top. Of Ichazo she writes that "his enneagon of personality types was even further beyond the original. He knew of the seven deadly sins, but due to the fact that there were nine numbers, he arbitrarily placed lust as number 8 and anger as number 1" (Bakhtiar 2013a: 6). Bakhtiar is unaware of, or does not mention, the writings of Raymund Lull in which there are unmistakably nine vices and nine virtues, which we know Ichazo had read about.

Bakhtiar calls Ichazo's amendment a "catastrophic decision, done without reference to the works of the early Jewish and Christian scholars and theologians on ethics such as Thomas Aquinas and Moses Maimonides who both speak of the three-fold division of the soul into lust and anger ... and reason" (Bakhtiar 2013a: 7). She goes on to say:

> "Gurdjieff and Ichazo's versions are missing the following essential elements of the original Sufi Enneagram:
>
> 1. The center point in the circumference of the circle that symbolizes justice....
>
> 2. There is no mention of the four cardinal virtues: wisdom, temperance (or self-esteem or self-restraint), courage and justice.
>
> 3. Ichazo's Enneagram of Personality Types continues to place anger and lust on the circumference, each one being one of the nine points whereas in all traditional writing it is clearly stated that we are all created with the passions or animal soul that consists of anger and lust. Therefore, the passions are not specific to an individual, but are held by all people. The passions or ego are the enemy that requires spiritual warfare to overcome.
>
> 4. With the Enneagram of Personality Types there is less emphasis upon the Line of the Spirit as continuously moving through the circle, whereas this is the key to healing in the original Sufi Enneagram.

5. A person is fixed or 'typed' to a number whereas in the original Sufi Enneagram, we all exhibit all of the possibilities of too much, too little in terms of quantity of one of the cardinal virtues, or none at all in terms of quality at any and every moment of time. The numbers on the circumference, then, are important in indicating the Line of the Spirit, not in being any one special number.

6. The original Sufi Enneagram is called *wajhullah*, The Presence of God. That is, with the original image, one heals in the Presence of God, the goal being to become a fair and just person. This goal is not emphasized in the Enneagram of Personality Types and, as a matter of fact, is not possible when one is "typed" because a "type" has both positive and negative traits that a person then tries to hold on to. With the original Sufi Enneagram, one engages in spiritual warfare to rid one's "self" (body, soul and Spirit) of the negative traits or vices and replace them with the positive traits or virtues" (Bakhtiar 2013a: 7-9).

In order to better understand these deficiencies that Bakhtiar points out, we must look further at the explanation she gives of the Sufi Enneagram. Lets try to do so, although readers should be aware that her books need in depth study to locate the contributions of this tradition. This is one more area awaiting resolution.

At the end of her preface to *Rumi's Original Sufi Enneagram*, Bakhtiar relates the moment in which, while reading the *Masnavi*, Book I:2253, she found what she calls the confirmation of the original Sufi Enneagram in a story called "The Argument Between a Husband and His Wife". As Samuel Bedeck Sotillos states in the introduction, what Rumi does with this story is use "down-to-earth language to articulate the dynamic nature of the nine-pointed symbol" from various facets that take place in human relations and through "the dialectic that occurs between the Intellect and the ego" (Bakhtiar [Bedeck Sotillos], 2013: 29).

For the Western reader to grasp the implicit elements in the argument between the spouses,   in her first chapter, Bakhtiar presents the familiar symbol of the Enneagram[67] and places elements of the Koran within it. The circumference is divided into three equal parts. The first third (bottom left) has the following characteristics:

Physiological: Liver

Psychological 1: Affect (A)

Psychological 2: Attraction to Pleasure

Spiritual/Biological: Preserve the Species

Cognitive: Unconscious

Quranic 1: half of animal souls (*nafs ammarah*)

Quranic 2: Counseling to the positive (*amr bil maruf*)

The second third (bottom right) has the following characteristics:

Physiological: Heart

Psychological 1: Behavior (B)

Psychological 2: Avoidance of harm/pain

Spiritual/Biological: Preserve the Individual

Cognitive: Preconscious

Quranic 1: half of animal souls (*nafs ammarah*)

Quranic 2: Preventing the negative (*nahy an al-munkar*)

The third third (top) has the following characteristics:

Physiological: Brain

Psychological 1: Cognition (C)

---

[67] Since Bakhtiar does not say that she found evidence of a symbol in Rumi's texts, we have to suppose that it is based on the symbol that Gurdjieff shared. We would have to confirm this with research and also consider the inclusion of the Koranic interpretations that Bakhtiar proposes.

Psychological 2: Intellect

Spiritual/Biological: Preserve the Eternal Possibility of Self

Cognitive: Capable of Consciousness

Quranic 1: Rational soul

Quranic 2: Reason (*aql*)

So here we have the three-fold division of the self[68]: the lower segments (A) and (B) symbolize the animal soul and refer to the passions. The upper segment corresponds to reason or cognition (C). In the tendency to satisfy desire there is unconsciousness and at the same time preservation of the species. In avoiding harm there is also preconsciousness and this contributes to our preservation as individuals. Conscience accompanies intellect and cognition, simultaneously making possible the eternal preservation of the self.

Bakhtiar offers an everyday example: when we have satisfied our hunger and want to eat more, we have to move away from the table to maintain harmony. This is, she writes, "the basic criterion used here to understand the position of those who commit to inner change. When we have succeeded in doing this, it indicates that we have attained the cardinal virtues of wisdom, temperance … and courage … centered in justice … but only if another confirms that he or she has benefitted from our virtue of justice" (Bakhtiar 2013a: 42). Consequently, we need to achieve a balance between our energies of anger and lust and our reason.

If the function of preservation of the species is balanced, this results in temperance; if the preservation of the individual is balanced, this results in courage; and if the function of preservation of the eternal

---

[68] Throughout her writings, we can note the use of different terms for the same elements. On page 41 Bakhtiar writes "the three-fold division of the self" whereas on page 7 she spoke of the "three-fold division of the soul" (2013a). The explanation for this undifferentiated usage is that the Sufis have four different terms to speak of the non-physical dimensions of the human being: *rub, nafs, qalb* and *aql* (Almaas 2004 : 517). The terminology for the intangible requires an explicit understanding of the cosmology that underlies it, as is the case in German for the concepts of "geist" (spirit) and "seele" (soul).

possibility of self is balanced, this results in wisdom. Thus Bakhtiar proposes another Enneagram symbol in which she places justice at the center, temperance in the lower left third, courage in the lower right third and wisdom in the upper third.

Being centered or balanced, according to this Enneagram, "is to return to the nature within, originated by God (*fitrat Allah*). This nature was actualized at out birth when we were a potential mirror image of the Divine Spirit within us" (Bakhtiar 2013a: 43) but the environment in which we grow up, the people we relate with and the knowledge we experience add dust and rust to the mirror so that after a time we can no longer reflect our original, inner, God-given nature.

Bakhtiar goes on to dedicate several paragraphs[69] to explaining the temporary imbalances of the physical elements that constitute a person. Based on the thirds into which she divides the Enneagram of cardinal virtues (temperance, courage and wisdom, with justice at the center) she numbers the nine points and groups them in threes: preservation of the species, the individual and the self.[70]   Within each of these three groups there are three numbers, one of which corresponds to a qualitative imbalance (depraved negative states: 3, 6 and 9) and the other two are quantitative imbalances (1 and 2, 4 and 5, 7 and 8). Each number has defined characteristics depending on whether the temperament is dry or moist; all the quantitative imbalances are hot, whereas the qualitative ones are considered cold and dry.

---

[69] Pages 43 to 49 of *Rumi's Original Sufi Enneagram*.

[70] This categorization probably corresponds, with some variations, to what several contemporary Enneagram writers call subtypes, centers, triads or instincts.

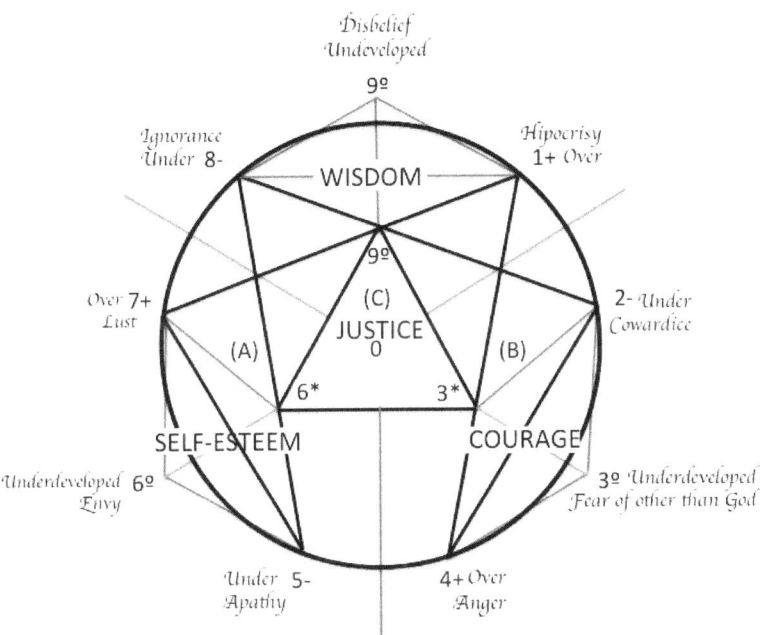

Figure 2: The Sufi Enneagram: the sign of the presence of God, *Wajhullah.* Reproduced, with permission, from cover illustration of Bakhtiar (2013c).

If the physical elements of the body are balanced and harmoniously integrated, the person manifests "the energies of the virtues. While there are hundreds of virtues," she explains, "the original Sufi Enneagram has organized them under four classical[71] headings of temperance ... courage, wisdom and justice" (Bakhtiar, 2013a: 45). To explain the interaction between these, Bakhtiar turns to an 18th century scholar and theologian Shah Waliullah,[72] which is

---

[71] Bakhtiar does not make explicit what she means by "classical", which can generate confusion given that on page 7 of the same book she makes reference to Christian writers such as Thomas Aquinas.

[72] Shah Waliullah wrote *Altaf al-quds* which means *Sacred Knowledge* (Bakhtiar 2013a: 46).

somewhat disconcerting since she is apparently explaining Rumi's 13th century Enneagram.

In order to pass from lust in its three forms (A: 5-, 6°,7+)[73] to temperance, a person must move through seven stages. One of these is tranquility, which requires an enhancing of spiritual power, promotion of spiritual heart and postponement of our desires for pleasure. How? She does not explain, in this stage nor for the other six. To move from anger to courage she indicates another seven stages, and a further seven in the transition from reason to wisdom.

Once a person has left behind the imbalances caused by the different kinds of negativity they are "morally healed ... [and] ready for the world of intuition [which] is entered through the center point or zero" of the Enneagram (Bakhtiar 2013a: 48). She attributes all the above to Rumi but does not give specific references for us to locate it in his writings. She concludes saying that "in order to enter that world [of intuition] you have to leave reason behind", the very method that you used to attain centeredness (Bakhtiar 2013a: 49).

This first chapter ends with a couple of paragraphs that need further explanation. The first refers to the fact that the line that moves through the symbol is called the "Line of the Spirit" and is based on a recurring decimal. The author attempts to delve further into this concept but does not manage to explain it. It appears to be a similar proposal to that which John G. Bennett gives us on the subject:[74]

> "It was observed at the time that a new kind of number appeared when one was divided by three or seven. This we now call a recurring decimal.

---

[73] The three signs of depravity of the temporary qualitative imbalances are marked with the symbol for degree (°), while the numbers 3, 6 and 9 have an asterisk (*) beside them when a virtue has been attained.

[74] It is important to remember that this English writer made an exhaustive study of Gurdjieff's sources and even interviewed Shaykh Abd Allah al-Faiz Daghstani who had taught Gurdjieff.

When one is divided by three an endless succession of threes is obtained, thus:

$1/3 = .33333...$ written $.\,3\,\dot{}$

The addition of another third part to this produces endless sixes, thus

$1/3 + 1/3 = 2/3 = .66666...$ or $.6\dot{}$

When the final third part is added also, endless nines result, thus

$1/3 + 1/3 + 1/3 = 3/3 = .99999...$ or $.9\dot{}$

Hence we obtain a symbolism for one as an endless recurrence of the number *nine.*

When one is divided by seven, however, another and more complex pattern of numbers appears, which contains no threes, sixes or nines. Thus

$1/7 = .142857142857...$ or $.1\dot{}42857\dot{}$

and successive additions of seventh parts reproduce this pattern, but start from different digits thus

$2/7 = .2\dot{}85714\dot{}$

$3/7 = .4\dot{}28571\dot{}$

$4/7 = .5\dot{}71428\dot{}$

$5/7 = .7\dot{}14285\dot{}$

$6/7 = .8\dot{}57142\dot{}$

When the final seventh part is added, this sequence disappears and is replaced by the recurring nines once again. Thus

$7/7 = .9\dot{}$

These properties[75] were combined into a symbol that proved to have amazing significance. It could be used to represent every process that maintains itself by self-renewal, including

---

[75] This is the same definition of the Enneagram by Bennett that we spoke of in the introduction, but now with a context which enables us to understand it better.

of course, life itself. The symbol consists of nine lines and is therefore called the Enneagram" (Bennett 1983: 2).

Another paragraph of Bakhtiar's that requires specification about the sources is the final one in the chapter and refers to Al-Ghazzali (1058-1111 CE) and his book *The Alchemy of Happiness (Kimiya-yi sa'adat)*. Although the quotation has a close relation to suggestions for healing the self, the problem lies in that the reader cannot discern whether Rumi, writing a century later, was aware or took up the ideas of Al-Ghazzali, or whether the quotation is a contemporary inclusion of the modern author's.

Perhaps for a reader who is well acquainted with Laleh Bakhtiar's complete works —which are extensive[76]— it is easier to grasp her ideas with a greater understanding of concepts that she assumes we know, but for those who are only aware of her more recent work on the Enneagram there seem to be some detailed explanations missing that could contribute to better framing her assertions.

Her discovery of the Enneagram in Rumi's *Masnavi* was, as she relates it herself, a moment of inner illumination that enabled her to confirm the Sufi Enneagram in a story in which a couple accuse each other of negative treatments, moving through fear, anger, lust and reason to arrive at a self-restriction which allows them to find balance and brings them toward justice. Similar situations can probably be found in other texts and by other authors who also apply the Sufi moral practice, but for Bakhtiar this episode was paradigmatic. In any case, prudence obliges us to take account of what she herself says: "there is not just one way to understand and interpret the original Sufi Enneagram, but several depending upon the analyst's intuitions and his or her understanding of the major points along the way towards moral healing" (Bakhtiar 2013a: 5-6).

In *The Argument Between a Husband and His Wife,* Rumi's interventions between the paragraphs in which the two spouses speak, clarify the nature of what is happening. The accusations take place between the man and woman, he says, in the external world, but in each of their *selves*[77] a

---

[76] Laleh Bakhtiar started publishing her writings in the 1970s and has covered subjects from Sufism and classical Arab authors, such as Avicenna and Al-Ghazzali, to healing with the name of God and mysticism. She turned 77 in 2015.

[77] *Self* corresponds to the Arab word *Nafs* and, according to Frager and Fadiman, "refers more to a vital process than a static structure of the psyche" (Frager and Fadiman, 2005: Chapter 15). These authors cite Ozak, M (1981) *The Unveiling of Love*, Inner Tradition, NY.

process takes place that we cannot know and which refers to the temporal nature of internal imbalances.

Bakhtiar's interpretation of what happens within the couple appears interspersed with verses from the Koran and the imbalances are classified according to the masculine principle of reason and the feminine principle of passion. These principles are not explained.

In order to understand how this Enneagram works in Rumi's plot about the spouses, we have to remember that the starting point is the idea that the unit is nine. If this unit is divided in seven (four cardinal virtues and three centers) it gives us a series of numbers without the digits 3, 6 and 9. These three numbers form the triangle of the Enneagram, but in this case it is a smaller triangle. The numbers 3, 6 and 9 are balance points within the Line of Change or Spirit and correspond to the positive traits of wisdom (9), courage (3) and temperance (6). When accompanied by the symbol of degree (°) they represent the lack of quality of the segment's characteristic and there is an imbalance which is referred to as undeveloped (Bakhtiar, 2013b:56).

Each passage in the story acquires numbers according to the vice or the virtue that applies and according to its location in the circle. Once this is clear, four levels of treatment apply and can be selected according to the strength of the negative trait: diet, medication, poison and surgery (Bakhtiar, 2013a: 88). The four levels are applied to the negative traits to reduce them and, in reducing the ego, give way to beauty and justice.

All of the above, which remains somewhat obscure in *Rumi's Original Sufi Enneagram*, gains more clarity in *The Sufi Enneagram. The Secrets of the Symbol Unveiled*, which Bakhtiar published in the same year (Bakhtiar 2013b). In this book she develops the Sufi concepts that are needed to understand not only what Rumi proposed but also the bases of Islamic philosophy, with special attention to the Sufi theses. She explains the relationship between the microcosmos and the macrocosmos in order to be able to understand the relation and correspondence between the elements of nature and of the human being. First she explains that in order to understand how the Enneagram works, one needs a spiritual hermeneutic, which "is the bridge over which one intuitively passes between the quantitative and the qualitative, between form and meaning" (Bakhtiar 2013b: 9). From there she continues with the concept of space, rhythm, shape, the relationship between mathematics and nature, the   planets and constellations, until, in Chapter 5, on Matter - after a presentation of humors and temperaments - we find the link to the Sufi Enneagram.

Having come this far, it is important to recall that the goal of Arabian alchemy was the dominion of corporeal matter in order to penetrate the intangible essence of human beings, or their divine aspect. Starting from terrestrial substances, they sought the transformation of the seven body metals, for which it was necessary to find their perfect combination in order to reach the spiritual alchemy. "Transformation comes from the unveiling of the Light of the nature originated by God… [This process] requires … the direction of a master (outer or inner) who is the equivalent of the 'Philosopher's Stone'," writes Bakhtiar, "but none of this can be done without the Presence of God, symbolized by the Sufi Enneagram. The method of spiritual alchemy is based in cosmology rather than metaphysics or theology. … Change takes place through corresponding the external body … with internal psychological states" (2013b: 93). This path of learning cannot be travelled without a language of symbols, in which "the main signs… are the 'hidden' sciences of numbers, geometry and letters" (Bakhtiar 2013b: 93). At the beginning of this path, self-awareness is confused, disorganized, but through spiritual practices like invocation, meditation and self-examination, concentration emerges. "Through spiritual practices, the seeker turns away from the outer world to the inner" (Bakhtiar 2013b: 94).

In Laleh Bakhtiar's explanations to understand the complexity of the Sufi Enneagram we perceive an attempt to give this version priority over any other historical account of the origins of the

Enneagram such as we know it in the second decade of the 21st century. Her superficial disqualification of Gurdjieff and Ichazo leads us to perceive hers as a defensive perspective that does not seek inclusion or complementarity.

There are other authors who take into account Gurdjieff and Ichazo in speaking of the Sufi Enneagram, which strengthens our hypothesis that there is not a single line of continuity in the so-called Sufi Enneagram. This is the case for Abdul Karim Baudino, who writes that, "One of Gurdjieff's missions was to bring spirituality to the sceptical westerner. So, what did he do? He took a spiritual tradition like Sufism, captured its essential concepts, stripped it of emotional connotations and presented it with a technical terminology which would not suggest religious associations" (Baudino, 2014: 67). This quotation is controversial because the historical evidence points to the Christian Churches in the East as the main source for Gurdjieff, as we shall see.

One who did make the effort, throughout his life, to find the similarities and differences between the Sufi and the Christian visions is an outstanding scholar of the 13th century, Raymund Lull, who designed several symbols which, without a doubt, can be considered proto-Enneagrams, and which he may well have enriched during his travels among the Sufi communities around Armenia.

Chapter 6

Raymund Lull: the origin of the virtues and vices in the Enneagram

The contemporary Enneagram of the nine personalities does not make sense without Raymund Lull. Gurdjieff did not work on the nine virtues and nine passions that we now find in many books on the subject. These come from Western Christianity and it was Lull who placed them in a circle with a nine-point star.

This took place in the 13th century, important years both in the Muslim world and in medieval Christian Europe. In that century, in spite of public animosity towards the peoples then referred to as Saracens,[78] among the more learned populations there was an exchange of ideas: from the military to the mystic. This is the time of most of the crusades. Lull, among others, was convinced that in order to stop the Arabs, the Christians had to know them. The Arabs had already translated Aristoteles and amongst their intellectuals there were those that had inherited the learning of the Chaldeans and the Persians. Scholasticism was at its height, in the Islamic Golden Age, and it was this dominant theological-philosophical thought that the Islamic scholars attempted to compare to the Koran. One Western scholar spent much of his life doing the same thing; having once learned Arabic he applied himself to comparing Christianity and Islam. His name: Raymund Lull (in one English variant), Raimundo Lulio (in Spanish), Ramon Llull (in modern

---

[78] Before the 17th century the words Islam or Muslim had not been translated into Latin, Catalan or other European languages, so that medieval Christians used the term Saracen.

Catalan) or Raimundus Lullus (as he signed his texts in Latin).[79] He may well have been the most prolific of all medieval authors: he wrote some 300 works.

Raymund Lull, born in 1232, in Palma de Mallorca, is a central figure in the history of the Enneagram. His obsession to understand, explain and memorize the origins and composition of the universe, including humans, in addition to his mission to convert the Arabs to Christianity, lead him to penetrate the philosophy of some Sufi brotherhoods and Arab scientists until he discovered common areas in both philosophical systems. It is possible that some of the many diagrams he drew were inspired in this convergence, this syncretism may have led eventually to his proto-Enneagrams.

Lull's determination and independence enabled him to set aside something that was typical of his time: the antithesis between Christianity and all that was then considered pagan. On the one hand, he openly fought the Saracens with his weapons of reason, and through his supposedly redeeming speeches, while on the other hand, he showed great curiosity for their philosophy.

We are here facing an Arab-Sufi-Christian bridge who, in collating all that he found most transcendent in the three traditions, can be considered within the legacy of the perennial philosophy. Even if we set aside the Arab influence and only consider what he called his "art" or the ordering of all knowledge, even then we could argue that what he wrote remains applicable today. Lull set out, in the words of Heinrich Cornelius Agrippa, to order all knowledge according to truth.

Two Lullian scholars are invaluable to understand who we are dealing with, the English historian Frances A. Yates (1899-1981)

---

[79] Translator's note: Raymund Lull is remarkable in many ways but also for the variety of translations there have been of his name in different European languages. In addition to those given in the text: Raymond Lulle (French), Raimondo Lullo (Italian). English variants include Raymund Lull and Raymond Lully. We have chosen the former for this publication but in citations we maintain the spelling used by each original author.

and the Italian philosopher Paolo Rossi (1923-2012). On the works of Raymund Lull, Yates has written: "Lullism is no unimportant side-issue in the history of Western civilization. Its influence over five centuries was incalculably great. Lull was much in Italy and manuscripts of his works were early disseminated there and may have been known to Dante... The Renaissance seized on Lullism with intense enthusiasm; in fact, it is perhaps hardly an exaggeration to say that Lullism is one of the major forces in the Renaissance. The Lullian medical theories were known to Paracelsus. ... The system was definitely known to Descartes, who recognized that it was present in his spirit when he conceived his new method of constituting a universal science. There was a large-scale revival of Lullism in eighteenth-century Germany, the end product of which was the system of Lullism" (Yates, 1982: 67).

For his part, Paolo Rossi, like Yates, in addition to studying parts of his oeuvre in great depth, makes some more general comments: "The Lullian art was presented then, as inextricably bound up with the understanding of the objects which constitute the world. Unlike formal logic, it deals with things, and not with words alone. It is concerned with the structure of the world, and not just the structure of discourses. An exemplaristic metaphysics or universal symbolism is at the root of this technique which claims to be able to speak simultaneously of logic and metaphysics, and claims to set out not only the rules which are the bases of all discourses, but the rules according to which reality is structured. ... Lull considered God and the 'divine dignities' to be the archetypes of reality, and he saw the entire universe as a gigantic ensemble of symbols which had their ultimate reference outside the physical world of appearances in the structure of divine being: *'the similitudes of divine nature are impressed in every creature according to their ability to receive them, which varies according to their proximity to the superior level, which is man, so that every creature carries, to a great or lesser extent, the mark of its Maker within itself'*" (Rossi, 2006:

32).[80] Anyone well acquainted with the objectives of the Enneagram needs no further comment. Lull is referring to what, in the Jesuit Enneagram, is called Essence.

It is not possible to know which part of Lull's writings Oscar Ichazo read to create his enneagons of passions and virtues, which he later shared with the 57 participants of a retreat in Arica. Once he had declared his knowledge of Lull's work, as we shall see later, there can be no doubt he was drawing on an infinite source.

If one of the 13th century proto-Enneagrams was created jointly by Lull and a Sufi scholar, this fact should already be recorded in one of the many studies of Lull's work. The Raimundus Lullus Institut at Freiburg University in Germany and the Archivium Lullianum at the Autonomous University of Barcelona have been operating since 1957; both are institutions where there may be someone interested and able to clear up any of doubts brought up here. It would be very positive to unite this task with the search for answers about the origins of the Enneagram.

This does not mean that the history of the Enneagram starts in the 13th century. As we have already said, the ancient cultures settled between the Tigris and the Euphrates, and others in the surrounding regions, contributed to that extraordinary mixture of Chaldean, Helenistic, Egyptian, Persian and Hebrew that connected the mathematical, the corporeal and the intangible, and which then expanded geographically until it reached the scientific-spiritual communities of Europe and also Central Asia, that Raymund Lull also visited in 1301.

---

[80] The italics in this paragraph correspond to the text taken by Rossi from Lull's *Compendium artis demostrativae*, in R. Lulio, *Opera*, Maguncia 1721-1724, vol. III, p.74.

Before coming to that historical event, it is necessary to briefly review Lull's biography.[81] His father was Catalan, born in Barcelona, and had fought for the King of Aragon, James I, the Conqueror, against the Arabs settled in Majorca. For his services in this war of re-conquest which ended in 1229, he was given lands on the island, where Lull was later born into a family with economic and cultural resources. He married young, left the island to serve at the court of James II, where he organized festivities and by association took to wine, women and music. He would later write about this period of his life in *Liber Contemplationis in Deo*: "for thirty years I brought forth no fruit in this world, I cumbered the ground, nay, was noxious and hurtful to my friends and neighbors. Therefore, since a mere tree, that has neither intellect nor reason, is more fruitful than I have been, I am exceedingly ashamed and count myself worthy of great blame" (Zwemer, 1902: 28). Lull had great talents as a poet, writer, sailor, observer, philosopher, horse rider, mystic, mathematician and student of the skies. Each of his biographers highlights some of his facets. In his writing, the German scholar Adolph Helfferich places him at the beginning of Catalan literature.[82]

By 1257 Lull was seneschal at the court of the infant James, who later became James II of Majorca. In that year he was married to Blanca Picany with whom he had 2 children. After a long period at the Court of Aragon, at the age of 32 he returned to Palma de Mallorca and, according to scholars, one day, while writing a love letter, he had a vision of Jesus Christ, an event which recurred several times from 1263 onwards (Ausejo, 2004: 21). For this

---

[81] Several biographies of Lull have been written since the 17th century: by Seguí in 1606, Colleter in 1646, Hauteville in 1666, Parroquet in 1667, Anon 1700, Delécluze in 1840 to name just the first ones. The data given here were taken from a 1902 text published by Samuel M. Zwemer at the Funk & Wagnalls publishing house in New York. The most recent biography of Lull is: *Raimundus Lullus. An Introduction to his Life, Works and Thought*, by Alexander Fidora and Josep Rubio, Turhout, Brepols Publications, 2008.

[82] Helfferich, Adolph (1858), *Raymund Lull und die Anfänge der Catalonischen Literatur*, Berlin: Verlad Von Julius Springer.

reason he decided to renounce everything to dedicate himself to converting the infidel, to record the errors of the Arabs and to found monasteries. Converting Muslims to Christianity has a sociopolitical reasoning: the re-conquest of Majorca had required a major military action which now prevented the ethnic integration of Muslims, who made up a third of the population of the island.

In 1266 the holy man[83] went to a cave on Puig de Randa, a mountain some 20 km East of Palma de Mallorca, where he remained for nine years, while he prepared the structure of his prolific and varied life work. How in a cave? readers might ask. Frances Amelia Yates, the English historian and professor at the Warburg Institute of the University of London, asked herself the same question. She based her research exclusively on primary sources and thus consulted Lull's original manuscripts in several countries. Her conclusion was that in the cave the Majorcan received information which he later systematized in the writing of much of his books. She says, "It was in the year 1274 that Lull had the vision on Mount Randa in which the two primary figures of the Art, the 'A' figure and the 'T' figure, were divinely revealed to him" (Yates, 1982: 112). The important thing here is how the historian reports that Lull received the information: by divine revelation. The historical record indicates that there, in the cave on a mountain in Majorca, Lull visualized, among other things, diagrams that look similar to our contemporary Enneagram.

After his voluntary retreat on Majorca, Lull spends his time writing and taking the Christian message to the Saracens, as the Arabs or Muslims were known in medieval Christianity. To this end he studied not only Christianity, but also the doctrines of Mohammed and the theories of the Arab philosophers, which he read in Arabic, which he had learnt in nine years studying with a slave he had

---

[83] He was beatified by immemorial cult in Majorca but without following the official Vatican paperwork. On various occasions the Bishops of Majorca have attempted to propose his canonization. Most recently, and in recognition of the 700th anniversary of Lull's death, in February 2015 a Majorcan delegation visited the Vatican; but were told that his supposed beatification had to be ratified first.

bought in 1265. While he studied, he wrote texts that allowed him to show the truth of Christianity, but at the same time he started to know the most conspicuous Muslim philosophers in order to have arguments with which to refute them. His texts refuting Averroes[84] date from this time: *Liber de reprobatione errorum Averrois, Liber de existentia et agentia Dei contra Averroem, Ars Theologi et philosophiae contra Averroem.*

The more he studied the Koran, the more he realized that Mohammed had taken elements of Judaism and Christianity but, according to him, without preserving the aspect of love. The more he studied Averroes, the more he wanted to be able to discuss with Arabs who knew his work, and the more he was convinced that, instead of using force, it was possible to reason with them to accept the coincidences between the two religions and to convert some to Christianity or to an acceptance of peaceful co-existence. The more he studied the Canon of Medicine by Avicenna, the more he wanted to know how to reach the perfect equilibrium of humours and natural elements that control the temperaments.

Lull did not consider the Crusades a sure way to recover the holy places of Christianity and he said it with these words: "I see many knights going to the Holy Land beyond the seas and thinking that they can acquire it by force of arms; but in the end they all are destroyed before they attain that which they think to have. Whence it seems to me that the conquest of the Holy Land ought not to be attempted except in the way in which Thou and Thine apostles acquired it, namely, by love and prayers, and the pouring out of tears and of blood" (Zwemer, 1902: 53). While he wrote these reflections he made great efforts to perfect his grasp of Arabic and to build the structure of a book that could strictly and formally demonstrate the Christian doctrine and its cosmogony, seeking always to support his arguments with incontrovertible evidence. As

---

[84] Averroes is the latinized form of Ibn Rushd (1126-1198) an Andalusian Arab scholar. He wrote on many subjects including logic, philosophy, theology, jurisprudence, psychology, politics, music, mathematics, medicine, physics and astronomy.

he progressed he gave his texts to priests and intellectuals around him, asking them to point out any weak arguments they found. He mentions this in the introduction to his *Necessaria Demonstratio Articulorum Fidei*. Eventually, in 1275, he completed a system of logic and philosophy which he called *Ars Major Sive Generalis*. He had begun to replace known scholastic methods with a new art of acquisition, demonstration and confrontation that could encompass all possible knowledge. For this purpose he traced a great many circles and made numerous tables in order to find the different ways in which categories are applied to things. In terms of the Enneagram of personalities, we might say that he was looking for the correlations between human beings and their virtues and vices, as well as the way to return to the absolute. The diagrams were a mnemonic tool that he never abandoned; in his books we can find several circumferences whose interiors are crossed by lines which go to and from nine points indicating human and divine attributes. Paolo Rossi explains, "Each of these nine divisions of the universe corresponde to one of the nine letters of the Lullian alphabet (BCDEFGHIK) in its double significance as absolute and relative predicate, although, according to Lull, some of the significances of these letters change according to the different spheres to which they are applied" (Rossi, 2006:34).

Lull was a master of combinatory art, which, as Elena Ausejo, a researcher at the University of Zaragoza writes, "puts him in direct relation with the Arab sources of combinatory'ics" (Ausejo, 2004: 26).[85] She continues, "Lull proposes a system of combinations of dignities and attributes which, taken two by two, or three by three, can be represented in a triangle or circle, which facilitates the calculation of combinations of 9 elements…" (Ausejo, 2004: 26).

Lull was determined to convince the Saracens that rational Christianity had better arguments, but he knew that the theories of

---

[85] To make this statement Elena Ausejo cites Ahmed Djebbar (1987), L'analyse combinatoire au Maghreb entre le XIIe et le XIVe siécle, *Cahiers d'Histoire et Philosophie des Sciences*, 20: 232-239.

Avicenna, Al-Ghazali and Averroes were then at the centre of Muslim culture and that they were very solid.

In order to study these Arab philosophers and those of Iranian Islam, as well as deepen his own understanding of the cosmogony that he had constituted, Lull undertook a series of journeys. He went to Montpellier, a city in the south of France that in the 13th century was an important cultural center, in which several ecumenical councils were held and where, in 1292, Pope Nicholas IV founded a university. He remained in France for several years, writing, studying and teaching. In 1286 he travelled to Rome, where he convinced Pope Honorious IV to found a school of oriental languages in Paris. Lull could not stop proclaiming the need for Europe to understand the Arabic language. Around this time he published his *Ars Generalis*, in which he affirmed that "A month's practice in the Art would enable one not only to trace the common principles of all the sciences, but also to achieve greater results than those possible through studying logic..." (Rossi, 2006: 32).

At the age of 56, Lull traveled for the first time to Tunis, a western centre of the 13th century Muslim world. There he invited the ulemas and Arab intellectuals to present evidence for and against Christianity and Islam in an open and reasonable comparison. He even promised that if they convinced him he would embrace Islam as his religion. In public places he presented his theory about the lack of love in the being of Allah and the absence of harmony in the attributes that the Koran grants. He claimed that the Koran recognized two active principles of divinity: will and wisdom, but that it excluded goodness and greatness. Christianity, on the other hand —Lull told the Muslims— recognized in God the highest attributes. The Sultan heard of Lull's speeches and suggested the preacher avoid presenting the supposed errors of Islam if he wished to avoid imprisonment. He was soon detained, but not for long, because one of his adversaries, who recognized the intellectual skills of the prisoner, pointed out to the Sultan that it was convenient to prepare Muslims with solid arguments. Lull was expelled from Tunis. From there he went to Naples, Rome and

Genoa where, among other things, he taught and studied Averroes, of whom he always spoke with great respect. He spent much time thinking and writing about the theories of this philosopher on the irreconcilable opposition between faith and knowledge.

He also wanted to read the books of another great Muslim man: Al-Ghazali or Algazel, who had taught at the Nezamiyeh school, in Nishapur, in what is now north east Iran, a place where celebrities like the astronomer and mathematician Nasir al-Din al-Tusi taught. By then Lull had been contact with these Arab scholars who had long conversations with him and shared their knowledge of medicine, astronomy, mathematics and jurisprudence. Lull developed diagrams on the basis of several of these exchanges. He was particularly interested in the point of view of certain Saracens, known as Sufis, with regard to the divine. It is relevant to include an eloquent academic quotation on this subject: "I am indebted to Mr. Robert Pring-Mill[86] of Oxford for a textual quotation from Lully's *Blanquerna*,[87] in which he states that he has adopted devotional methodology from the 'Sufies', called by him religious men among the Saracens" (Shah, 1999: 388).[88]

There can be no doubt that Lull learns of Sufi philosophy. Yates writes of *Blanquerna*, "In his novels of *Felix* and *Blanquerna* we meet with jongleurs and knights, but also with that attractive figure, the Lullian hermit, a solitary who dwells in forests and is found under a tree, contemplating Bonitas, *et alia*, in nature and cancelling out vices with virtues" (Yates, 1982: 116). This action, of canceling vices with virtues appears explicitly in the Enneagram that Laleh

---

[86] English academic who studied Lull.

[87] *Blanquerna* is a religious novel in four volumes. It is titled after the protagonist who wishes to be a friar but falls in love. However, the lovers decide to remain ascetic and their searches make up the body of the novel.

[88] Shah records that Pring-Mill's communication was dated June 26, 1962, quoting the Els Nostres Classics edition of Lull's *Llivre de Evast e Blanquerna*, Vol 3, pp.10.

Bakhtiar attributes to the Sufis, and it is also one of the objectives of the current Enneagram.

Lull becomes so interested in Sufi philosophy that, in 1301, he decides to travel to the area where he knows they continue to teach the work of Al-Ghazali and Nasir al-Din al Tusi, (a celebrated mathematician, theologian and doctor who had died 25 years earlier). He is particularly interested to make contact with the disciples of Tusi because in the visions on Mount Randa there were issues of geometry, arithmetic, music and astronomy. Tusi had been the most important mathematician and astronomer of the 13th century, he knew the work of Euclides, developed original tables on the movements of the planets and wrote a book about the attributes of God: *Awsaf al Ashraf.* Laleh Bakhtiar writes "It is unclear who first formulated the nine points on the circumference of the circle of the Enneagram. It might have been Nasir al-Din Tusi (1201-1274) a contemporary of Rumi or Rumi himself, yet an instrumental facet of the enigmatic origins of the Enneagram has been unveiled" (Bakhtiar, 2013a: 30). In any case, this is a highly relevant aspect for future researchers on the history of the Enneagram.

Lull embarks, then, on a journey to Cyprus and then from Syria he continues to Armenia[89] where he stays for more than a year. This was a year dedicated to study and conversations with everyone who could complement his understanding. "It was in Armenia where he wrote the book titled *The things man should believe concerning God.* Written in Latin it was later translated to Catalan... " (Helfferich, 1858: 86). We know that in his visit to Cilicia (as the Mediterranean coast of Anatolia was then called, now in Turkey) he had a companion; finding out who this was and whether that person left any written text is another subject for future researchers.

---

[89] The information about Lull's travels are taken from Samuel M. Zwemer's text, written in Bahrein in 1902. On page 132 of his book he gives the eight books which he has consulted and cited, Helfferich's publication among them.

Armenia was a principality where a Christian majority was resisting Islam and where the inheritance of the ancient Persian scientists still circulated. Among the non-Christians who were aware of the breadth of Lull's knowledge of the Arab philosophers were some Sufis who knew the life and works of Al-Ghazali; it is highly likely that he also came into contact with the followers of Yalal al-Din Muhammad Rumi or with Rumi himself, since they were contemporaries for 38 years, but we need further research of primary sources in order to be able to confirm this. There is also no empirical evidence of an encounter with the mathematician al-Tusi or his students, but some historians feel that it is still possible to find the information in manuscripts since "Lull was one of the most prolific authors who ever lived. Only a small proportion of his work is generally known, and much of it is still unpublished" (Yates, 1982: 30).[90] In his voyage to Armenia and surroundings Lull had a very precise objective to research and exchange information. Yates is convinced by his Arab sources and that for him some of them were valid interlocutors. She points out that some of them are natural philosophers and writes: "This seems to suggest that Lull knew of a Saracen sect well-versed *in logica et in naturalibus* the members of which were also mystical theologians well-versed in drawing moral and spiritual analogies from material things" (Yates, 1982: 61).

It is important to keep in mind that in the region around Armenia are the places in which Gurdjieff would be born, live and travel seven centuries later and where he would find the symbol of the Enneagram. It is an area in which the inhabitants have been influenced by various traditions and ethnic groups. It would be important to find out where Lull stayed in Armenia that year and who he met. We know he had a great interest in Al-Ghazali, who, at the end of his life, taught at the Nezamiyeh school in Nishapur (now Northern Iran). Rumi was also in Nishapur for time and it was there

---

[90] Yeats was doing her research in the late 1970s; his complete works are now known.

that Nasir al-Din al-Tusi studied philosophy, medicine and mathematics, gaining great prestige.

The quest for disciples or people with knowledge of Al-Ghazali or Algazel arose because he was a learned Sunni who had taught at a madrassa in Baghdad and had engaged in discussion with the Arab elders at the end of the 12th century. He wrote several books, among them some in which he refutes Avicenna. At the age of 37 he left his privileged place as a recognized intellectual to join a Sufi circle and become a dervish,[91] initiating a 10-year spiritual journey. Lull had studied his life and work, and perhaps wished to meet people who belonged to Al-Ghazali's school. Given his eagerness to understand the Sufi philosophy through direct exchange with the people who knew it, it seems feasible that during that year in Armenia he should have encountered people from whom he learned of the 99 divine qualities[92] and was able to compare and contrast them with the attributes of the Christian God. Lull must have applied his method of learning and teaching to all that he came across: the tables with different points of view from which propositions can be formed about an issue, and the diagrams. One of Lull's essays is titled *On the Squaring and Triangulation of the Circle*. His *Ars Major* "is a mnemonic, or, rather, a mechanical contrivance for ascertaining all possible categories that apply to any possible proposition. Just as by knowing the typical terminations or conjugations of Arabic grammar, for example, we can inflect and conjugate any word; so, Lull reasons, by a knowledge of the different types of existence and their possible relations and combinations we should possess knowledge of the whole of nature and of all truth as a system" (Zwemer, 1902: 123).

It is appealing to think that Lull and some of the scholarly Sufis and Arab mathematicians that he encountered in the region could have

---

[91] Sufis who make spinning movements as part of their spiritual practice.

[92] Number which comes from personal notes taken during a course on Sufi tradition given by Dr. Carlos de León, 19th September 2007.

designed the proto-Enneagrams that we know. Why not look for a reliable historical record of a meeting between Lull, Rumi and al-Tusi, since it is chronologically and geographically possible? Why not propose that in the contents of the symbol there is a Christian and a Sufi inheritance? Why are the different parties interested in the Enneagram determined to attribute its origin to their faction, when it may well have been a collective work, as is perennial wisdom?

Is it possible that the diagram with human passions and virtues, in addition to the movements of the celestial bodies and interactions between them and other metaphysical elements, was so convincing that it was conserved and distributed among other Sufi scholars or Arab scientists who integrated it with diagrams of their own design or inheritance and thus could it have passed down generation after generation until it came into Gurdjieff's hands? This is an alternative hypothesis to that of the Chaldean seal lost in eastern Turkestan or of the 9-point symbol traced in rubies on white marble in an Afghan monastery - a point we will return to in a moment.

For us, finding the precise origin, with exact dates and participants, is very meaningful because of the importance the Enneagram has gained in the modern day; but for them, for Lull or Rumi, or for the mathematician and astronomer al-Tusi, the design of the symbol would have been one more activity in their busy days. Rumi was writing his poetry and in a state of ecstacy, while Lull studied, made diagrams and travelled to convert Muslims to Christianity and al-Tusi was absorbed by his work at the observatory of Maragheh. None of them would have given it the historical importance that it has today, perhaps for them it was an explanatory drawing they could all agree on. Whether it was in fact Rumi, al-Tusi or some other Sufi master or Iranian Muslim master who captured Lull's concerns, what matters now is that in the contents of the Enneagram there are indisputable synchronicities in the quest for the highest degree of perfection that a human being can reach while in his body.

Rumi sought to make his way through the 70 thousand veils of darkness and the 70 thousand veils of light that separate the human soul from God, a process which the Enneagram also tends towards from a different cosmogony. A Sufi order in Mexico, the Nur Ashki Yerrahi, in speaking of the end of Rumi's life, makes a reference to the breaking down of all the frontiers, "even those of his own religious or cultural tradition. All the false identities of his limited nature".[93] Precisely this, the false identities of the enneatypes, is what the Enneagram aims to transcend.

The medieval German mystic and dominican preacher Eckhart (1260-1328), of neoplatonic influence, offers testimony of Lull's link to the Sufis. Guraieb writes that Lull was "an intrepid traveller and a no less indefatigable writer, an expert of Arab philosophers, whose language he knew well; who studied Averroism in depth to 'combat' it; he was a Third Order Franciscan, inflamed by love: the Majorcan Raymond Lull, theologian, apostle, missionary and mystic... Meister Eckhart met with him and from his lips heard speak of the Arab Sufis and of their philosophers" (Guraieb, 1976: 143).

There are many angles of this Sufi-Christian relationship that remain to be examined. In his first discussions with the Muslims, Lull used to put forward the description of the seven cardinal virtues and the seven capital sins in relation to the behavior of the Saracens. The seven virtues and sins have been known since the 6th century in *Moralia on Job*, the work of Pope Gregory I, 60th supreme pontiff of the Catholic Church, but let us recall that in the 4th century Evagrius mentions eight *logismoi*, as does another desert meditator and later Church Father, John Cassian, in the same century.

When Lull starts preaching he mentions seven sins and virtues; we can argue that he is a son of the Scholasticism of his time, although

---

[93] Leaflet: *Rumi: monarca del amor divino* [Rumi: monarch of divine love] written by Sheija Amina Teslima al-Yerráhi of the Sufi Order Nur Ashki Yerráhi in Mexico: Sinaloa 213, Colonia Roma, Mexico City. Undated.

on occasions he declares himself against it, but in some of his books he writes not of seven but of nine, as they appear in his diagrams. We would have to discover if, after his exchanges with the Sufis, he decided to increase the virtues and vices to nine, a number which, as we see in the description, he had already used. "'The great art, accordingly, begins by laying down an alphabet according to which the nine letters from B to K stand for different kinds of substances and attributes. Thus in the series of substances B stands for God, C, angel, D, heaven, E, man and so on; in the series of absolute attributes B represents goodness, D, duration, C, greatness; or, again, in the nine questions of scholastic philosophy B stands for *utrum*, C, for *quid*, D, for *de quo*, etc'. By manipulating these letters in such a way as will show the relationship of different objects and predicates you exercise the 'new art'" (Zwemer, 1902: 124).

In his book *Arbor scientiae* (*Tree of Science*), which he started writing in Rome in 1295 and finished a year later, Lull asserts that the principles of the General Art that form part of the moral conception of man are nine, and the rules are also nine, and he illustrates this with a table that contains the keys for the nine letters which are placed around the circumference_(see book cover). On page 86 of the online version of this text (a 1664 print, translated to Spanish), digitized by the Spanish Virtual Library of Bibliographic Patrimony,[94] there are three tables. In the first he included the nine transcendent principles that start with B for *Bondad* (goodness). "This transcendentality of good is based on the transcendent Good in God which is Goodness and Love itself" (Briancesco, 1986: 20). What Lull does with these divine attributes is show where man should be going, by means of their virtues, to reach God. The interesting thing about this table, in terms of showing the connection with the Enneagram, is that it shows the following nine vices or privations of good:

---

[94] http://bvpb.mcu.es/es/consulta/registro.cmd?id=397951 consulted 11/02/2016 - facsimile of a 1664 Spanish translation of Lull's 13th century text.

B: Avarice
C: Gluttony
D: Lust
E: Pride
F: Sloth
G: Envy
H: Anger
I: Deceit
K: Inconstancy

These nine vices that Lull includes correspond to the nine passions of the present-day Enneagram of personalities. If we review Oscar Ichazo's diagrams we find that he mentions: anger, pride, falsehood, envy, avarice, fear, greed, lust and sloth (Ichazo, 1982: 18). And in the Enneagram of passions that Claudio Naranjo offers we find: anger, pride, vanity, envy, avarice, fear, greed, lust and sloth (Naranjo, 1994). The notable difference between what we use now and the 13th century proposal is the addition of Fear, which Lull calls Inconstancy. This is a fundamental difference which would be worth reflecting on and on which we need more precise data. Was Ichazo the one who made the substitution of Fear for Inconstancy at number 6 on the Enneagram? He claimed to know the Lullian diagrams and after his retreat in Arica, Fear appears as one of the vices. In his own words: "In 1943, I inherited my grandfather's library from my uncle Julio, who was a lawyer and a philosopher. It was in an ancient text (a medieval grimoire) about the Chaldean Seal (enneagram) where I first came across this diagram which, for the Chaldeans, was a magical figure. At the same time, I also found the Chaldean seal (enneagram) in the books of Ramon Llull, who … [was] directly influenced by the Sufi theologists".[95]

---

[95] *Enneagram Monthly*. "An interview with Oscar Ichazo by Andrea Isaacs and Jack Labanauskas". Part I: November 1996. Part II: December 1996 and part III: January 1997. Business WorldPress Themes. Portola Valley, Ca. Also online http://www.enneagram-monthly.com/setting-the-record-straight.html consulted 11/02/2016

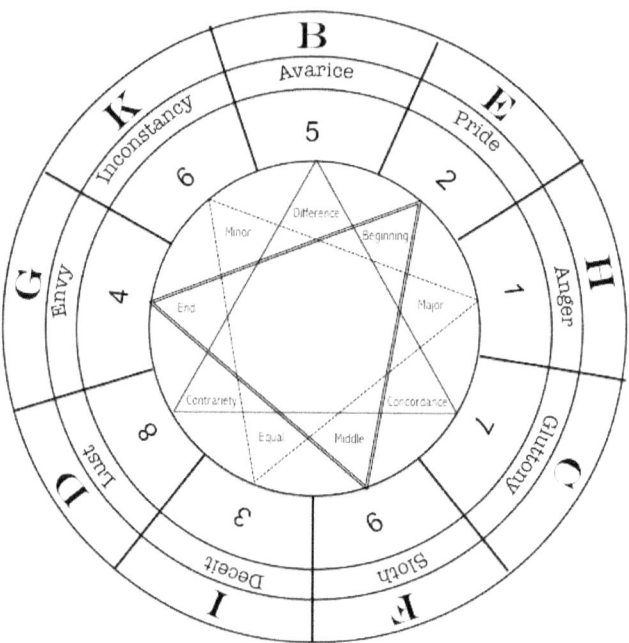

Figure 3: Lull's proto-Enneagram from *Ars Brevis* (1432) reproduced on the cover, transposed into modern English by Adelaida Harrison Lafuente.

Of what there appears to be no doubt is the fact that through Scholasticism, Lull received concepts from the Catholic Church and, although he may have interspersed some Muslim elements, he then bequeathed these to the medieval and Renaissance Christian tradition (although it may not have had a direct, explicit or Church-approved pathway).

Towards the end of his life, Raymund Lull makes a synthesis of what he considers most relevant in his life: "I had a wife and children; I was tolerably rich; I led a secular life. All these things I cheerfully resigned for the sake of promoting the common good and diffusing abroad the holy faith. I learned Arabic. I have several times gone abroad to preach the Gospel to the Saracens. I have for the sake of faith been cast into prison and scourged. *I have laboured fortyfive years to gain over the shepherds of the church and the princes of Europe to the common good of Christendom.* Now I am old and poor, but still I am intent on the same object. I will persevere in it till death, if the Lord permits it" (Zwemer, 1902: 64). He died on 30th June 1315, apparently stoned to death in the public market at Bejäia, formerly known also as Bugia, in modern Algeria, after insisting that the Muslims embrace Christianity, or so legend has it.

This early encyclopedist, as Lull is known, left a vast body of work in Catalan, Arabic and Latin. His original manuscripts were consulted in Rome, Milan, Paris, Munich, at Innichen Abbey and in Venice by the English historian Frances Yates, a specialist in the period. She writes: "Lull was a tremendous system-builder. He built his systems, so he believed, on the elemental patterns of nature, combined with the divine patterns formed by the Dignities, or divine attributes as they revolved on the combinatory wheels" (Yates, 1982:4). In his *Tractatus novus de astronomia*, she finds a correspondence between the four elements, the planets and the characteristics of the temperaments combined with different terms to those commonly known. The element air corresponds to hot and moist; fire to hot and dry; earth is cold and dry and water, cold and wet. Just as the Sufis classify the elements that constitute the human body (Bakhtiar, 2013b:83). Yates, referring to Lull, adds: "Astrological theory involves, of course, that not only the complexion of man (choleric, sanguine, melancholic or phlegmatic) depends on stellar influences, but that all things in nature - stones, metals, plants, animals - must be grouped in accordance with these influences" (Yates, 1982: 16). The Sufi scholars agree on this point also, like Almaas, who speaking of Rumi says that the latter believed that the soul also exists in the mineral, vegetable, animal, human and angelic levels, having various attributes according to the dimensions of reality (Almaas, 2004:520). Lull's manuscripts are illustrated with diagrams, seals and figures that integrate and contrast the elements presented in them.[96]

Frances Yates, also gives account of another influence on Lull which is present in the Enneagram: the Jewish Kabbalah. "Pico della Mirandola knew the Art of Lull, which he associated with the Cabala, and Lullist syncretism and universalism were to prove very congenial to many Renaissance thinkers and magi" (Yates, 1983: 82).

In Lull's original manuscripts, studied by Frances Yates, and in the dozens of books that have been published about him, there are several symbols which could be considered antecedents of the present-day Enneagram. She reproduces them in *Lull & Bruno - Collected Essays*, published in London in 1982. Framed in a great circumference we see nine-pointed stars, one of them with latin labels which indicate nine virtues and another of the different phases of a process of spiritual alchemy.[97] She also mentions another circumference developed by Lull and taken from *Electorium Remundi* by Thomas Myésier,[98] which she describes as follows: "This circle of the universe is divided into nine segments, and in the segments are written the two meanings which BCDEFGHIK have" (Yates, 1982: 76). These same letters appear around the nine-point stars in other Lullian circumferences and signify the nine attributes of God (in Latin: *Bonitas, Magnitudo, Eternitas, Potestas, Sapientia, Voluntas, Virtus, Veritas, Gloria*) and gain greater meaning when we know that, in his dialogues with the Saracens, Lull sought to demonstrate that the

---

[96] For example on page 57 of *Lull & Bruno* (1982), Yates reproduces one of Lull's diagrams elaborated within a circle in which 12 signs are mentioned, the seven planets, the four elements, the temperaments showing contrasts and concordances.

[97] The historian gives them the title of Figures for Lull's *Ars Brevis* taken from his *Opera*, Strasbourg, 1617.

[98] Thomas le Myésier was Lull's disciple in Paris in 1311 and wrote, dictated by Lull, *Vita Beati Raymond Lulli*, which is considered to be practically an autobiography, according to a note by Elena Ausejo (Actas del Octavo Congreso de la Sociedad Española de las Ciencias y de las Técnicas, 2004, page 21).

Christian God was greatly attractive so that they should come to him. With regard to this Yates says, "in each book, elemental theory leads immediately to theological analogies, often accompanied by lamentations that these things are not demonstrated more clearly to the Saracens so that they may thereby be converted to the Catholic faith" (Yates, 1982: 35). Hypothetically, we can suggest that in his attempt to approach the Islamic cosmogony, in order to illustrate his theory, Lull aligned himself with the nine-pointed star of the Sufi Enneagram: "In forms of the Art later than the *Ars demostrativa*, Lull changed the number of Dignitates on which the Arts were based from sixteen to nine" (Yates, 1982: 99).

Lull held in his hands a symbol with some elements of the Enneagram. How much was there of Sufi and how much of Christian Scholasticism in the design of the symbol? In relation to Yates' remarks, did he design the symbol himself? Rohr and Ebert think so.[99] They both state that Lull was determined to find points of coincidence between the religions and he considered the understanding of the human vices and virtues as a property common to both. The starting point that these Enneagram scholars find in Lull's texts[100] or the shared question of truth in the principle religions are the nine names of the characteristics of God that Lull distributes clockwise around a circumference, joined by lines that cross the circle, passing through the center which represents the ineffable mystery of God. Lull elaborates a second figure, a circle with three triangles inside it, which represents the relative principles which describe the proximity and the difference between God and his creatures. About these circles Rohr and Ebert write, "The closeness of both these figures to the Enneagram figure is

---

[99] Richard Rohr and Andreas Ebert wrote *The Enneagram: a Christian Perspective*, first published in English in 1995; the original was in German and was published as *Das Enneagramm: Die neun Gesichter der Seele* in 1989.

[100] Lull's book cited by Rohr and Ebert is: *Vom Freund und dem Geliebten: Die Kunst der Kontemplation*, Zurich and Dusseldorf, 1998. (Apparently a compendium of two of Lull's books *Book of the Lover and the Beloved*, and *The Art of Contemplation*.)

unmistakable. Like the figures of Evagrius, Lull's schemata could also be called 'proto-Enneagrams'" (Rohr and Ebert, 2001: 15-16).

There is another aspect to resolve, however: Lull's symbols are made up of a circumference and within it three closed triangles, that is to say they do nos contain a hexad, hexagram or six-line figure (which unites the numbers 1-4-2-8-5-7) with the exact inclination of the lines that we find in the modern Enneagram, whereas the Sufi symbol in Bakhtiar's book does, although her triangle is smaller than in the contemporary Enneagram figure. How does Gurdjieff get to the symbol as we know it today? Yet another question that remains unanswered.

The interest in the evolution of human beings is the important thing in the Enneagram; the rest, where the original seal came from, or the nine-pointed star is not essential, although the search for the origins and the trajectory of the symbol that represents the Enneagram is important, not only because its genesis is not reliably documented, but —above all— because the lack of empirical evidence has led to competition between different schools of thought interested in the Enneagram.[101] It has also, and this is worse, increased the resistance on the part of some academics, to include it in university studies on characterology,[102] which is one way to begin to know about a series of processes of much greater scope. Even if it only stops at the game of the nine personalities, the instrument is useful because, from the start, the equilibrium between vices and virtues produces elements which shed light on action and communication which are helpful for a better

---

[101] This competition over the source of knowledge has even become legal wrangling. In 1992 the Court of Appeal of the United States received a case presented by the Arica Institute Inc. against H. Palmer and Harper & Row Publishers, No. 771 Docket 91-7859. It was dismissed.

[102] Gradually, the number of clinical psychologists emerging from universities who include the Enneagram among their techniques is increasing. The testimony and work of Jerome Wagner Ph.D. at Loyola University in Chicago is interesting. He writes, "A typography I've found specially useful is the Enneagram" (Wagner, 2010: 18).

understanding of the messages we receive from others and for a greater awareness of the messages we emit.

After his death, Lull's work began to cause concern and enthusiasm in Spain and reached the ears of the Tribunal of the Holy Office of the Inquisition. The Inquisitor General of the Crown of Aragon, Nicolau Eimeric (1316-1399) went to great lengths to demonstrate that Lull was a heretic. His efforts made their mark and by the 15th century his books circulated mainly in convents, monasteries and some universities. The following century Philip II of Spain read some of Lull's texts and made himself a protector of his work, while the Dominican order continued to point out the heresies the 14th century inquisitor identified. Lull's work provoked great controversy and this encouraged its diffusion, although many of his students were being processed by the Inquisition at the same time. This was the case for Sebastian Riera, scholar of Lullian theology at the General Study in Majorca in the 1660s.[103] Although the ecclesiastic tribunals threatened those who were interested in Lull's work, three centuries later, in the heart of Christian Europe, the symbol re-appeared, with the incline of the lines as we know it today, in the writings of a Jesuit called Athanasius Kircher, three centuries before Gurdjieff. To understand Kircher, we need to go back to the origins of the Society of Jesus to which the orientalist scientist belonged.

---

[103] The inquisitorial process is described in Ramis Barceló, R (2013) El proceso inquisitorial al catedrático lulista Sebastián Riera, *Revista de la Inquisición (Intolerancia y derechos humanos)* (2013) Vol. 17, 107-139, ISSN 1131-5571. The journal is open access and the article can be obtained at this website: https://dialnet.unirioja.es/descarga/articulo/4616704.pdf

Chapter 7

The intermittent
contribution of Ignatian spirituality

In this chapter we will take a look, *grosso modo*, at some moments of the visible history of the Society of Jesus, from its beginnings to the present, with a very specific objective: to identify how and to what extent the Jesuit spiritual quest coincides with the content and practice of the Enneagram. The questions that frame this inquiry are: why did so many Jesuits develop a great enthusiasm for the Enneagram in the 1970s? Why did Pope Francis take the trouble to mention the Enneagram at a conference of Latin American Bishops? Could it be because many Jesuits who teach it have grasped that self-knowledge is an essential step in any altruistic endeavour? Is there an area of convergence for the Enneagram and Ignatian spirituality?

Trying to answer these and other questions calls for a historical review to locate enneagramatic elements in Jesuit writings. In the 17th century, Athanasius Kircher, S.J., leaves documentary evidence in the proto-Enneagrams he creates, but even before that there are other philosophical texts which shed light on our questions.

As a starting point, let us go back to Ignatius Loyola, founder of the order. The Society of Jesus began in 1540 in Spain and spread gradually to several countries. One of the central documents, written by Loyola[104] himself, and which has remained current since the 16th century, is about the spiritual exercises. As we shall see in a

---

[104] In addition to the *Spiritual Exercises*, Ignatius Loyola wrote an *Autobiography*, *The Constitutions*, *The Spiritual Diary* and many letters which have been published in several volumes.

moment, it is very probable that Pope Francis had the first week of these spiritual exercises in mind when he mentioned the Enneagram.

The Jesuits are known for their interest in studying the world around them, for their polished intellect and for their involvement in social actions. Some members have left a significant mark in the places where they worked, suggesting that this line has continued over the centuries. Before Ignatius Loyola's death, two Spanish Jesuits were born who would contribute, with their studies and writings, to give strength and visibility to the work of Ignatius in the 16th and early 17th centuries. They were Luis de Molina (1535-1600) and Francisco Suárez (1548-1617). They are both part of Jesuit Scholasticism, which already had some modern elements, given that in their writings they participate in the scientific debates of the time.

Luis de Molina introduced the notion of mediate knowledge (*scientia media*) in between intellect and divine grace, distancing himself from the prevailing Thomists around him. He opposed determinism and supported free will. In his writings we find a precedent which might explain the proclivity of some Jesuits for the Enneagram. Jesuit philosophy at the time stressed human liberty alongside the action of divine grace, that is to say, they underlined the effort that human beings had to make to eradicate their vices and reach virtue, while the Dominicans had a more deterministic view. This led to a controversy known as *De auxiliis* which lasted from 1582 to 1607 and "which developed between Spanish theologians, Jesuits and Dominicans, who debated passionately on the subject of human liberty and the designs of an omniscient and omnipresent God" (Zermeño, 2003: 61). To date, a numerous group of Jesuits — who have found in the Enneagram an apt instrument to know their own weaknesses and improve upon them— know that human beings must make an effort to achieve their personal evolution and for that purpose they must exercise free will.

Historian Guillermo Zermeño writes that Jesuit philosophy was viewed with suspicion by the Spanish Inquisition, but in Portugal it was well received, which is why it was in Lisbon, in 1588, that Luis de Molina published *Concordia liberi arbitrii cum gratia donis*, in which he systematized the contributions of other Jesuits which highlighted the purpose of free will.

Francisco Suárez, for his part, writes a text about the principle of individuation which would later by cited by Descartes, Spinoza, Vico and Hume, among others. He generates much controversy in ecclesiastic and intellectual circles, for which he feels obliged to explain the basis of his thesis to the General of the Society of Jesus. He writes a letter saying, "People have the custom of reading by sections, reading out of tradition, one for the other, without looking deeply, and removed from the sources, which are our sacred and human authority and also reason, each thing in its place. I have tried to step away from this path and look at the roots of things, which leads to my things ordinarily appearing somewhat novel" (in Bergadá, 1950: 1923). Suaréz was named *Doctor Eximius* by the Pontiff.[105]

The influence of Molina and Suárez on 17th century thought was enormous. One example is their contribution to Leibniz: "His early training at Leipzig was scholastic, and reflections on Molina and Suarez become his distinctive intellectual ammunition" (Collins, 1998: 592). We mention these two cases because they demonstrate the continuity of Jesuit thought through the centuries. This is a religious order that thinks, questions, decides and acts from free will, while also appealing to divine grace.

Another Jesuit whose work deserves more research is Matteo Ricci, born in Macerata, Central Italy, in 1552 and student of another

---

[105] Several of Francisco Suárez's books, edited at the beginning of the 17th century in Germany, are currently held at the Palafoxiana Library in Puebla, Mexico. He was "probably the most consulted author for philosophy students at Jesuit Colleges" writes Zermeño (2003). This was before the expulsion of the order in 1767.

Jesuit, Christopher Clavius, who taught mathematics and astronomy. Ricci lived in China for 28 years. While he learnt the language he prepared a *mapamundi* with the European concept of cartography, which caused great surprise and recognition among the scientific community. He soon realized that in order to teach people about Christianity he had to understand the religious cosmogony of the Chinese and this led him to learn about Taoism and Confucianism. He understood that his interlocutors saw the world as an organized whole which emerged from the nature of the universe, in which each part acts in relation to the other parts. As he observed the intrinsic and not causal capacity of the game of interweaving and opposing all existing elements, he gradually adopted a Taoist vision of life that became a background to his writing. A century later, this would influence Leibniz and through him the first traces of organicism emerged in Europe, which is a similar perspective to that of the Enneagram.

Matteo Ricci is admired and followed by another notable Jesuit who lives for most of the 17th century: Athanasius Kircher (1602-1680) was born in Hessel, Germany,[106] near Fulda Abbey where the Society of Jesus had a college, which he attended. He was ordained in Paderborn, where he learnt Greek and Hebrew and later studied philosophy in Cologne. In 1630, "he asked the Superior General of the Order to send him as a missionary to China, but his request was rejected and he had to make the best of collecting materials sent to Europe by other missionaries" (Gómez de Liaño, 2001: 36). Among these missionaries, was Matteo Ricci, to whom Kircher pays homage in his iconography.[107] In 1635 Kircher traveled to Rome, where he stayed for the rest of his life, studying an enormous variety of subjects and phenomena from antediluvian fossils and

---

[106] Information taken from the chapter on the life of Kircher in: Gómez de Liaño, Ignacio (2001) *Athanasius Kircher. Itinerario del Éxtasis o Las Imágenes de un Saber Universal*, Madrid: Siruela.

[107] Among the 520 Kircher illustrations in Gómez de Liaño's selection, two are dedicated to Ricci. See pages 160 and 173; in both he exalts Ricci's understanding of Chinese philosophy.

volcanic eruptions to questions of high theology.[108] Among his published works, two seem pertinent for the history of the Enneagram. The first, dated 1652, is titled *Oedipus Aegyptiacus*[109] and includes a drawing of the Tree of Life from the Jewish *Kabbalah* with a description of the *sefirot* in Hebrew. In his study of Kircher's images, Gómez de Liaño writes of the Tree of Life: "Given that the Tree is a diagram of maximum universality, it serves as a key to open the potentialities of all the levels of the Universe" (Gómez de Liaño, 2001: 236). This would be Gurdjieff's objective also, three centuries later.

A contemporary Kabbalist describes the Tree of Life as follows: "It expresses the connection between man and the Infinite Light, which is the plane of essence, faced with the multiplicity of its manifestations.... Through the symbolism of the Tree, the Kabbalah postulates that all the gigantic network of the Manifestation[110] is structured like an organic whole which participates of one life" (Madirolas, 2005: 21). We are dealing with a map of conscience, continues the same author, which is not only a creative effusion, but also a return path. Just as in the case of the Chaldean Oracles or the Enneagram, we might add, which is why it would be worth delving a little deeper into Kircher's affirmations that "all the ancient wisdom of the Jews, was received in Egypt, via Moses" (Gómez de Liaño, 2001: 236).

---

[108] An illustrated sample of the variety of subjects touched upon by Kircher can be found in a review by Ignacio Gómez de Liaño (2001).

[109] This text by Kircher is in the Palafoxiana Library in Puebla, Mexico. The full title is *Oedipus aegyptiacus, hoc, est, Universalis hieroglyphicae veterum doctrinae temporum iniuria abolitae instauratio opus ex omni orientalium doctrina & sapientia conditium, nec non viginti diversarum linguarum authoritate stabilitum.*

[110] The *manifestation*, according to a footnote in Madirolas' text, is the totality of existence; it is a broader term than *creation*, which it includes, and has an additional component signifying awareness.

In Gómez de Liaño's explanation of this Tree of Life, there is another important element which should lead Enneagram researchers to further investigate the Jewish Kabbalah: "From the cosmological point of view the seven inferior *sefirots* are the seven planets of the Chaldeans, whereas the superior triad signifies - according to Kircher - the sphere of the fixed stars, the *primum mobile* and the empyreal. They also corresponde with the ten names of God, the ten archangels, the nine angelic orders plus the souls of men and the human constitution" (Gómez de Liaño 2001: 236). We would have to find out if the seven *sefirots* mentioned by Kircher have any correspondence with what Gurdjieff and his direct disciples call the Law of Seven, which they use to explain the evolution of the universe and human beings, in the same way that the three superior *sefirots* could be related to the Law of Three, that talks about the three forces involved in any act of creation.

The other book by Kircher that could be important for us, is one that was distributed in 1665 with the title *Arithmologia sive de abditis Numerorum Mysteriis*. At the beginning, in one print, it shows all the central elements of the current Enneagram symbol, that is to say the sphere, the triangle, the hexad and lines between the nine points of a star. It is surprising that the lines of the hexad are shown with the same angles as the modern Enneagram symbol, which is not the case in Lull's proto-Enneagrams. The question that arises could lead us to another hypothesis: Did Kircher find, in some old Egyptian papyrus that he studied, a nine-pointed star like the one he draw in his *Arithmologia*? Did he modify one of Lull's diagrams? I hope someone will come up with the empirical evidence to answer these questions in the near future.

Figure 4: Detail of Kircher's proto-Enneagram on frontispiece of *Arithmologia* (1665). (Zentralbibliothek Zürich NE 898)

Kircher carries out research in areas of human knowledge as dissimilar as acoustics, magnetism, vulcanology, optics, egyptology, sinology, biblical archaeology, arithmology, and musicology. "Determined, as he was, to find a universal science and writing —a project that would enthuse a young Leibniz— Kircher placed as the foundation of this singular edifice, if not as the dome that would crown it, Platonic-Pythagorean metaphysics, the combinatory logic of Raymond Lull and the gnosis of the hermetecists" (Gómez de Liaño, 2001: 9). Lull appears to have been a definitive influence for him, as was Nicholas of Kues (1401-1464), one of the first philosophers in whom we can detect the transition from medieval to Renaissance thought.

It is important to emphasize the point that Kircher knew the work of Lull. In fact, almost four centuries later he also developed a Tree of Science similar to Lull's, but allocating the branches not to the medieval sciences but to those of the 17th century. In his writings the elements of the Enneagram are evident: "For the Platonian", writes Kircher, "the triad is the exemplary idea of the triple world, it is the true equilibrium of Pythagorean justice, the triangle of divine nature, the complement of all imperfection and of one-armed nature, the only centre of the driving passion of Proteus' forms, the foundation of the mystic pyramid, the source and origin of bodies, and nothing is more fecund than the triad for all mystic meanings and the deepest explanations of things" (Gómez de Liaño, 2001: 20).

Kircher ventured into all the traditions he had access to in his quest for a way for humans to return to the Absolute, which he identified with God. In an attempt to synthesize his work, Gómez de Liaño writes, "Here we have a system of thought, Kircher's philosophy: in well proportioned fusion, he presents us with the Platonic theory of archetypal ideas, the Unity and the procession of beings from the Unity by Plotinus, the mysticism of numbers from Pythagoras and the Kabbalah, the syncretism of the hermeticist texts, the Lullian scale of being and the theology of pseudo-Dionysius the Areopagite. It is, without a doubt, the last great flare of Renaissance syncretic philosophy,   whose exaltation of the Mind and the World propitiated the mundane investigations, the development of mathematical and physical studies, at the same time as it exalted the values of imagination and the mystic union with divinity through love. This philosophy saw in the universe the hieroglyph or the talisman of divinity, a magical reality that unites the superior and the inferior in the same way that magic is the art of creating links between different planes of reality" (Gómez de Liaño, 2001: 23). This union of the superior and the inferior is an element of continuity that has not been lost from the Chaldeans to the present.

Gómez de Liaño assures us that the Jesuits of the 17th century, and in particular the superiors of the Society of Jesus, were proud of the fact that a distinguished member of their Order, who was publicly identified with the uses and objectives of the Order, was also a visible leader in the study of hermeticism and in the understanding of the sciences, knowledge and human occupations.

Kircher's texts were also known to Jesuit priests in various provinces of the Americas. One example is Mexico, for which we have documentary sources. Carlos de Sigüenza y Góngora, who was ordained in 1662 at the monastery in Tepotzotlán, was one of the great intellectuals of the Viceroyalty of New Spain. His work included diverse subjects and one text stands out, his *Libra Astronomica y Philosophica*, in which he refutes the thesis of another Jesuit, Eusebio Francisco Kino, on the subject of comets and related matters.

There is evidence that the Jesuit Sigüenza worked on Kircher's texts. In his *Manifesto against the comets stripped of their power over the timid*[111] Sigüenza mentions two of Kircher's works: *Mundus Subterraneus*[112] and *Itinerarium Exstaticum*. Sigüenza's writings and books, along with some mammoth bones that he appreciated, were bequeathed in his will to the Colegio Máximo de San Pedro y San Pablo.[113] That packet included the copies of Kircher's work that Sigüenza had studied. It included the frontispiece of the *Arithmologia* which contains the antecedent of the Enneagram symbol. Charles III of Spain ordered the expulsion of the Jesuits from all Spanish territories in 1767 and when they were deported part of the libraries in their colleges and monasteries were left to what is today the Palafoxiana Library in the historic center of Puebla. The library is today the depository of 14 books in Latin by Kircher, attractive study material for any researchers who wish to search for details about this 17th century proto-Enneagram, and evidence also of the Jesuit interest in Kircher's work.

---

[111] See complete text in: Trabulse Elías (1992) *Historia de la Ciencia en México*, Mexico: Fondo de Cultura Económica, pp. 146-152.

[112] *Mundus Subterraneus* is in the Palafoxiana Library, Puebla, Mexico, classified as follows: Kircher, Atanasio, *Mundus Subterraneus, in XII libros, Amstelodami, apud Joannen Janssonium á Waesberge & filos,* 1678.

[113] Information drawn from Guillermo Tovar y de Teresa (1991) *La Ciudad de los Palacios: Crónica de un Patrimonio Perdido*, Editorial Vuelta, Mexico, Vol. II: p. 183

The Society of Jesus expanded significantly beyond the boundaries of Europe and in some countries it came to have considerable power, not only in its daily labors with the people, but also in administrative and political affairs. This is the case in Mexico, where the Jesuits arrived in 1572 and very soon founded colleges and expanded; by the 17th century there was evidence that a group of priests were devoted to the humanistic defence of indigenous peoples, and some, like Francisco Javier Clavijero, spoke Nahuatl, and translated the Meshica codices and had studied the situation of the Spanish Crown.

Some authors consider these Jesuits precursors to Mexican independence. This episode is not unimportant because it is part of what some consider the "1814 restoration" or the second phase in the history of the Society. In 1767 Charles III of Spain expelled the Society of Jesus from Spanish territory, with a special mention for the Jesuits in the American colonies. Six years later the Pope in Rome issued a Decree of Suppression of the Jesuit Order. It was only in 1814 that this decree was rescinded and the Jesuit Order "restored". One historian writes, "In the 1830s, in the heat of debates about the relevance of the Society of Jesus returning to Mexico, some distinguished publicists and historians promoted the representation of the Jesuits as precursors to the country's independence" (Fabre et al, 2014: 234). Four decades after the Decree of Suppression, when Mexico had already initiated the process of independence from Spain, the full legal Restoration of the Society of Jesus took place on 7th August 1814.

The repercussions were felt at this time and not only in the American colonies. The Decree of Suppression in 1773 also affected the Society in Europe. With the passing of time, things returned to normal, reaching the highest point of the Restoration in the mid 20th century, before entering another phase of concerns and projects that clashed with the Second Vatican Council. An account of these events seems necessary to understand how a considerable number of Jesuit priests become involved with the Enneagram in the last three decades of the 20th century and the first two of the 21st century.

The Jesuits and the Enneagram in the 20th century

Before we embark on the account of the late 20th century, it is important to mention a Jesuit, born in the 19th century, who wrote, in the first decades of the 20th century, a book which has several areas of coincidence with the Enneagram: he places the Absolute as creator of the universe and proposes that the tendency of the universe is to return to the Absolute. He was Gurdjieff's contemporary, yet their paths do not appear to have crossed. His understanding was generated little by little, through travel, study, meditation and inner-reflections throughout his life. He came to similar conclusions to those of the Enneagram that explains the universe and even surpassed them. His name was Pierre Teilhard de Chardin (1881-1955). This Jesuit was born in the French village of Sarcenat, in the Auvergne. In 1899 he began his novitiate in Aix-en-Provence. He studied natural sciences, philosophy and mathematics, then theology in Sussex, United Kingdom, and continued with a Doctorate in Natural Sciences at the Sorbonne in Paris. He participated in the First World War as a priest and a stretcher bearer; from 1923 to 1946 he lived in China and his books were censored by the Vatican from then on. Later he dedicated himself to a series of scientific investigations which would continue until his death. In 1957, two years after his death, the Congregation for the Doctrine of the Faith prohibited his texts and they were removed from libraries and bookshops. It was only in 1962, with the opening of the Second Vatican Council, that Pope John XXIII lifted the prohibition on Teilhard de Chardin's works, but the damage had been done and the fear of reading them was already widespread. His complete works were saved thanks to a few young Jesuits who convinced Jean Mortier, Teilhard's secretary, that she should inherit all his papers; the will was made and nothing was lost.[114]

What does Teilhard de Chardin say? His oeuvre is vast. Ediciones du Seuil has published his original texts in French in 13 volumes, made up of 187 long essays, without counting his diaries and letters. If we had to summarize them in a few words, we would say that what he writes about is the quest to explain how and to what extent both matter and human thought are profoundly involved in the evolution of all that exists. This evolution progresses towards greater complexity, and "as I understand it here, complexity is an organized, and consequently centred heterogeneity" (Teilhard de Chardin, 1966: 222). Since he never stopped being a Jesuit with Christian faith, he tried to unite, in his words, the phenomenon of man, the universe and the divine milieu.[115] He never mentioned, as far as we know, the word Enneagram, but he did write about the noosphere, which is also studied by one of the most lucid exponents of the contemporary Enneagram: Anthony Blake.

What is the noosphere and what relationship does it have to the Enneagram? The noosphere, writes the Jesuit, is "the Earth's thinking envelope" (Teilhard de Chardin, 1980: 31). Elsewhere he writes, "Impossible still to form an idea of the modes or appearances that might be adopted by this formidable hyper-cell, this brain of brains, this Noosphere woven by all intelligences at once on the surface of the earth" (Teilhard de Chardin, 1966: 230).

Teilhard takes the term noosphere from the Russian scientist Vladimir Vernadsky (1863-1945) whom he cites. This physicist and mathematician from the University of St. Petersburg considers that the Earth is made up of five integrated areas: the lithosphere or solid

---

[114] The detailed and documented narration of these events can be found in J.A. Franco Esparza (1997) *Teilhard de Chardin, una cosmovisión para el año 2000*, Mexico: JGH Editores SA de CV.

[115] *The Phenomenon of Man* (1976) Harper Perennial, and *The Divine Milieu* (2001) Harper Perennial, are two of Teilhard's published works.

sphere, the atmosphere, the biosphere, the technosphere (produced by all that is made by mankind) and the noosphere, or sphere of human thought.[116] He also proposed that the three stages of Earth's evolution are: geological evolution, biological evolution and cultural evolution. Teilhard de Chardin perceived this with Christian enthusiasm because everything in existence had to advance towards the Omega Point (a term coined by him) or the highest point in the evolution of conscience, pre-existing the appearance of human beings and the universe and towards which everything would tend to return.

This is where Blake's ideas —the Enneagram scholar and practitioner— converge with Teilhard's. In the diagrams the Englishman presents of the Enneagram of nine points of evolution there is a first octave that corresponds to the biosphere, a second octave that corresponds to the technosphere, and a third octave that corresponds to the noosphere (Blake, 1996: 208). See Figure 5, Blake's *Nine Points of Evolution*. In the center of the diagram is the symbol of the Enneagram and in each octave we find his elements placed in the hexad, leaving the triangle free, whose three parts represent the movements of the octaves: point 3, the human disturbance in the global ecosystem, point 6, the beginning of the solution and at point 9 the collection of all the interpretations about the origin of man forming part of the knowing mind or noosphere.

---

[116] This sphere of human thought appears not only in the work of the Russian scientist Vernadsky, but also we can also perceive it in Chinese philosophy: the theory of Zhineng Qigong, where the Noosphere is called Yi-yuan Ti: "Thus the chi of unified human consciousness (Yi-yuan Ti) occupies a higher level in the evolutionary spiral than original Hunyuan chi...", in *Life More Abundant. The Science of Zhineng Qigong, principles and practice. Based on the original teachings of Ming Pang* (1999) p. 104.

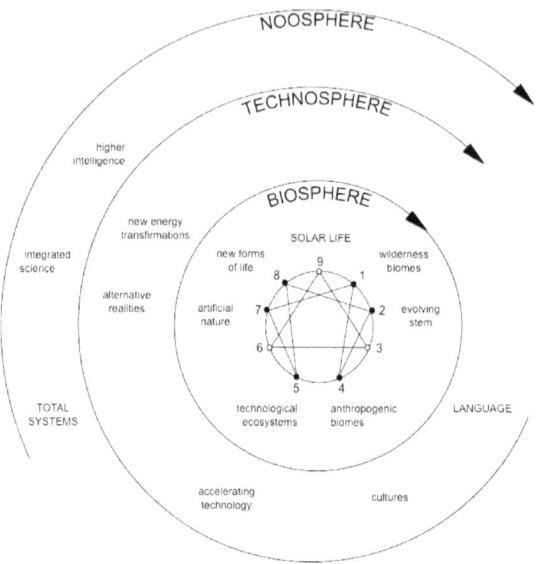

Figure 5. Blake's *Nine Points of Evolution*.
Reproduced, with permission, from *The Intelligent Enneagram* (Blake, 1996: 208).

In the section on the disciples of Gurdjieff's disciples (in Chapter 9) we will see more of Blake's arguments. For now we will just transcribe a paragraph by Ouspensky which inevitably leads us to associate him with the thesis of the Jesuit Teilhard: "In right knowledge the study of man must proceed on parallel lines with the study of the world, and the study of the world must run parallel with the study of man. Laws are everywhere the same, in the world as well as in man. Having mastered the principles of any one law we must look for its manifestation in the world and in man simultaneously. Moreover, some laws are more easily observed in the world, others are more easily observed in man. Therefore in certain cases it is better to begin with the world and then to pass on to man, and in other cases it is better to begin with man and then to pass on to the world" (Ouspensky, 2001[1949]: 122). In the case of Teilhard's scientific endeavour, he preferred to seek out the workings of the world, to understand man in it. This extraordinary Jesuit died in 1955, leaving a body of work as vast as it was unknown.

At this point we must return to the objective of providing some elements to explain why the Enneagram was so popular among Jesuits.

In the second half of the 20th century two parallel events take place: the Second Vatican Council and the beginning of Jesuit interest in the Enneagram. 1962 was a year of renewal in the Catholic Church and its religious orders. Let us remember that the Council ends in 1965 and the complete official documents begin to be published. In the same year the Jesuits name a new Superior called Pedro Arrupe, who will remain at the head of the Society of Jesus until 1983.

Arrupe embodied the post-Council life of the Catholic church. He was president of the Union of Superiors General of Religious Orders and as such participated in various synods of bishops (1967, 1969, 1971, 1974) to prolong the Council. The synod of 1974 dealt with the subject of the relationship between evangelization and human promotion, that is to say, it was about subjects related with human beings of flesh and blood, just as they are. We have to remember that it is precisely around this time that the Enneagram gains ground among the Jesuits. The first documented record is from 1971, when the Jesuit Patrick O'Leary states that he learnt about the Enneagram on a course given by another Jesuit, Bob Ochs, at Loyola University in Chicago.

The atmosphere at that time within the Society of Jesus encouraged great openness and a sustained attempt to apply the Council's documents. Many Jesuits, used to thinking for themselves, found in the Enneagram a concrete way to work with the faithful, with a view to linking the human condition with evangelization, starting with an exercise of self-knowledge and personal growth. This, in addition to the fact that their Father Superior, Arrupe, was concerned to make the explicit link between the Second Vatican

Council and the mission laid out by their founder Loyola. "The Second Vatican Council has helped us to better understand the thought of St. Ignatius" (Madrigal, 2014: 29).

These are enthusiastic and receptive times for the Jesuits. During the 1970s they read the Council documents and renew their own territories of action. In 1980 Father Arrupe, writes a document entitled *The Trinitarian Inspiration of the Ignatian Charism* in which he said: "The thesis I propounded [last year at the Ignatian Center of Spirituality] was that a proper understanding and application of 'our way of proceeding' enables the Society today, in a line of historical continuity, to attain the double objective that Vatican II has set for religious institutes: a return to the sources of their particular charism and at the same time an adaptation to the changed conditions of the times" (Arrupe, 2001 [1980]: 1). In their General Congregations XXXI and XXXII the members of the Society of Jesus make a great effort to adjust and adapt to what is happening in the world.

Some Jesuits in the 1970s called the Enneagram "the Sufi numbers" with full understanding that they were referring to a system that came from a different tradition to the Catholic church, but they also had in mind that the Second Vatican Council propitiated dialogue with other religions. It would seem that their conscience was not only at ease but also enthusiastic.

Forty years after this moment of renewal, the Catholic church is now facing old and new problems that led Pope Francis to see the Enneagram with less enthusiastic eyes than the Jesuits of the 1970s. Later on we will analyze what he had to say on the subject in 2013. Let us continue with the account of the Jesuit pioneers of the Enneagram.

In the second half of the 20th century several Jesuits have written about the Enneagram. Robert Ochs, S.J., studied with Claudio Naranjo in the early 1970s at the Esalen Institute, and then spread the word among several other Jesuit priests. He shared his notes and diagrams of the symbol he had received from Naranjo, who had in turn received it from Oscar Ichazo. Amongst the Jesuits who heard from Ochs and who later wrote about the Enneagram themselves, was Tad Dunne, who wrote a book the following decade in which he offers a contemporary version of Ignatius Loyola's spiritual exercises.[117] In 1999 he published another text entitled *Enneatypes*. It is quite likely that Dunne associated the Jesuit maxim of "Agere Contra" (to act against temptation) with the Enneagram personalities and that this gave rise to an interpretation of the arrows which now appear on the symbol to indicate against which temptation, vice or passion each enneatype should struggle. This probability is based on the "General Pattern of Arrows" which appears in a book which seems to be the first in which the Enneagram is presented as a theory of personality. "Figure 14 portrays Dunne's general pattern of movement in moving against the arrows" (Beesing et al., 1984: 158). On the same page they explain the movement as follows: "Self-help in being redeemed centers on 'moving against the arrows' of compulsion. This involves moving against the arrow by moving *toward the pride* of the other personality type" (Beesing et al., 1984: 158).

This idea of "struggling against" appears in Gurdjieff's Enneagram in several forms. An obvious one is transcribed by Ouspensky: "In the sphere of the emotions it is very useful to try to struggle with the habit of giving immediate expression to all one's unpleasant emotions. ... Besides being a very good method for self-observation, the struggle against expressing unpleasant emotions has at the same time another significance. It is one of the few directions in which a man can change himself or his habits without creating other undesirable habits" (Ouspensky, 2001 [1949]: 112). This is, then, another form of *Agere Contra*, without necessarily signifying any point of contact between what Ignatius Loyola wrote in the 16th century and what was known at that time of the Enneagram in Central Asia and Renaissance Europe. However, we

---

[117] Dunne, T (1991) *Spiritual Exercises for Today: A contemporary Presentation of the Classic Spiritual Exercises of Ignatius Loyola.*

should not altogether discard the possibility of a connection. We continue with the Jesuits and their contributions to the Enneagram.

Patrick H. O'Leary, S.J., coauthor of the cited text referring Dunne, mentions that he was first introduced to the Enneagram at a course about Religious Experience given in 1971 by Bob Ochs and, the same year, he also participated in a seminar specifically about the Enneagram, led again by Ochs.[118] He writes that "They sought to test its validity in the light of their own experience and background in Ignatian spirituality" (Beesing et al., 1984: 1). His statement seems important because it raises a relevant question: apart from *Agere Contra*, what elements of Ignatian spirituality coincide with the Enneagram that these Jesuits were practicing?

In the same 1971-1972 generation of Enneagram studies there was another classmate who later left the order: Jerome Wagner, author of several books on the Enneagram.[119] At the same Loyola University in Chicago, another Jesuit priest who was present at Ochs' classes was Paul Robb. He taught at that university and also at the Jesuit School of Theology in Chicago. He wrote *Passage Through Mid-Life* and founded the Institute of Spiritual Leadership which functioned as a ecumenical community. He died in 2010.

During those years, the proof of the validity of the Enneagram in light of a Jesuit education underwent a review, submitted to one of the instruments Ignatius Loyola left to his order: the spiritual exercises. The relationship of *Agere Contra* —or the inner movement of the enneatypes within the circumference of the Enneagram— to one of the Contemplations of the Ignatian Exercises seems to be a fact that the Jesuits could easily validate in

---

[118] In the introduction to the book he wrote with Maria Beesing and Robert J. Nogosek, entitled *The Enneagram: A Journey of Self Discovery.* The first edition, in English was published in 1984 by Dimension Books Inc.

[119] Jerome Wagner's publications are: *The Enneagram Spectrum of Personality Styles: an Introductory Guide* (1996); *Wagner Enneagram Personality Style Scales* (1999); and most recently *Nine Lenses on the World, the Enneagram Perspective*, published in 2010.

practice. Later on we will give an example of a Jesuit contribution to the contemporary Enneagram.

After Ochs, Patrick H. O'Leary began to teach the Enneagram and, along with Maria Beesing, he developed a series of seminars at the Jesuit Retreat House[120] in Cleveland, Ohio and in other places. In the book they write together, along with Robert J. Nogosek, they start by pointing out that to reach authentic personal freedom it is necessary to undertake a journey inside the self, which begins with the discovery of the driving force of our personality. In each one of the nine personality types, the authors assure us, there is a compulsion, "a kind of 'hidden sin', where sin is understood as a kind of paralysis or hindrance in becoming one's true authentic self" (Beesing, O'Leary and Nogosek, 1984: 6). The second chapter is titled "The Enneagramatic Jesus", written as an antidote to the first, that is, to avoid privileging negativity. Here they study the personality of Jesus, taken from the gospels, to demonstrate the positive aspects of the nine personalities. Some young Jesuits recall this content as something learnt at some point in their studies.[121]

Don Richard Riso, a prolific author who has his own following, writes that the first brief notes about the personality types were written and distributed in 1972 and 1973 at informal seminars in Jesuit Theological Centres, especially at the University of California in Berkeley and at Loyola University in Chicago. Riso heard of the Enneagram for the first time in Toronto in 1974,[122] when he was a

---

[120] Maite Melendo, who writes the prologue to the Spanish translation of Empereur's book (Empereur, 2000), and was a student of Empereur and Helen Palmer in the 1970s, calls this place by a slightly different name: the Jesuit Renewal Center, but we assume that they are both speaking of the same place. The first book by this Spaniard was *En tu Centro: el Eneagrama* (1993) published by Sal Terrae.

[121] For example Juan Carlos Henríquez, S.J. , academic at ITESO, the Jesuit University in Guadalajara, Mexico.

[122] In his book *Discovering your personality type,* published in 1995, Riso claims to have encountered the Enneagram for the first time in 1973, that is to say, one year earlier.

Jesuit seminarist and he writes that the "Jesuit material" were nine sketches about personality types which were also called the "Sufi numbers" (Riso and Hudson, 1996: 16). Riso originally wrote this in 1987;[123] seven years later in another book he describes in more detail how the Enneagram expanded among the Jesuits (Riso, 1995). He mentions that Ochs transmitted his interpretation of what he learned from Naranjo to other Jesuits in North America and "They in turn made use of it for spiritual counselling and added their insights to the steadily growing and constantly changing core of oral and written material. The 'Jesuit tradition' is thus an offshoot of the 'Naranjo tradition' and both are offshoots of the original 'Arica tradition' and are somewhat different from it" (Riso, 1995: 110). One of their insights was the connection with the Ignatian Spiritual Exercises.

Riso was always concerned about the origin of the Enneagram. He explored that history as much as he could, without neglecting the great contributions[124] he continued to make until the year he died.[125] He was a Jesuit priest for 13 years and within the order he knew the notes of Robert Ochs and the drawings of Ichazo's enneagons. He writes, "it consisted of nine one-page impressionistic descriptions of the personality types along with several pages of Enneagrams labeled with the names of the ego fixations, the passions, the virtues, the traps, and other material that had been transmitted more or less intact from the Arica tradition. The Jesuit tradition also included oral teachings of its own, some of which made sense, some of which did not" (Riso, 1995: 111). It is highly likely that these "oral teachings of their own" included the link that was made to Ignatius Loyola's Spiritual Exercises.

---

[123] *Personality Types: Using the Enneagram for Self Discovery* (1987) Houghton Mifflin, Boston.

[124] He himself lists 13 of them in *Discovering your Personality Type*, pages 115-116.

[125] He died on 30th August 2012.

As far as Riso is concerned, when he stops being a Jesuit he takes on the task of untangling the Enneagram from the religious aspects that it contained, without overlooking the fact that the teachings had a high spiritual value. In his own words: "On September 2, 1975, I began full-time work on the Enneagram, interpreting the Jesuit tradition in the light of Freud, Jung, Karen Horney, Erich Fromm, and other modern psychologists. Because I had been introduced to the Enneagram in the Jesuit tradition, I continued to work in it, although I eliminated the overtly religious tone and content of that interpretation. I was and am convinced that the Enneagram is neither primarily religious in nature nor merely another psychological typology, but an all-encompassing psychology of personality that, among other things, has profound spiritual implications" (Riso, 1995: 112). In 1991 Russ Hudson joined Don Riso in his work and contributed to the development of a questionnaire to identify a person's enneatype, which has become known as RHETI or the Riso Hudson Enneagram Type Indicator.

James Empereur, S.J., also belonged to the group of North American Jesuits in the Province of Chicago who learnt about the Enneagram from Bob Ochs in the early 1970s. He writes: "When I began my journey with the enneagram, there were, as noted earlier, no published books available. There were handwritten and typed notes of various kinds, many of which had their origin with Robert Ochs, S.J. But once Ochs shared the system among many Jesuit communities, books began to appear…" (Empereur, 1990: 6). This first channel of distribution that Ochs established, which must have been accompanied by a personal explanation highlighting the importance of the material he had found, also explains the enthusiasm within the Society of Jesus. Empereur agrees with what we said earlier about the Second Vatican Council: "The importance of the Ignatian tradition and the *Spiritual Exercises* in the history of spiritual direction is well known. Space does not allow adequate comment here. A discussion of the *Exercises* could constitute a study in itself. Suffice it to say here that since Vatican II there has been a recovery of the authentic shape of Ignatian spirituality and the purpose of the Exercises" (Empereur, 1990: 26).

In effect, we could do with another book in which the Jesuits who took up the Enneagram so enthusiastically in the 1970s express the reasons that it so captured them. For now a reading of the first and second weeks of St. Ignatius' Spiritual Exercises raises some data which allows us to see something that the Jesuits dwell on in their relations with the Enneagram: the direction of integration and disintegration of the enneatypes. To analyze for example, the book by Don Richard Riso and Russ Hudson, *The Wisdom of the Enneagram* (1999) we find that at the end of Chapter 6, Dynamics and variations, the authors show patterns of growth with which each personality can work and they also point out the difficulties of each enneatype. For this they use arrows between the numbers. Each number is related to two others and this is indicated by two arrows, one that leaves the number and another that comes towards it. In the words of the authors: "The arrows on the [...] Enneagram indicate the Directions of Disintegration for each type. For example, Type Eight represents the Two's Direction of Disintegration. The arrows for the Direction of Integration move in the reverse order, so that the Direction of Integration for Type Eight is toward Two, and so forth, for all the types" (Riso and Hudson, 1999: 88).

In another book, Riso explains it like this: "The numbers on the Enneagram are connected in a sequence that denotes each personality type's Direction of Integration (health, self-actualization) and the Direction of Disintegration (unhealth, neurosis). In other words, as individuals of each type become healthy or unhealthy, they change in different ways..." (Riso, 1993: 13). This last remark is one of Riso's contributions, said and emphasized by him, to make openly explicit what he discovers and develops with regard to what he had learnt with the Jesuits.[126]

---

[126] See pages 142 and 143 of *Discovering your personality type* (1995).

The Jesuits work with the Enneagram of nine personalities without forgetting their own teachings, without overlooking one of the basic instruments left to them by their founder: the spiritual exercises which contain precise indications for each of the four weeks during which they should be completed.

From the first week of the exercises we perceive something that is fundamental to understand where the Jesuit enthusiasm of the Enneagram came from. The exercises are organized according to a numbering system that runs from beginning to end. Number 13 indicates that one must struggle against temptation in the opposite sense to that suggested by the temptation. Once again, this is *Agere Contra*, which we will explain in more detail when we speak of the pronouncement about the Enneagram made by the Argentine Jesuit who has been at the head of the Catholic church since 13th March 2013.

The second week of the Exercises presents the "Meditation on the Kingdom of Christ in light of the call a king makes to his subjects to go to war".[127] This war has been interpreted by some Jesuits in a more precise or functional way for the current times and they express it as the war against the inertias of the ego, the war against temptations and vices that belong to each of the Enneagram personalities. This daily struggle is represented by the arrows between the numbers which appear in the modern symbol of the Enneagram. The direction of the arrows enables us to undertake a very concrete job of freeing ourselves from the obstacles which present themselves to every enneatype in any interaction or daily communication with others.

Richard Rohr, a franciscan who began to give seminars about the Enneagram in the 1970s makes an affirmation about the Jesuits without revealing his sources: "After long years of testing and theological scrutiny many Jesuits decide to adopt the Enneagram as

---

[127] *The Spiritual Exercises by St Ignatius of Loyola* in modern Spanish translation by Pablo López de Lara, Ediciones Paulinas, 7th edition, Mexico D.F., 2005, p. 93.

a tool for spiritual counseling and as a model for retreat work" (Rohr and Ebert, 2001: 20). We would just need to find out not only when this took place, but —and above all— who, within the Jesuit order, gave this approbation.

Pope Francis and the Enneagram

Unlikely as it may seem, the current leader of the Catholic Church made an explicit reference to the Enneagram, shortly after he became Supreme Pontiff. It was 28th July 2013, at a meeting of the Coordinating Committee of the Latin-American Episcopal Council (CELAM).[128]

To understand the sense of his remarks we have to remember that Jorge Mario Bergoglio is a Jesuit priest and also Argentine, a country where the Enneagram has spread quite widely. As a Jesuit provincial in Argentina it is highly likely that he was aware of courses which were given on the subject by certain priests, he may even have attended some. On the other hand, it is essential to know in what context the Pope mentioned the Enneagram. It was not a forced declaration in an interview or conversation in which someone interrogated him on the subject. It was a deliberate mention on a subject he was knowledgable about. He made his remarks while reading a speech directed at the Bishops in charge of CELAM for the four-year period 2011-2015. The printed text of Pope Francis' speech (without improvisations) was 9 pages long and is available online (Bergoglio 2013). The video of him giving the speech, including improvisations, lasts 43 minutes and 33 seconds.[129]

His speech was divided into five parts:

---

[128] The meeting was held at the Sumaré Study Center, in Rio de Janeiro, Brasil, as part of the trip to attend the 28th World Youth Day.

[129] The speech was available as a video on www.ewtn.com but may no longer be accessible.

1. Introduction
2. Particular characteristics of Aparecida[130]
3. Dimensions of the Continental Mission
4. Some temptations against missionary discipleship
5. Some ecclesiological guidelines

The general objective of the speech was to reflect on what happens within and without the Church and to offer some paths of action to the Latin-American Bishops for the renewal of each of the dioceses in the region. His starting point was the work carried out during the 5th Episcopal Conference, a conference that did not begin with a prepared document to be approved by all, but rather each participant contributed a diagnostic document and a plan of action in relation to the situation in their country. The resulting document was called the "Continental Mission". What Bergoglio did at this gathering in 2013 was to rethink some of the questions about how to carry out an internal renewal of the Church and how to establish, in the present, a dialogue with the people in their daily life.

In the 4th point of his speech, the Pope introduces a mention of the Enneagram. To capture the sense of his words, we have to highlight that in the previous paragraph he had alluded to words from the Second Vatican Council in which he affirms that "The joys and hopes, the grief and anguish of the people of our time, especially of those who are poor or afflicted, are the joys and hopes, the grief and anguish of the followers of Christ as well (Gaudium et Spes, 1965: 1).[131] Here we find the basis for our dialogue with the contemporary world". A few paragraphs earlier he had said that followers of Christ "are not individuals caught up in a privatized spirituality, but persons in community, devoting themselves to others" and "The

---

[130] Aparecida is a city in the state of Sao Paulo, Brazil, where the 5th Conference of Latin American and Caribbean Bishops was held in May 2007.

[131] Gaudium et Spes, refers to the only pastoral constitution of the Vatican II, promulgated in 1965. It deals with man in the modern world. The full text is available on the Vatican website: http://www.vatican.va/archive/hist_councils/ii_vatican_council/documents/vat-ii_const_19651207_gaudium-et-spes_en.html

Continental Mission thus implies membership in the Church". He gives the two current challenges of missionary discipleship as the Church's inner renewal and dialogue with the world around them (all quotations from Bergoglio, 2013: part 3).

He warns that the decision to opt for missionary discipleship will encounter temptation, that is to say that temptation will present itself and will require "clear-sightedness and evangelical astuteness" to overcome. He mentions some attitudes of "a Church which is 'tempted'"[132] and this is when he recommends "recognizing certain contemporary proposals which can parody the process of missionary discipleship and hold back, even bring to a halt, the process of Pastoral Conversion". He goes on to make three specific such proposals. The first, which is the one we are interested in, was called "Making the Gospel message an ideology" and he then describes four ways of making the message an ideology: sociological reductionism, psychologizing, the Gnostic solution and the Pelagian solution. The Pope placed the Enneagram in the second of these four (all quotations from Bergoglio, 2013: part 4).

These four ways of making the message an ideology which, according to Pope Francis, could pertain as much to Bishops as to lay people, are temptations which can distract from the central mission of the Church. On the subject of psychologizing he says that it is "an elitist hermeneutics which ultimately reduces the 'encounter with Jesus Christ' and its development to a process of growing self-awareness... It ends up being an immanent, self-centred approach. It has nothing to do with transcendence and consequently, with missionary spirit" (Bergoglio, 2013: part 4b). When he finished reading this paragraph the Pope made a long pause, without taking a drink as in other pauses and seemed to think about what he is going to say. He seemed to remember a concrete case but did not quite have the right words for his improvisation, so he began with a doubt about which terms to use and then continued:

---

[132] Inverted commas from the original speech.

"No... I don't have anything against the Enneagram... no, it's as if... but when you find yourself on a course of Spiritual Exercises and the first week of those exercises is based on the Enneagram to get to know yourself, tell me where does the dialogue of compassion with the Resuscitated Christ end up? Do you see where the temptation lies? It is a psychologism. It is then a psychologistic hermeneutic that ends up in a good thing; self-knowledge is not bad, it's a good thing, but it is not the missionary discipleship we are looking for and that is when we are being tempted" (Improvisation number 29 in Pope Francis' speech).[133]

When Pope Francis says that the Enneagram is a psychologistic hermeneutic it is most likely that he is only referring to the Enneagram of nine personality types, that is little more than an ego-game, and not to the Enneagram whose objective is the return to the Absolute. It is also extremely probable that when he mentioned the first week of the Spiritual Exercises, the Pontiff was thinking of the Spiritual Exercises of Ignatius Loyola, which he is well aware of because Jesuits have to complete them at least twice in a lifetime.

A detailed reading of the original Ignatian Exercises[134] casts some light on the temptations that a Jesuit might identify if they know the Enneagram. In the general instructions, both for those giving the exercises and for those receiving them, at number 13[135] it says: "in order to act against the desolation and conquer the temptations, [the

---

[133] The author listened to the recording of the Pope's speech at least a dozen times and the counting of the improvisations is hers, in relation to the official text, as published by the Vatican on their website.

[134] Some courses, instead of taking place over 4 weeks, as orthodoxy would have it, are sometimes offered in one, for example at the Jesuit Exercise Center (Celamex) in Colonia Legaria, Mexico City, and several other places.

[135] Numbering is continuous throughout the 4 weeks of the Exercises.

person who is exercising himself] ought … to accustom himself not only to resist the adversary, but even to overthrow him" (St. Ignatius of Loyola, 1914 [1548]). The sense of acting in opposition is of great importance to understand the link that the Jesuits found to the Enneagram. We highlight the plural (Jesuits) because, although it may have been the discovery of one at first, the fact is that many others adopted it also, in successive generations, because it corresponds with that key piece of Ignatian spirituality. In this early part of the spiritual exercises there is a substantial element, as mentioned, which any well-informed member of the Society of Jesus can recognize: the *agere contra*[136] or acting in the opposite direction. One of the great Jesuit interpretations of the Enneagram is synthesized in the phrase "to act against the desolation and conquer the temptations". The arrows, within the circle linking numbers indicate precisely how it is that each human being should undertake the action of moving against temptation. What the first Jesuits to work on the Enneagram achieved, was to find a concrete way of applying the Ignatian maxim of *agere contra*. They gave it immediate viability, they personalized it, found an apt instrument so that not only Jesuits, but anyone, could better understand which are the specific temptations in daily life against which we should struggle to find the path to transcendence that Pope Francis was speaking of.

Perhaps some of the people with personal experience and direct knowledge of this application of the Exercises should set up a dialogue with the Pope. They might be able to express their conviction that the temptation is not a psychologism, but rather something quite concrete that we all stumble across on a daily basis, each of us finding their own stumbling blocks, as the Enneagram indicates. This makes it a suitable instrument to exercise otherness to gain awareness of the other, starting, of course, with an understanding of our own vices and virtues which, in our Essence, form the basis of each of us.

---

[136] *Agere* means: to take, to lead, to guide. Taken from Latin-Spanish dictionary by Editorial Ramón Sopena, Barcelona, 1999.

In the First Week,[137] after the Principle or Foundation, there is a Particular and Daily Examen which must be practiced three times each day. The first one says "... in the morning, immediately on rising ... one ought to propose to guard himself with diligence against that particular sin or defect which he wants to correct and amend" (Ignatius of Loyola (1914 [1548]: 20). If we know the basic enneatype in which we move, the sin or temptation becomes something quite specific within each person's tendency, and can be identified as something very concrete to be overcome each day. This Ignatian intent for the early morning is corresponded in the Enneagram with a very precise form of application. If we did not have such a path, it would be very hard to make progress.

If we immerse ourselves in the atmosphere of renewal that pervaded the Jesuit communities of the 1970s and 80s, a reading of the previous paragraph, with the Enneagram in mind, leads us immediately to an association with the enneatypes that describe the "hidden sin" or the compulsion in each of us, as O'Leary and his co-authors would have it (Beesing et al, 1984). Beyond making a mistake that could hurt your neighbor, there is an attitude that provokes negativity and which drags on permanently if there is no awareness of its source or cause. What the Enneagram does is show "that particular sin or defect which he wants to correct and amend" in a clear way, as a product of the personality we have. In addition, it also points out the antidote. This is an example of what the priests who know the Enneagram can achieve. It is understandable, then, to add the techniques of self-knowledge to what Ignatius Loyola instructed his order to carry out, especially in the first and second weeks of the Exercises. But let us allow those who have experienced both to speak for themselves.

Richard Rohr, who considers himself a follower of Ignatius Loyola and practices his Spiritual Exercises, says that these make possible "'the discernment of spirits' of those inner and outer voices and

---

[137] Page 20 of the digital publication of Fr. Mullan's 1914 translation of Ignatius Loyola's original Spanish text, approved by the Pontiff in 1548.

impulses that continually influence us… The Enneagram is a related tool, and in some ways a still more precise tool, for reaching this goal. That is one of the reasons why a series of retreat masters have begun to introduce the Enneagram alongside traditional Ignatian Exercises" (Rohr and Ebert, 2001: 22).

A Canadian Jesuit called Jean-Marc Laporte, born in 1937, was provincial superior of the Jesuits in English Canada from 2002 to 2008. Two years later he wrote a text entitled "*A Christian Transposition of the Enneagram: With Paul of Tarsus and Ignatius Loyola*",[138] in which he takes another look at Ignatius Loyola's Spiritual Exercises and shows what he considers to be a contribution to the Enneagram. He focuses on the meditation in the second week, a meditation that implies two dynamics: that of sin and that of grace. Laporte assures us that the Enneagram helps us to experience the power of sin and the power of grace that act on our lives and which cause confusion in the path towards God because "Enneagram work is a helpful instrument in our opening ourselves [sic] to this grace" (Laporte, 2010: 29). He also adds that it is a useful aid so that our talents and gifts may fructify and not get buried in the illusion of our self-sufficiency.

Another opinion, which we could imagine might be a reply to the Pope's words about the first week of the Spiritual Exercises and the Enneagram, comes from the Spanish writer Maite Melendo, who learnt about the Enneagram in the US from the Jesuits who started teaching it in the 1970s. Since then she has directed Ignatian Spiritual Exercises and taught the Enneagram in Spain. She asserts that we cannot know God if we do not know ourselves, and that "This substantial truth of all spirituality was recognized by Ignatius Loyola as a principle and foundation of the Spiritual Exercises" (in Empereur [Melendo] 2000: 13).

---

[138] http://orientations.jesuits.ca/ennea%20spexx.pdf Accessed 16 December 2014 and 4 March 2016.

In the second decade of the 21st century there are many Jesuits using the Enneagram, not only in the United States where the original group emerged, but also in Mexico, Argentina, Colombia and Spain. For example, Fr. Julio Jiménez, S.J., who identifies himself as a promotor of Ignatian spirituality and has a Masters from the Universidad Javeriana in Bogotá, gives a course at the Meeting House of Santa María de los Farallones in Cali, entitled "The Enneagram Jesuit-style with Ignatian spirituality". There are many others like him.

As we have said, the dynamic of the nine personalities is just one aspect of the Enneagram, the most useful for making genuinely meaningful modifications to our personal behavior and in our relations with others. Seen in isolation, that is without connection to the concrete change that it can facilitate, the game of personalities in its most primitive form can seem —as the Pontiff said— immanent and self-centred, since it does not get to the essence of the human being, nor participate in the spirituality that seeks to transcend through love of others. If the Pope knew this, perhaps he would have referred to it, or perhaps he would not have included the Enneagram in his paragraph about psychological ideologization.

The Enneagram's detractors have edited the Pope's words to spread them out of context and use them to show that the position of the Catholic Church is to break all ties with the practice of the Enneagram. This is not the sense in which Bergoglio spoke.

It is highly likely, that some Jesuits who teach the Enneagram in the second decade of the 21st century do not have the same clarity that their predecessors had in the 1970s and 1980s when, knowing how the Enneagram worked on the spiritual plane, they decided to study it in depth and dedicate their professional lives to its promotion. Perhaps a partial reminiscence of all this, an unenthusiastic inertia, is what reached the ears of Jorge Mario Bergoglio in Argentina.

What seems clear is that the Ignatian spirituality contains a component that resonates with the Enneagram that seeks self-knowledge for a return to God. In answer to the question, What is Ignatian spirituality? the Mexican province of the Society of Jesus replies: "it is that which leads the human family to channel its deepest energies.... the Ignatian spirituality is a spirituality that faces the world, where God speaks and at the same time calls us to respond to him. It is a spirituality to search for, find and do God's will in his creatures, using all the means within our reach".[139] One of those means, according to a wide group of Jesuits, has been the Enneagram.

---

[139] Sitio de la Provincia Mexicana de la Compañía de Jesús en Internet, con su última actualización el 15 de agosto de 2013. http://sjmex.org/espiritualidad/espiritualidad-ignaciana.html

Chapter 8

Gurdjieff: his roots and sources

Gurdjieff was a very great enigma in more ways than one, as John Bennett writes in the opening of his book about this extraordinary character (Bennett, 1975). Of all his followers, Bennett is among those who spent the most time with Gurdjieff over many years. He was even with him in his final days and he claims that of all those who knew Gurdjieff, there are no two with the same opinion of the man. "Another enigma connected with Gurdjieff", Bennett continues, "concerns the sources of his teaching and methods... Anyone who takes the trouble to examine his teaching and his methods, can assign nearly every fragment to some known tradition" (Bennett, 1975: 1). In effect, it would take a deep understanding of the roots of several ancestral traditions, including their secret aspects, to locate the complete composition of the Enneagram and its applications. It is quite probable that even Gurdjieff did not have this breadth and depth of knowledge, but he inherited, assimilated and tried to put into practice the information that he found during his life. Which is why he has such a central place in the contemporary Enneagram.

His refusal to be explicit about the origin of some of his knowledge, led to speculation and conjecture. In general he kept quiet about the names of people and places where he acquired his knowledge. Ouspensky writes: "About schools and where he had found the knowledge he undoubtedly possessed he spoke very little and always superficially. He mentioned Tibetan monasteries, the Chitral, Mount Athos; Sufi schools in Persia, in Bokhara, and eastern Turkestan; he mentioned dervishes of various orders; but all of them in a very indefinite way" (Ouspensky, 2001 [1949]: 36). His students mention some places and traditions that can be placed and others of which there is no trace, such as the Monastery of Subari in Therhzas, mentioned by Nott (1990: 10).

George Ivanovitch Gurdjieff has gone down in history essentially for two reasons: first, he made the symbol of the Enneagram known in the West and thus initiated the search for its meaning; and second, for having founded, in 1912 in Moscow, a highly demanding school for personal development, the Institute for the Harmonious Development of Man, based on an ancient cosmogony. The Russian Revolution forced him to emigrate towards the Caucasus with his students, and from there to Tiflis, now capital of Georgia. Ten years later they established the school again at the Chateau Prieuré in Fontainebleau, 55 kilometres from Paris, and remained there for about ten years until they were obliged to leave because they could not pay the rent. Although the institute failed,[140] it gave rise to notes, books and testimonies by several of his disciples, which are conserved today and serve as a source of information and learning about the reach of the Enneagram.

Gurdjieff was born in 1872[141] in Alexandropol, a small town near Kars, which was Russian-Armenian territory until 1918, and now belongs to Turkey. He lived in Kars from the age of six. His mother was a native of this region, which not only belongs to the land between the Black and the Caspian Seas, but is also a "coherent and well-defined geographical unit", as John Bennett said, shortly after

---

[140] This is not a personal judgement, we are simply sharing Bennett's opinion on the subject: "His initial attempt in France, at Fontainebleau, failed…" (Bennett, 1975: 96).

[141] Some biographies also suggest he was born in 1873 or 1877. James Moore places his birth in 1866, with some documentary evidence. The year 1872, cited here, is the date given by John G. Bennett in the book *Gurdjieff: a very great enigma* after consulting several sources and Gurdjieff's family.

studying it *in situ.*[142] As important as the geography of the region, so also is the hybrid culture, which is the result of the meeting of so many peoples here over the centuries. The region is protected by the Mountains of the Caucasus and those of Kurdistan, at the foot of Mount Ararat. The passage from Asia to Europe, or viceversa, is constrained to a few narrow channels in this area, writes Bennett, "the most important [of which] runs northwest from Tabriz to Kars and then almost due west through Erzurum where it joins the valley of the Euphrates River", that is, to the north of the area of the ancient Assyrian and Babylonian Empires. This means that Gurdjieff lived and grew up at a cultural and linguistic crossroads, but with very defined roots of his own.

To describe where Gurdjieff's father came from, let him speak for himself: "My father came of a Greek family whose ancestors had emigrated from Byzantium, having left their country to escape the persecution by the Turks which followed their conquest of Constantinople. At first they settled in the heart of Turkey, but later, for certain reasons, among which was the search for more suitable climatic conditions and better pasturage for the herds of domestic cattle forming a part of the enormous riches of my ancestors, they moved to the eastern shores of the Black Sea, to the environs of the town now called Gumush Khaneh. Still later, not long before the last big Russo-Turkish war, owing to repeated persecutions by the Turks, they moved from there to Georgia. In Georgia my father separated from his brothers and moved to Armenia, settling in the town of Alexandropol, the name of which had just been changed from the Turkish name of Gumri" (Gurdjieff, 2010 [1963]: 40).

The dialects of the regions in which Gurdjieff grew up varied, so Turkic-Tatar was adopted as the common language, in addition to Armenian. He himself explains that as soon as they settled in Kars his father sent him to a Greek school and then to a Russian College.

---

[142] Bennett makes this statement in one of the conferences he gave at Denison House in the summer of 1963, after returning from the region where Gurdjieff was born, grew up and traveled (Bennett, 1975).

This is relevant because later on he would be able to communicate in these languages with a variety of interlocutors.

Because of the region in which he grew up, he came into contact in one way or another with a variety of religious traditions. Some more directly, like the Russian Orthodox Christian Church, through Fr. Borsh, Archpriest of the church in Kars, and Fr. Evlissi, who became assistant to the superior of the Essene monastery, as Gurdjieff himself describes. Meanwhile there were always Muslims and some Sufis around him; he always knew the Armenian traditions, he visited the sacred city of Nakhichevan and was intrigued by its origins and by the Bagratid kings whose royal city was Ani, close to where Gurdjieff was born and grew up. He felt Armenian and the conflicts within the ethnic group moved him in 1890 to participate in secret societies that sought to bring an end to the Ottoman Empire. In Rome, according to his biographer Moore, he even participated in the Armenian Social Revolutionary Party. The rites of the Greek Christian Church were also familiar to him.

For 20 years he travelled in Egypt, India, Tibet, Afghanistan, the Caucasus region, around Tiflis (modern-day Georgia), to the monasteries that still exist along the southern shore of the Black Sea[143] and on the Pamir plateau, in what is now Tajikistan, highlands where several mountain ranges begin like the Hindu Kush, which crosses the borders of Afghanistan, Pakistan, China and Kyrgyzstan. In 1896, according to another of his biographers, he went to Crete in search of the Imastun Brotherhood and was sponsored by a Greek 'Spartacist' Society (Shirley, 2004: 83). Everything suggests that during this time he discovered and lived with different teachers and in communities of different traditions.

As a young man he visited Istanbul, Jerusalem, Alexandria and Abyssinia, places which contributed to opening his mind, although it was his travels in Central Asia, in the last decade of the 19th

---

[143] For example the Monastery of Sumela, in the Pontic Mountains, 54km south of Trabzon, in modern Turkey. It dates back to the 4th century C.E. and during the Ottoman Empire was run by the Greek Orthodox Church.

century and the first decade of the 20th, that defined the focus of his activities and his transcendence to the present. Gurdjieff left his native land with a two-fold baggage: on the one hand the stamp of the Eastern Christian Churches which, as Bennett writes, place much weight on the resurrection, the transit to another life; and on the other hand, an interest provoked by childhood experiences of observing spiritualists, fortune-tellers and yezidis.[144] At the age of 21 he read the theosophist Madame Blavatsky and travelled to India looking for the places she spoke of. He was intrigued, then, by a class of phenomena related to the intangible, the transcendent, with the secrets of traditions. One influence that he himself highlights is that of Bogachevsky, or Fr. Evlissi,[145] who had a high position of trust in the Essene Monastery, close to the Dead Sea, where — tradition dictates— Jesus received his first initiations.

What exactly Gurdjieff may have learnt from the Essenes, via Evlissi or directly, is another mystery to be explored. We must remember that at the beginning of the 20th century this group was not as well known as it has become since the discovery of the Dead Sea scrolls between 1946-47. According to the experts, these scrolls were part of the Essene library: "…it has [been] determined that of the three best-known groups of Judaism in the mid-second century BCE until the time of the destruction of Qumran in 68CE (the Sadducees, the Pharisees and the Essenes), the group most closely resembling the Qumran group is indeed the Essenes" (García Martínez, 1996: lii). Amongst the texts found, some reveal an interest in what was happening between the Tigris and the Euphrates, for example one fragment says, "Words of the prayer which Nabonidus, king of the land of Babylon…" (García Martínez, 1996: 289). This person governed the region where the Chaldean Magi lived between 556 and 539 BCE; it would be interesting to see

---

[144] The *yezidis* are a Transcaucasian sect from the area of Mount Ararat, whom Gurdjieff calls "devil-worshippers" (Gurdjieff, 2010 [1963]: 64).

[145] Bennett writes that this name, like many that figure in *Meetings with Remarkable Men* may have been made up by Gurdjieff.

if it is possible to discover a certain continuity between them and the Essenes.

We must keep in mind that Gurdjieff feels connected to the Russian Orthodox Church, which, before the 9th century, after separating from the Roman Church, preserves certain primitive Christian traditions.[146] Bennett, who was with Gurdjieff just before he died writes: "It is probable that Gurdjieff retained his contact with the Greek and Russian Orthodox tradition throughout the whole of his life, and certainly when I saw him at the end of his life, the sense that he was a member of the Russian Orthodox Church was quite strong with us" (Bennett, 1975: 32). The Armenian always considered himself an esoteric Christian.

On his mother's side, the traditions of the Armenian Church were also formative. This church had an original Christian legacy since the time that Saul of Tarsus (or Paul the Apostle) preached in its territories. In the 8th century it was invaded by Islam, which provoked a diaspora and those who followed the teachings of Nestorius, who came from Alexandria and had been Archbishop of Constantinople, moved in whole communities to northern Persia and Kurdistan and neighboring regions. In the 4th century the Armenian Church had a similar importance to the Greek or Russian Orthodox Churches; its full name was the Armenian Apostolic Gregorian Church, that is to say that it was not loyal to Rome but rather faithful to the teachings of Jesus' apostles. This Church was attacked at several moments in history, but especially during the Armenian genocide which began in 1915. Gurdjieff's father was killed in Kars, on 25th April 1918, as part of this extermination of Armenian Christians by Ottoman Turks.

The Nestorian communities, which began in Syria and expanded to Armenia, continued to exist into the 20th century. By then they had

---

[146] After the death of Jesus, Andrew (brother of Peter and also a disciple of Jesus) preaches in Scythia, or what is now Kazakhstan, southern Russia and the Ukraine.

less power and prestige that they had had in the Middle Ages,[147] but still enough identity that Gurdjieff was able to recognize them on his travels across the plateau of the Pamir and the Hindu Kush.

Bennett, who retraced the route Gurdjieff followed in the first decade of the 20th century, was convinced of the openness the latter had had towards several traditions whose origins probably lie with the Chaldeans. He claims that the Greek and Russian churches are commonly termed "Eastern" and "we tend to forget the importance of the Armenian, Assyrian, Nestorian and other churches of those early days. But certainly Gurdjieff did not forget this, and he was powerfully influenced by the realization that something had been preserved in the Armenian Church and also among the Assyrians and Nestorians, which was connected with the process of spiritual transformation of man, which they, in their turn, had probably inherited from the earlier traditions of the Chaldeans, with which, to a great extent, we have lost contact" (Bennett, 1975: 33).

Just around the time of Gurdjieff's travels, at the beginning of the 20th century, new texts by Evagrius come to light: "The first was the Armenian corpus of Evagrius, which included a biographical note on Evagrius as well as an extensive collection of his most important works. This was published in 1907 by Sarghisian" (Introduction to Evagrius Ponticus [Bamberger], 1972: xxx). If these rediscovered texts were well received anywhere, it was in the monasteries of the Greek and Russian Orthodox tradition, several of which had for centuries guarded various documents which would later form part of the *Philokalia*.[148]

---

[147] In the 13th century the Italian Franciscan Catholic Giovanni da Pian del Carpine reported to Pope Innocent IV the existence of Nestorian communities in Central Asia. C.fr. Joao de Pian del Carpine et al. (2005) *Cronicas de viagem. Franciscanos no Extremo Oriente antes de Marco Polo (1245-1330)* Porto Alegre, Brasil: Braganca Paulista, Pensamiento Franciscano VII.

[148] The *Philokalia* was first published in Venice in 1782. It is a collection of works about mysticism and ascesis by priests of the Christian Orthodox Church. It includes texts by Evagrius about the discernment of passions and thoughts, as well as others by John of Damascus about human virtues and vices.

Between 1897 and 1915, Gurdjieff spent a few seasons in some of the dozens of inhabited monasteries in the region, and also living with some of the Sufi communities near by. He may have found some of the teachings he later shared in his school in these religious communities, but it would be useful to do more precise research on the subject.

Mount Athos, which Ouspensky recalled Gurdjieff speaking of, is now in Greece. There are still many ancient monasteries on its slopes, which were home to Byzantine theologians and mystics. One of these was Gregory Palamas, born in Constantinople in 1296, whose spiritual descendants, Nicodemus the Hagiorite (1749-1809) and Macarius of Corinth (1731-1805), were among the compilers of the *Philokalia*. Of Palamas we know that he "entered the Athos monastic community and became a disciple of Gregory of Sinai" (in Evagrius Ponticus [Bamberger], 1972: lvi). As we have said, Evagrius was part of the 18th century *Philokalia* and these treasures of the Greek and Russian Orthodox tradition are also cited by Oscar Ichazo.

In May 1955 John Bennett travelled to Central Asia with a very specific objective: to find informants who could give him an account of those people with whom Gurdjieff had learnt the Enneagram (Bennett, 1974: Chapter 24). He recounts the results in his books,[149] not without stating the proviso that it is very difficult to follow Gurdjieff's autobiographical accounts because they seem to be written in code, encrypted and some fragments are deliberately altered and the stories muddled. For this reason the Englishman traveled a great deal, comparing what he had heard from his teacher over many years with what he found along the way. One thing does seem clear: Gurdjieff found some knowledge and techniques that have remained intact through the centuries. Bennett maintains that some come from the ancient traditions of Zoroaster and they travelled to the regions where Gurdjieff encountered the teachings of the Enneagram. This assertion leads us to an

---

[149] Mainly in *Witness* (1974) and in *Gurdjieff, a Very Great Enigma* (1975).

extraordinary research challenge: to find out how this knowledge was transmitted over the centuries. A reconstruction is complicated but not impossible.

As we said in relation to the Essenes, what is most difficult to discover is how the knowledge was conserved and passed on from the Chaldean Magi to the community that later welcomed Gurdjieff. Bennett reports one revelation that Gurdjieff shared with him: "One such clue given by Gurdjieff is the mention in several passages of the Sarmoun or Sarman Society. The pronunciation is the same for either spelling and the word can be assigned to old Persian. It does, in fact, appear in some of the Pahlawi texts to designate those who conserve the doctrines of Zoroaster" (Bennett, 1973: 56).

In about 1895 Gurdjieff founded a group who called themselves the Seekers of Truth. With them, he travelled through Turkestan to Tabriz and Baghdad (Shirley 2004: 84). Bennett followed what he calls clues, left by his teacher so that someone who studied his texts intelligently could reconstruct his steps. The first clue was the existence of a sect called the People of the Truth or the Ahl-i-Haqq in a region of Northern Persia and into part of Kurdistan. Bennett conducted his research both in libraries and on the ground, but above all analyzing in detail the only book Gurdjieff published during his lifetime, *The Herald of Coming Good* (1934),[150] "In it he writes openly of his contact with a brotherhood in Persia, and says that he sent a number of his pupils to their monastery" (Bennett 1975: 40). Bennett supposes that it is the same as that of the Ahl-i-Haqq; it was founded in 1316 by Sultan Sahaq, not only as a religious group but rather as guardians of ancient traditions. This Persian brotherhood called Ahl-i-Haqq could have inherited and become, for centuries, the custodians of the teachings that were later handed down to Gurdjieff.

---

[150] This is the only book by Gurdjieff in which Bennett is confident of the literal facts because, he writes, it belongs to a phase in which his teacher had not yet started to alter the data. In fact, as soon as he published *The Herald of Coming Good*, Gurdjieff requested the suspension of its distribution and withdrew the copies that had been given out (Bennett 1975: 74).

Bennett suggests that 1316 was "more a fresh start or reform than a true beginning" for this group. "This is evident from the fact that they preserved, through the coming of Islam, not only Nestorian Christian traditions, but also much earlier Chaldean or Zoroastrian traditions that had belonged to the time of the greatness of Babylon, which is now 4000 years before the present" (Bennett, 1975: 40). This Persian brotherhood is key for future research because it supports the hypothesis that there is a direct line of continuity from the Chaldean Magi to the Enneagram.

In his book *Meetings with Remarkable Men* (2010 [1963]), Gurdjieff constantly introduces fictitious elements and mixes them with facts. He plays with the names of people and places. Bennett was able to observe this, not only in the years with his teacher, but also on his travels. One line of pending research would be to decant these two types of elements, which would not be an idle exercise because the general framework in which the episodes that Gurdjieff narrates take place is entirely compatible with the genesis of the Enneagram among the Chaldeans. In a chapter entitled "Mr. X or Captain Pogossian" some interesting facts emerge in a novelistic plot about the finding of some ancient parchments amongst some old ruins. What he writes is not very plausible. This is the way Gurdjieff chose to cover up a fact: the existence of the Sarmouni community.

In this episode about the rolls of parchment, Gurdjieff introduced the same historical facts that we can find in the historiographies of the region between the Tigris and the Euphrates. A transcription of the whole paragraph: "What struck us most was the word Sarmoung, which we had come across several times in the book called Merkhavat. This word is the name of a famous esoteric school which, according to tradition, was founded in Babylon as far back as 2500 B.C., and which was known to have existed somewhere in Mesopotamia up to the sixth or seventh century AD; but about its further existence one could not obtain anywhere the least information. This school was said to have possessed great knowledge, containing the key to many secret mysteries" (Gurdjieff, 2010 [1963]: 90). The mention of Merkhavat and Mesopotamia are important; the first takes us back to a Jewish mysticism prior to the Kabbalah, which probably did have contact with the Chaldean Magi in ancient Mesopotamia. The Babylonian civilization is a constant reference point, both for Gurdjieff and for those of his followers who concerned themselves with the origins of their master's teachings.

Later, in the same account Gurdjieff writes: "About the sixth or seventh century the descendants of the Assyrians, the Aisors, were driven by the Byzantines out of Mesopotamia into Persia... The Aisors, who, as I have said, are descended from the Assyrians, are now scattered all over the earth. There are many of them in Transcaucasia, north-western Persia and eastern Turkey, and one finds groups of them throughout the whole of Asia Minor. ... Most of them are Nestorians, that is, they do not acknowledge the divinity of Christ" (Gurdjieff, 2010 [1963]: 91). These types of references are very frequent in Gurdjieff's writing: the Nestorian Church, the Armenian archimandrites, the Essenes, the Greek and Russian Orthodox Churches. There is no sign of Muslim influence, not in the geographical references, nor in the content of his texts.

Deciphering what Gurdjieff really found in the Sarmouni community was one of Bennett's objectives, which he advanced but did not fully resolve. In his book *Gurdjieff: Making a New World*, he says that the word *sarmoung* can be interpreted in three ways. The first: "It is the word for bee, which has always been a symbol of those who collect the precious 'honey' of traditional wisdom and preserve it for further generations"; the second is the title of a collection of legends, written by a Nestorian Archimandrite in the 13th century, about "a mysterious power transmitted from the time of Zoroaster and made manifest in the time of Christ"; the third interpretation is that *sar* means head (both literally and in the sense of principal or chief) and *Man* is Persian for the quality transmitted by heredity to a distinguished family or race (Bennett 1973: 57).

In another chapter of *Meetings with Remarkable Men*, Gurdjieff takes up the subject of the Sarmoun once again, in the same way he usually constructs his accounts: mixing fact and fiction. He writes that, while he was in Bokhara, a friend told him he had just met "an old man … [who] is a member of a brotherhood, known among the dervishes by the name of Sarmoung, of which the chief monastery is somewhere in the heart of Asia" (Gurdjieff, 2010 [1963]: 148). It is worth mentioning here that the word dervish is Persian, *darvish*, and that it was originally used to refer to the mendicants who had withdrawn from the material world to dedicate themselves to an ascetic life. In the quotation above, Gurdjieff deliberately hides the location of the Sarmoun monastery and after describing his encounter with the old man, he says he was invited to spend a period at the monastery "on condition that I would take a solemn oath never to tell anyone where the monastery was situated" (Gurdjieff, 2010 [1963]: 148).

All those who have written on this subject present similar accounts. In the words of one of Gurdjieff's biographers: "Four Kara-Kirghiz riders met Gurdjieff and Soloviev at the ruins of the fortress of Yeni-Hissar. The Kara-Kirghiz put blindfolding hoods called *bashliks* over the heads of the seekers so they would not know the way —should it be decided that they were not suitable to remain in the monastery— and took them on a long horseback journey through the mountains of Turkestan. The blinding hoods remained until they camped at night and were taken off en route only twice, once when they needed all their attention to cross a narrow swinging bridge of rope and creaking, rotting planks… there was simply a vertiginously deep abyss, a creaking and uncertain old bridge, and no handrails" (Shirley, 2004: 88).

Another of Gurdjieff's biographers spent decades trying to trace his life and when he comes to the subject of the Sarmoun monastery he writes, "Gurdjieff was obliged to make the journey blindfolded; contemporary maps were defective; and above all he was sworn to eternal secrecy" (Moore, 1993: 31). Everything suggests that Gurdjieff never told anyone.

So on the subject of Gurdjieff's stay at the Sarmoun monastery, there is no documentary evidence and therefore, for almost seventy years,[151] personal interpretations have been made. It is time to turn opinions into hypotheses based on some hard facts. There is one document, published for the first time in 1965, about the Sarmoun brotherhood,[152] without any reference to Gurdjieff - an important point because the author was not looking for a lost fact, nor for a trace of the teacher, but rather stumbled across the monastery by accident. Major Desmond R. Martin, gives the following account of an experience he had in northern Afghanistan:

> "Not so long ago I found myself walking through a mulberry grove in what might have been an English garden—if one did not look upwards to the frowning crags of the Hindu Kush, or at the robes of the monks of the Sarmoun community… The Sarmouni (the name means 'The Bees') have often been accused of being Christians in disguise, Buddhists, Moslem sectarians, or of harbouring even more ancient beliefs, derived, some say, from Babylonia. Others claim that their teaching has survived the Flood; but which flood I cannot say" (Martin, 1966: 22).

This information collected by a traveller about the origins of the Sarmoun community, without being terribly precise, follows the hypothetical line of Babylonian and Christian roots that Gurdjieff taught. Martin does not mention the exact location of the monastery, and if this event took place in the 1960s, it does seem surprising that in the next 50-odd years no-one has been able to verify the coordinates or the information that he observed. Martin continues that one night they allowed him to see the treasures of the

---

[151] Since Gurdjieff's death, in October 1949, until now.

[152] By Desmond R. Martin, "Below the Hindu Kush" in: The Lady, vol. CLXII, No. 4210, 9 December 1965 p. 870, reprinted in a leaflet published by Roy Weaver Davidson (1966) *Documents on Contemporary Dervish Communities*, p. 22.

community, which they assured him had not been seen before by any non-initiate. They told him that they had been "'deconsecrated' … because a new phase of teaching, somewhere to the westward, had superseded the ritual to which they belonged" (Martin, 1966: 22). Amongst these treasures was an unbelievably beautiful articulated tree, of gold and other metals, which resembled a Babylonian work of art which Martin had seen in the Baghdad Museum. They had used the tree to indicate the postures assumed by the dervishes, to a special music, for self-development. There was also "A tall pillar of lapis lazuli, about nine feet high by two feet in diameter … which the devotees circle round, one hand on the pillar, to achieve a particular state of mind" and, most interesting of all,

> "On a wall faced with white Afghan marble, delineated in polished rubies glowed the symbol of the community. This is the mystical 'No-Koonja',[153] the ninefold Naqsch or 'Impress', an emblem which I was later to see in various forms embroidered on clothes. This figure 'reaches for the innermost secret of man', I was informed" (Martin, 1966: 23).

Is this the symbol of the Enneagram? It is time, as we were saying, to construct a hypothesis that goes beyond subjective accounts.

Over the years, in trying to pin down the origin of the symbol, researchers have come back to a phrase by Gurdjieff about Bokhara: "'If you really want to know the secrets of Islam', he said, 'you will find them in Bokhara'" (Bennett, 1975: 59). He did not say the secrets of Sarmoun, he was referring specifically to Islam, which certainly has an important centre in Bokhara.

Bokhara has been inhabited for at least the last 7000 years. It was part of the Persian Empire and was on the Silk Road, so that, for

---

[153] In the glossary of the publication the No-Koonja is given to signify "Nine-sided: enneagon".

centuries, all kinds of people have passed through the city including, of course, Gurdjieff.

In fact, in the second of Bennett's hand drawn maps (Bennett, 1975: 69) he places Bokhara at the centre, signifying an important place on his teacher's route. Today it is in Uzbekistan, like Samarkand, another city with similar features, also mentioned by Gurdjieff. But there is another route which is more important for the purposes of the Enneagram: the Royal Road, traced in the 5th century BCE by Darius I, king of Persia to improve communication across his domains. This route, also known as the "aqueduct of ideas" began in Babylonia and went either east towards Turkestan, or northwest through Nineveh, and into the regions familiar to Gurdjieff and continued to Izmir in modern Turkey. It is a probable route for the ancient Chaldean wisdom.

Bokhara is important in the history of the Enneagram because it generates controversy among those who have tried to locate the origins of the symbol. It is the cradle of the Naqshbandi Sufi tradition, and therefore of the Sufi Enneagram. The most serious scholars of the subject[154] consider it to have originated in this region: "The Naqshbandiyya derives its name from Baha'uddin Naqshband, the epithet of the fourteenth spiritual master Muhammad al-Uwaysi of Bukhara" (Weismann, 2009: 14). Another academic confirms the facts about this Sufi master, "Baha ad-Din was born in 1318 in the village of Qasr-i Hinduvan (later renamed Qasr-i Arifan) near Bukhara, and it was there also that he died in 1389" (Algar, 1976: 134). Bokhara is then, for the Sufis, a city unequivocally associated with the Naqshbandis, and at the same time, from the perspective of Western historians, it is a very ancient site that has been inhabited by many cultures before the existence of Sufi brotherhoods.

---

[154] There are two very complete historiographies on the subject of the Naqshbandi Sufis: one by Hamid Algar, Professor Emeritus of Persian Studies at the Faculty of Near Eastern Studies, University of California, Berkeley. The other is by Itzchak Weismann, professor at the Department of Middle Eastern History and Director of the Jewish-Arab Center, at the University of Haifa, Israel.

John Bennett introduced the name of this Sufi brotherhood to the history of the Enneagram. He mentions it openly in the second of three conferences he gave in the summer of 1963 at Denison House. Bennett starts by saying, "I have to tell you a very interesting sort of detective story" and goes on to describe his interpretation of a remark of Gurdjieff's in *Meetings with Remarkable Men* but he does not present any historical evidence of the supposed contact between Gurdjieff and the Naqshbandi (Bennett, 1975: 55). He concludes with quite careful phrasing, "So I think it is pretty certain that when Gurdjieff writes about the Bokharian Dervish Bogga-Eddin, he is putting us on to the Naqshbandi Order of Dervishes". He then explains that he has encountered the Naqshbandi Order of Dervishes on his travels and they "have fascinated me for many years" (Bennett, 1975: 56).

In another book, in a compilation prepared by A.G.E. Blake, we find that cautious language again when Bennett gives his version of the origin of the symbol: "It is indeed a wonder that this remarkable symbol should have been produced and great respect is due to the people who devised it. It is worth mentioning here that the great Bahauddin Shah of Bokhara was called Nakshband or sign-maker and that he is said to have expressed his teachings by means of symbols" (Bennett 1983: 31). He speaks of the production of the symbol without specifying who produced it and indicates that Bahauddin Shah "is said to have expressed" without giving a source of the saying, but the fact that he includes the meaning of the Sufi's name, sign-maker, can be read to mean that he —the sign maker— designed the Enneagram symbol. There is no evidence that this was the case. More research is necessary.

Laleh Bakhtiar also links Gurdjieff with the Naqshbandi but she goes further in suggesting that Gurdjieff met Shaykh Abd Allah al-Faiz ad-Daghestani[155] of the Sufi Order Naqshbandi "and learned about the Enneagram through this encounter" (Bakhtiar, 2013a: 12). The Iranian American scholar makes this assertion without

---

[155] The spelling of this name varies from one author to another.

demonstrating knowledge of the content of Gurdjieff's Enneagram. A study of the complex underlying cosmogony is precisely what could tell us the true origin of the Armenian's knowledge. Later Bakhtiar refers to one of Bennett's conferences, in which he recounts how Gurdjieff said that if they really desired to know the secrets of Islam they would find them in Bokhara. Bennett added: "This is equivalent to saying you will find them if you can find the centre of the Naqshbandi" (Bennett, 1975: 59), but Gurdjieff did not say this, it is Bennett's interpretation.

As we embark on the history of the Naqshbandi we have to be clear about our sources. In the studies about this Sufi community we find conflicting accounts and, without wishing to discredit any of them, we have to stick to the hard facts. An example of different sources on the same subject: two researchers seek to study the history of the Naqshbandi. The first, Hamid Algar, published his research in 1976 with the title *The Naqshbandi order: A preliminary survey of its history and significance*; the second is Itzchak Weismann, who published his research in 2007: *The Naqshbandiyya, Orthodoxy and Activism in a Worldwide Sufi Tradition*. Algar begins the history with the Prophet Mohammed in the 7th century and he is interested in showing the original connections between the Naqshbandi and the *silsila* or the prophet's genealogy. The second begins his account in the 13th century without making any connection to Mohammed. What I wish to show with this example is that on these subjects, both for Sufi brotherhoods and for the Enneagram itself, it has become essential to locate the sources of our information because the texts are often strongly partisan and favour one tradition over others.

There is no doubt that there is a Sufi Enneagram of Naqshbandi origin, but that does not mean that it is the same Enneagram that was used in Gurdjieff's teachings. According to one of his biographers, the Enneagram application that Gurdjieff taught in 1916 to his groups in Moscow and Petrograd was "a dynamic model for synthesising, at macrocosmic and microcosmic level, his 'Law of Three' and 'Law of Seven'. Later at Fontainebleau in 1922 he

choreographed and taught the first of those many Sacred Dances or
'Movements', whose beautiful but rigorously prescribed evolutions
enact the enneagram ... as a moving symbol" (Moore, 1993: 344).
As we shall see later on, Gurdjieff's direct students give accounts of
those two laws and sacred dances. We are not talking about the
dances of the Sufi whirling dervishes, but others, described
according to what happened to Gurdjieff on that trip to the
Sarmouni monastery: "In a side court, called the Women's Court,
young priestess-dancers learned sacred dances. Twice a day those
who lived in the second and third courts assembled to take in the
sacred dances of the priestesses and the Sarmoung's sacred music.
The priestesses were taught, from childhood, dances that were
thousands of years old, each one a sort of complex somatic
semaphore transmitting, to those who could read their
choreographed symbology, 'one or another truth' encoded into the
dance in antediluvian times" (Shirley 2004: 90).[156]

Given the high level of scholarship and recognized cultural level of
Gurdjieff's students who have written about him, it is not believable
that they could have omitted to mention the Naqshbandi teachings,
if these had been given by Gurdjieff. What drew many of the
intellectuals who were enthusiastic about his teachings, was the
coincidences with their own positions and personal searches.
Several of them, for example, had had some contact with the
theosophy of Helena Blavatsky, who constantly cites the Essenes,
who Gurdjieff was also very interested in. The Essenes are another
pending item of research.[157] There is evidence of their existence at

---

[156] At the SAT IV (Seekers After Truth courses, Level 4) that Claudio Naranjo
directed 21- 25 March 2007 in Tonalli, Zumpahuacan, Estado de México, the first
thing students had to do each day for one hour at dawn was to learn one of these
dances with teacher Rafael Ruiz. The mind must be fully concentrated to
complete the dances; if another thought intervenes, even for a moment, the dancer
will make a mistake.

[157] The now widely known Dead Sea scrolls, or Qumran manuscripts, attributed
to the Essenes, and now available in digital format, would be an important
primary source.

least 2 centuries before the Common Era[158] and it is highly probable that they had contact with the knowledge of the Chaldean Magi.

James Moore, Gurdjieff's English biographer wonders "was Gurdjieff ever tempted to present his teaching explicitly in Christian terms? It is undeniable that Gurdjieff reverenced Christ, and all his life strove to braid together diverse strands of Christian pietism. As a youth his precocious visits to Echmiadzin and the monastery of Sanaine[159] had preceded longer journeys: searching in Cappadocia the origins of Christian liturgy; in Mount Athos the legacy of Hesychasm,[160] in Jerusalem the link with the Essenes; and in Coptic Abyssinia the roots of Christian Gnosis" (Moore, 1993: 76). For this scholar of Gurdjieff's life, who for years pursued every testimony or documentary evidence he could find about the man, there is no trace of Sufism in his ideology; Gurdjieff's roots were, without a doubt, Christian.

Bennett, referring specifically to Gurdjieff's search writes that "a very central feature, or theme, of Gurdjieff's teaching and methods is that man is destined, or required, during his life on earth, to transform energies. One way of looking to see the reason of man's existence on the earth, is that he is able to produce, by his way of living, certain substances required for very high purposes" (Bennett, 1975: 42).

What are these substances? Bennett refers to the work of Ouspensky and Nicoll for the technical study and mentions a Table of Hydrogens in which there is a range of these substances from the coarsest to the finest (Bennett, 1975: 50); however, for the purposes

---

[158] Titus Flavius Josephus and Pliny the Elder document the existence of the Essenes.

[159] An educational centre in Armenia, whose construction took place gradually between the 10th-13th centuries. It was a place of Christian worship, where manuscripts were copied and monks studied.

[160] Ascetic practice of Eastern Christian monks, initiated by Evagrius Ponticus in the 4th century C.E.

of making it accessible to the varied public that came to his talks that Summer 1963, he simply says that these substances are behind all human activities and he adds, "Gurdjieff was very clear about the importance for man of being able to produce and control the substances he requires in order to produce changes. He understood that you cannot improve the way something works if you continue to feed it with unsuitable fuel. You have to produce more refined fuel to get a more refined action" (Bennett, 1975: 84). In his autobiography Bennett adds, citing Gurdjieff, that it calls for a much greater concentration of Higher Emotional Energy than people have naturally. But, he continues, there are some rare people "who are connected to a Great Reservoir or Accumulator of this energy. This Reservoir has no limits" (Bennett, 1974: 116). In Oriental traditions, in China for example, specifically in the Zhineng Qigong, this refined fuel is called Hunyan Qi.[161] Ouspensky, of whom more later, writes that Gurdjieff said that the process of evolution began like this, "a certain group of cells gradually becomes conscious; then it attracts to itself other cells, subordinates others, and gradually makes the whole organism serve its aims and not merely eat, drink, and sleep. This is evolution and there can be no other kind of evolution. In humanity as in individual man everything begins with the formation of a conscious nucleus. All the mechanical forces of life fight against the formation of this conscious nucleus in humanity, in just the same way as all mechanical habits, tastes and weaknesses fight against conscious self-remembering in man" (Ouspensky, 2001 [1949]: 308). This paragraph refers to the Law of Seven, the phenomena that prevent the increase of conscience in human beings.

We should remember that in the second decade of the 21st century there is still much to decipher in what Gurdjieff transmitted to his disciples and there are also issues to correct and amend given that Gurdjieff wrote "in pencil, in Armenian; this is translated into Russian, and then into literal English by the Russians; it is then

---

[161] The Zhineng Qigong was articulated, on the basis of the most appropriate Qigongs of China, by Master Pang He Ming.

gone over by one or two English and American pupils at the Prieuré who have only a rough knowledge of the use of words" (Nott, 1990: 125). This is why the books written by his disciples are required reading to compare them with what Gurdjieff is said to have written. His disciples, especially those with higher education and who really wanted to understand what their Armenian teacher explained, give his teachings more coherence and logical order. Seen from the outside, the information transmitted at Gurdjieff's school provoked remarks, for example one reportedly made to A.G.E. Blake by a German philosopher: "Arnold Keyserling once remarked to me about Gurdjieff, 'He invented a different theory every day!'" (Blake, 1996: xvii).

The abundant literature, generated by the students who experienced the school in Fontainebleau and who compared their learning with other sources, as well as the books written in turn by *their* students, constitutes a poorly explored territory for new researchers on the origin of the Enneagram.

It is important to note that neither Gurdjieff's disciples, nor he himself, worked with the nine personality types. They do use the symbol that concerns us: a circle, with a superposed triangle and hexad or hexagram, which give a figure with nine points with 40° of separation between each point. This is to describe it in a simple sense, but in a more complex sense we perceive its representation of several processes that relate to the composition and dynamic of the universe, including human beings.

With regard to what we know today as personality types, the inheritors of Gurdjieff's school[162] have written descriptions of seven human 'types' whose names are associated with the planets, the Moon and the Sun, each of these in turn is associated to a gland in the human body: the Lunar, with the pancreas; the Venusian, with the parathyroid gland; the Mercurial, with the thyroid gland; the Saturnine, with the anterior pituitary gland; the Martian, with the

---

[162] See in particular Rodney Collin (1984) and Maurice Nicoll (1996).

adrenal gland; the Jovial (of Jove, or Jupiter), with the posterior pituitary gland; the Solar with the thymus (see Figure 6).[163] There is documented evidence that at Gurdjieff's school an association was made between body organs and personality types.

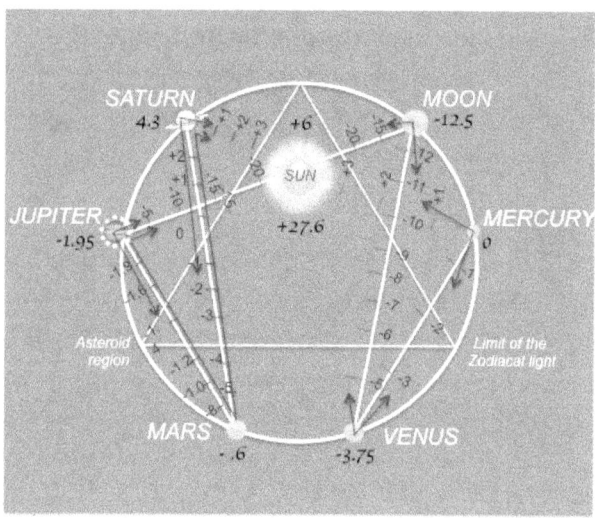

Figure 6: Collin's Circulation of Light between the planets and the sun. (Taken from Spanish version of Collin's *Theory of Celestial Influence*, published as *Desarrollo de la Luz* in 1952.)

Something that needs further research is why Gurdjieff breaks with the number nine to use the number seven, giving greater power to the musical scale.[164] The following quotation gives a sense of how

---

[163] Alfonso Ruiz Soto, a Mexican who formed part of the Fourth Way, used these terms in his teaching of the Enneagram. In the late 1980s he gave courses at the Benedictine Monastery of Santa María de la Resurrección, in Cuernavaca, Morelos, 85km south of Mexico City. In 2015 he continues with his teaching but it is now called the Heptagram and the types have other names coined by him: solitary, sensitive, acute, structured, energetic, expansive and charismatic.

[164] Alejandro Volpi, a versatile Enneagram scholar with mathematical leanings, claims that in passing from nine to seven the model loses scientific rigour.

Gurdjieff's work was perceived at the end of the 20th century by a good number of scholars and teachers of the Enneagram: "The system that Gurdjieff taught was a vast and complex study of psychology, spirituality, and cosmology that aimed at helping students understand their place in the universe and their objective purpose in life. Gurdjieff also taught that the Enneagram was the central and most important symbol in his philosophy. He stated that a person did not understand anything completely until he or she understood it in terms of the Enneagram, that is, until he or she could correctly place the elements of a process at the correct points on the Enneagram, thereby seeing the interdependent and mutually sustained parts of the whole. The Enneagram taught by Gurdjieff was therefore primarily a *model of natural processes*, not a psychological typology" (Riso and Hudson, 1999: 20).

Both Gurdjieff and Ichazo are heterodox figures for historians used to working with primary sources. They do not reveal the origin of what they taught and they do not cite any documents. Their legacy is, however, a relevant piece of the contemporary history of the Enneagram because it has become a knowledge base on which, in recent years, people have worked systematically and in increasing depth. Gurdjieff should be recognized for having recovered much of the meaning of the ancient symbol of the Enneagram, made it known[165] and for having tried to put it into practice for the understanding of human beings and the universe.

Gurdjieff died on 29th October 1949 at the American Hospital in Neuilly, near Paris. The funeral was conducted according to the liturgy of the Russian Orthodox Church (Moore, 1993: 317). He left relatively few written texts, but his students and followers took on the task of passing on the knowledge systematized by him, several of whom published books. We highlight four: Ouspensky, Nicoll, Bennett and Nott. Some of their students, in turn, later wrote valuable books on the subject.

---

[165] The Enneagram became more widely known in 1949 with the publication of Ouspensky's book *In Search of the Miraculous*.

Chapter 9

The legacy of Gurdjieff's followers

Ouspensky

Pyotr Demianovich Ouspenskii, or Peter D. Ouspensky, as he is better known in English, met Gurdjieff in Moscow in 1915. They had both heard of one another. Ouspensky had already published *Tertium Organum*, a book in which he made some harsh criticisms of the instruments of thought in Aristoteles and Bacon. He had been a member of the Theosophical Society and had travelled in search of masters. He followed Gurdjieff intermittently and also set up his own school. He left a large body of work.

It is interesting to record how Ouspensky responded to a question about the criteria with which to recognize whether the teaching of a given school is true. With regard to Gurdjieff's school he answered, "For me personally the first proof of *this* school being right was an undoubted and exact knowledge in psychology surpassing everything I had ever heard before anywhere, and making psychology an exact and practical science. This was a fact, for me incontrovertible, and I had a special preparation for judging this fact" (Ouspensky, 2008:154).

With regard to the Enneagram symbol, Ouspensky is unequivocal: "It was given such significance by those who knew, that they considered it necessary to keep the knowledge of it secret" (Ouspensky, 2001 [1949]: 287).

Many reasons may lead individuals or groups to keep certain knowledge secret. On occasion it is the conservation of valuable information. It may also respond to power relations, as was the case of the secret of the Holy Office of the Congregation of the Supreme and Universal Inquisition which forced lawyers, witnesses, experts, and litigants to remain completely silent on the subject of documents, discussions and votes related to the tribunal. "Even the prisoner (let us think, for example, of Galileo after his conviction of 1633) was obligated by the bond of secrecy of the Holy Office with regard to all the eventual complications of his process" (Redondi, 1990:183). It is undeniable that institutions have always reserved certain information, but when that knowledge is consistent with reality, as Norbert Elias writes, "it can be kept secret for a certain time from when it is discovered, but it can always be discovered by others and, in practice, rarely can be kept a secret... The priests and scribes of ancient Sumeria and ancient Egypt managed, for a long time, to reserve exclusively for themselves a wide body of knowledge including, among others, the art of reading and writing, a monopoly that was a powerful lever to reach their privileged position" (Elias, 1994: 230).[166] It is obvious that at various moments in the history of the Enneagram it was kept secret to preserve it and in others to control it. Even in the 20th century we have Naranjo's testimony on the subject: "In view of the secret with which these psychological ideas were being presented by Ichazo, after my own involvement with him, I, too, made such secrecy a requirement for admission to the groups that I taught —either directly or through delegates— in the decade following 1970. Not deeming a verbal agreement binding enough, I went so far as to obtain from every participant a signed contract, one item of which addressed itself to

---

[166] Translator's note: based in Mexico City, we have been unable to locate the original English text of this article by Elias, but the original reference is Elias N (1987) The Retreat of Sociologists into the Present, *Theory, Culture & Society*, Vol 4: 223-247. His complete works have recently been edited and published in numerous volumes by the Norbert Elias Foundation (for more information see http://www.norberteliasfoundation.nl).

an agreement not to disclose some of the ideas and the spiritual practices taught in SAT" (Naranjo, 1994: xxx).

In several passages of his book, Ouspensky puts paragraphs in speech marks to signal what he took down directly from Gurdjieff. For example: "Speaking in general it must be understood that the enneagram is a universal symbol. All knowledge can be included in the enneagram and with the help of the enneagram it can be interpreted. … The knowledge of the enneagram has for a very long time been preserved in secret and if it now is, so to speak, made available to all, it is only in an incomplete and theoretical form of which nobody could make any practical use without instruction from a man who knows" (Ouspensky, 2001 [1949]: 294).

As often happens in academic and intellectual communities, there are divisions and students break away from those who were they teachers[167]. Bennet recounts the moment in which Ouspensky informs them that he will no longer follow Gurdjieff: "Ouspensky began, 'I have asked you to come because I must tell you that I have decided to break off all relations with Mr. Gurdjieff. This means that you have to choose. Either you can go and work with him, or you can come and work with me: but if you remain with me, you must give un undertaking that you will not communicate in any way with Mr. Gurdjieff or his pupils'" (Bennett, 1974: 126). This was in 1924 and from then on Ouspensky continued writing his extensive works.

Nicoll

Another disciple of Gurdjieff, and also of Ouspensky, who leaves a documented text about the Enneagram, is Maurice Nicoll, a

---

[167] History shows us a great many breaks between students and teachers, where the student take his/her own path. In the realm of psychoanalysis and psychology there is Freud's case. Adler, Jung, Rank and then Reich, Erikson and Fromm — among the youngest in the group— broke with their teacher. Only Abraham, Jones and Ferenczi remained loyal.

Scotsman born in 1884 who studied medicine at Cambridge University, and gave his practice a psychological angle, mainly from a Jungian perspective, and specialized in cerebral diseases. His father was a minister of the Free Church of Scotland, from whom he learnt a love of writing. Nicoll was 37 when he met Gurdjieff and shortly afterwards he started writing what would be an large body of work. In it he transcribes a good deal of what he heard from Gurdjieff: "In speaking of the Enneagram, G. said that it formulated the whole of the teaching and that the more a man could read its meanings the more deeply he understood the Work. On one occasion, asked what it was all about, G. said that it represents the union of the Law of Three, or Law of the Trinity, and the Law of Seven, or Law of the Octave. Let us remind ourselves that the Law of Three states that in every manifestation three forces, active, passive and neutralizing, must take part, and that they are the creative forces which create the different orders of the worlds in a descending scale, increasing the number of laws as they duplicate themselves. Let us also remember that a second law exists, the Law of Seven, which relates to the *order of manifestation*. If there be a creative force there must also be *order* in creation, or all will be chaos. The interaction of these two laws in such a way that one does not hinder or stifle the other, and so that all possibilities are attained, is represented in the Enneagram" (Nicoll, 1996: 379).

In the second volume of his *Psychological Commentaries on the Teaching of Gurdjieff and Ouspensky*, Nicoll dedicates fourteen chapters to the Enneagram, none of them related to the study of personality. He does offer elements of a cosmovision that explain, with the use of mathematical laws, the connection between human beings and the matter that makes up the universe. He also says, "The Apparatus of the Universe is … for the purpose of Evolution. It is a vast distilling machine, to extract the finer from the coarser …" Individual evolution, he continues, requires "long, inner work, and then choosing the *finer*… How does [one] ascend in the Scale of Being? By means of something acting on it - something higher" (Nicoll, 1996: 431).

In his writings, Nicoll includes pictures of the Enneagram in which he explains, based on the laws mentioned above, the connections between some of the nine points of the Enneagram, with examples of actions carried out by a human being[168]. He writes: "You are probably looking at the mystery of life in the inner circulation of the Enneagram, whereas, looking at the outer series of numbers, you are perhaps looking at what corresponds to that powerful but erroneous form of thinking called thinking from appearances, from the senses. You notice that the higher must exist before the lower can undergo transformation" (Nicoll, 1996: 434). To synthesize and in Nicoll's own words: "What is the Enneagram about? The Enneagram depicts a series of transformations from lower to higher, from coarser to finer" (Nicoll, 1996: 434). He continues, "The object of this Work is to make us conscious in ourselves and to ourselves, to what is going on in us, to the vast inner traffic of thoughts and feelings that lies within, in the psychic invisible realm as distinct from the vast outer physical world of things and people that the senses reveal to us. Here, in this inner world, and in what we select and reject in it, lies the key to the Work, and so to evolution" (Nicoll, 1996: 441).

Bennett

John G. Bennett (1897-1974), born in England, was a versatile and passionate man, who studied Turkish at the School of Oriental and African Studies at the university of London and worked as a diplomat in Constantinople, where he met Gurdjieff in 1921. He later supported him in his failed attempt to set up a school in

---

[168] Nicoll gives examples with quantities of Hydrogens placed at the points that, on the Enneagram of personalities, correspond to numbers 1, 2 and 4 which appear connected according to several contemporary authors, since enneatype 4 integrates to enneatype 1 and disintegrates to enneatype 2. In Nicoll's diagram, the place that corresponds to 1 is called number 384 and represents the number of Hydrogens, the 2 has 192 Hydrogens, and at 4 there are 96 Hydrogens. When a person carries out an action in the sense of their own evolution it is said, from this perspective, that they fix Hydrogens.

London and lived with the study group around Gurdjieff at several moments in his life. In 1946 he founded the Institute for the Comparative Study of History, Philosophy and the Sciences in Kingston-upon-Thames, near London.

He accompanied Gurdjieff in his last days. As we have already said, Bennett always had a great curiosity about where Gurdjieff's teachings came from. First, he studied as much of the bibliography as he could find and then he travelled to some of the places mentioned by his teacher until he found some direct informants. He wrote books related to the context in which Gurdjieff lived and worked, but also others in which he reflects on the nature and reach of the implications of the knowledge received and generated not only by the Enneagram, but also of its complements which he found when he read the quantum theories of physicist David Bohm, first brought to his attention by his brilliant student Anthony Blake. On these subjects he wrote *Creative Thinking*, *Elementary Systematics* and *Deeper Man*[169].

Bennett's intellectual legacy is extraordinary and was ordered, studied, assimilated and completed by Blake from 1974 onwards, after Bennett's death. As a result of this period of compilation Blake published *Enneagram Studies*, a collection of Bennett's writings, in which he writes the preface (Bennett, 1983).

Given the precision with which he describes the application of the Enneagram to all types of processes, we transcribe what Bennett says in relation to this well known saying of Gurdjieff's: "Only what a man is able to put into the enneagram does he actually *know*, that is, understand. What he cannot put into the enneagram he does not understand" (in Bennett, 1983: 89)[170]. Bennett starts by stating that the Enneagram is, above all, a symbol of a cyclical process of

---

[169] These books are cited and studied by Anthony Blake in his book *The Supreme Art of Dialogue*, Du Versity Publications, 2009.

[170] This phrase is quoted from Ouspensky's 1949 book *In Search of the Miraculous: Fragments of an Unknown Teaching*.

development and then he describes its elements: circle, triangle and lines. Then he goes on to speak of the type of symbol it is, as well as its inner processes: "Whereas in the more familiar symbolisms there is a more or less one-to-one correspondence between symbol and meaning, in structural action symbolism the correspondences are one-to-many and correspondingly complex. Thus the inner triangle of the figure symbolizes the requirement that not one but three independently derived and mutually interacting processes of development are necessary to ensure that one single such process shall be enabled to reach completion. The triangle also serves to symbolize that the three processes must knit together according to the relationship of affirmation, denial and reconciliation specified by the three term system or triad. The first completing process transmits the affirmation in the relationship as the main process of the three. The second transmits the denying impulses to which the first is subject in consequence of hazard and uncertainty and contributed perforce by the environmental conditions through which it is required to proceed. The third process is concerned with bringing the development successfully to its intended conclusion through a reconciliation of these two oppositely-acting impulses" (Bennett, 1983: 92). In his conclusions to this final part of *Enneagram Studies*, Bennett assures us that the structure or pattern of the Enneagram is so general that it can help us to understand all kinds of situations and he ends by saying, "I have no doubt that this was one of the purposes for which it was originally created" (Bennett, 1983: 121). Bennett's ideas find a continuity in Blake's works.

Orage

There was one student of Gurdjieff's who died 15 years before him and was one of his favourites. At least, when he died, the teacher said that he had lost a brother. His name was Alfred Richard Orage (1873-1934), he was English, born in Dacre, Yorkshire. He spent a time at the school in Fontainebleau after being the editor of the journal *The New Age*, sponsored by George Bernard Shaw, who said that Orage was "the most brilliant editor for a century past". T.S. Elliot referred to him as "the finest critical intelligence of our age", according to a comment in the third part of the book of 15 essays he wrote, designed to increase the flexibility and scope of the mind in the process of increasing awareness. These essays were originally published in the magazine *Psychology* (in New York) between April 1925 and January 1926, and first published in book form with the title *The Active Mind: Adventures in Awareness* (in New York, 1954)[171].

It is important to understand that in *The New Age*, Orage promoted psychoanalysis and, without much publicity —like everything he did— he had formed a group to study the works of Freud from different points of view; Maurice Nicoll was also in this group.

Before being an editor, Orage was a school teacher in Leeds and was particularly interested in the work of Plato and Nietzsche. He got involved in politics and theosophy, just like many others who later joined the Fourth Way.[172] On his return from France and after his seven-year sojourn in New York, where he organized new groups to study the ideas of Gurdjieff, he founded the journal *The New English Weekly*, in which he published some of the articles which would be re-edited as a book after his death[173]. What is striking about Orage is that his interest was not so much to inform about what he had experienced in his life with Gurdjieff, whom he

[171] There are numerous editions of Orage's writings, in several languages, some are translations without copyright. Since its first publication in book form, *Exercises in Practical Psychology* has been re-edited in various volumes and translations. It was published in Mexico in Spanish in 2010 by Ediciones G.

[172] The Fourth Way is the name that Gurdjieff gave to the work he did with his students. The three known ways were the Way of the Yogi, the Monk and the Fakir, but none of these was practical in 20th century life, so Gurdjieff sought to follow a Fourth Way, which was based on the learning synthesized by him but also demanded a personal discovery on the part of each student.

[173] Most of his articles were first published in *The New Age*, the journal that Orage directed and edited from 1907 to 1922.

accompanied on his first visit to the United States and with whom he maintained a constant connection since he was organizing the study circles in New York. The interest of this refined, inquisitive and educated Englishman was to communicate *how*, in daily life, to change habits, strengthen the mind and increase awareness. He interspersed easy-to-understand practical exercises in his texts, convinced that little by little ordinary people were capable of generating changes at civilization level. He used to say that the transformations of our civilization could not depend "upon the ability of the half dozen or so minds that alone 'understand Einstein'" (Orage, 1930: 3). He did not have an apologetic attitude with regard to Gurdjieff, but —according to his friend Charles Nott — a week before his death, Orage repeated something that Nott had heard him say before: that the best thing that had happened to him had been to encounter the teachings of Gurdjieff. An Enneagram was carved on his tombstone.

Nott

Another follower of Gurdjieff was Charles Stanley Nott (1887-1978) another Englishman, born in Bedfordshire, dedicated to the translation and edition of books. He kept a diary, beginning in 1924 and filled it, over several years, with the events he observed and experienced at Gurdjieff's school. He records things that do not appear in the accounts of any of the other students. In writing of the dances and music that were practiced there, he mentions, for example, that some of the series of movements based on the Enneagram came from "a religious order seated near Mount Ararat, the Aisors, a Christian sect tinged with Sufism" (Nott, 1990:11). Another unusual reference, also about the movements that Gurdjieff taught at his school, was, "The series of movements was based on a very ancient symbol, the Enneagram, mathematically constructed like the movements of the order of the Pure Essenes, which was founded hundreds of years before Christ" (Nott, 1990:11). This mention of the Essenes confirms the powerful influence on a young

Gurdjieff of Father Evlissi, who had an important role in an Essene monastery in territory that is now occupied by the state of Israel. Gurdjieff was in contact with this group, which —after the immigrations provoked by the Maccabean rebellion in Jerusalem— ended up settling in the area of the Dead Sea. The Essene texts reached the areas of influence of the Russian Orthodox Church. It is likely that Gurdjieff never abandoned the link with Evlissi and that some aspects of what he learnt from him were amalgamated with the rest of the teachings that he acquired over the years.

Nyland

Willem A. Nyland (1890-1975) was born in Utrecht, Holland. He studied chemistry at university and then went to the United States to do a PhD at Columbia University. Nyland was in New York in 1924, when Gurdjieff made his first visit to the country, and heard him speak and attended a demonstration of the sacred dances. In June of the same year, Gurdjieff returned to Paris and Alfred R. Orage stayed in New York as his representative in the United States. Nyland studied with Orage for a time and then undertook several trips to France to meet Gurdjieff. Towards the end of his life, Gurdjieff gave Nyland several texts to organize a study group in the United States. Nyland did as requested and became one of the founders and trustees of the Gurdjieff Foundation. In the early 1970s he set up his own study groups.

Disciples of the disciples

Of those who visited Gurdjieff's school there were some, like Ouspensky, who made a break with the master after a few years and decided to study, write and spread the knowledge with their own students. Others wrote but did not found their own schools, and others abandoned the teachings and practice after Gurdjieff's death.

Three students of Gurdjieff's direct disciples stand out for the depth and practice of their teachings. The first is Rodney Collin, who was a disciple of Ouspensky. The second is Anthony Blake, disciple of John Bennett. The third is Richard Defouw, who studied with Nyland. They all follow Gurdjieff's line. In addition, there are several students of Gurdjieff's line who were initiated later, by Oscar Ichazo; among others, Claudio Naranjo, a South American, like his teacher. At another latitude, we find a Kuwaiti initiated in Ichazo's line, A. Hameed Ali, whose pen name is A.H. Almaas, who was a student of Claudio Naranjo.

These five disciples of Gurdjieff's disciples, Collin, Blake, Almaas, Defouw and Naranjo have produced serious, profound, well-researched texts with suggestions for applying the knowledge of the Enneagram. Here are brief accounts of the first four. We will come back to Naranjo in Chapter 11.

The disciples who stand out, Collin, Blake, Almaas and Defouw, have begun to make very pertinent contributions for our understanding of what appeared, in the original teachings, to be somewhat cryptic and complex.

Collin

Rodney Collin (1909-1956) was a student of Ouspenksy. He was born in Brighton, England, of a mother who studied theosophy and who taught him a love of reading. After studying at the London School of Economics, he travelled to Spain where he learnt the language and worked as an independent reporter. In 1930 he started to read Ouspensky, whom he met in 1936 and after that he decided to deepen his understanding of Russian's teachings. In 1937 he studied a number of texts in the British Museum Library and began to draft his first publications. When the Second World War began he travelled and practiced the dances that Ouspensky had learnt from Gurdjieff. In 1944 he went to Mexico and the following year he decided to work full time on the teachings of the Fourth Way and maintained a close relationship with Ouspensky until his death in 1947. A year later he finished his book *The Theory of Celestial Influence* (1997 [1954]) which includes all that he learned about the theory and practice of Gurdjieff's system in the ten years he spent with Ouspensky (first published in Spanish in Mexico in 1952). He moved to Guadalajara, Jalisco, where he finished *The Theory of Eternal Life*. In 1949 he began to translate Ouspensky's writings into Spanish, which he published at his own printing company called Ediciones Sol, which at the time offered 14 titles. In the mid-1950s he travelled to several other countries, as Bennett writes, "When we reached Cyprus, we unexpectedly met Rodney Collin-Smith and his wife. They had made a quick journey in the Near East, impelled it seems by much the same need as mine, to find evidence that the ancient traditional wisdom had not been lost" (Bennett, 1974: 315). Collin could have met Gurdjieff since between 1930, when he started reading about Gurdjieff's Work, and 1949, when Gurdjieff died, they were contemporaries. However, it seems that Ouspensky's writings were enough, together with — most importantly— his own discoveries.

Rodney Collin's work is original, serious, profound and referenced to all the sources he was able to find. In *The Theory of Celestial Influence* he combines the teachings of Ouspensky with treaties he consulted at the British Museum Library, several of them about the genesis of the universe and many others about human nature, both from a physiological and psychological perspective. He uses, of course, the Enneagram as a model to explain the universe and the human being within it, but he warns that his method is dual: inductive and deductive at the same time. This is the only way is he able to make the leap to the comprehension of unity, "For such true 'models of the universe' must not only display the inner form and structure of this universe, but must also reveal man's relation to it and his present and possible fates within it" (Collin, 1989: 2). He develops a detailed account of the function of each of the endocrine glands associated with each personality type, using the seven types of the Enneagram that Ouspensky worked with, and concludes that only by effectively and permanently overcoming the old personality, is it possible to acquire a new plane of consciousness.

Blake

A.G.E. Blake was a disciple of Bennett's until the latter's death and, together with Bennett's wife Elizabeth, he undertook the systematization of his writings into Bennett's last book[174]. Blake was born in Bristol in 1939. He studied physics at the university there and then went to Cambridge to study history and philosophy of science. For several decades he worked with John G. Bennett. In 1996 he published *The Intelligent Enneagram*, and in the preface he expresses his surprise that so few people who comment on the Enneagram take note of the astonishing hypothesis about the interconnections of the three octaves or worlds or types of action. What abounds, according to Blake, are the mechanical approximations which defeat the purpose of the Enneagram (1996: xv).

Although Blake was a student of someone who had been a direct disciple of Gurdjieff, he did not limit himself to that teaching. His academic background and his personal curiosity led him to investigate and practice his understanding beyond what Bennett himself proposed. His studies in physics meant he had no difficulty in understanding the exchange of letters that Bennett maintained with David Bohm[175] who, in 1950, published *Quantum Theory*. Blake had been Bohm's student at Bristol University and was able to integrate his quantum theories with the Enneagram. He claims that Bohm shows how it is necessary to progressively remove different veils to reach the essential and the true. He added that this is related to the foundation of the Enneagram in the "irreducible

---

[174] *Masters of Wisdom*, published in London in 1977 by Turnstone Books.

[175] The relationship between them was published as *The Bohm-Bennett Correspondence* by The DuVersity Publications.

idea of cosmoses: of the supersystem, and the subsystem, which form a quantum whole of action" (Blake, 1996: xvi).

Almaas

A.H. Almaas is of Kuwaiti origin and his full name is A. Hameed Ali. In January 1994, he recounts his own spiritual path after studying physics. "In 1971 I joined a group in Berkeley, where I was going to the University of California. The group was led by the Chilean Psychiatrist Claudio Naranjo. That group was the beginning of my direct contact with spiritual teaching, and the conscious launching of my inner journey. Dr. Naranjo, whom I related to as my teacher of the time, taught spiritual practice, mainly meditation, combined with psychological exploration. He combined his experience from Gestalt therapy and Karen Horney's self analysis with the map of the enneagram…The work I did with Naranjo extended the emotional openness I had experienced with Conant to the spiritual dimension, bringing about my first experiences of Essence, chakra openings and some development of the three centers as taught by Gurdjieff. Dr. Naranjo used the Gurdjieffian concept of the contrast of Essence with personality. This notion had a great impact on the direction of my journey" (Almaas, 2000: xi)."

With regard to the Enneagram, Almaas has not felt the need to repeat what has already been written throughout the 20th century. He recognizes the nine points of fixation of the ego that Ichazo proposes, the nine emotions of the ego that Naranjo studies, the nine forms of intuition according to Helen Palmer, the nine psychological structures we find in the books by Riso and Hudson, but beyond all these, Almaas conceives the Enneagram as an objective knowledge of all reality, not only of a human reality. He constructs a model of the Enneagram to show that "The Enneagram is a structure which facilitates the revelation of truth about Being and about human beings as part of this Being" (Almaas, 1998). With this author we move entirely into the realm of the essence. His quest is centred on going beyond the illusory points of view of egoic experience and of the sphere of fixations.

His writings surprise because his access to the subject was an interest in disentangling the nature of the real in Physics. He was writing his doctoral thesis at the University of Berkeley when he also started wondering about the reality of human nature. He is the creator of the Diamond Approach to self-realization. It is a spiritual teaching with modern psychology theories. He has written 17 books about spiritual realization. Among others, *Luminous Night's Journey: An Autobiographical Fragment* (2000[1996]), where he explains how the many Buddhist, Vedanta, Sufi, mystical Christian, and other sources influenced his spiritual path; *Facets of Unity* (1998) about the Enneagram of Holy Ideas, dedicated to Claudio Naranjo and with a prologue by Oscar Ichazo, and *The Inner Journey Home* (2004) about the soul's realization of the unity of reality, with enlightening appendices about the Western and Eastern concepts of the soul, as well as about the vision of the soul as an autopoietic system.

Defouw

Richard J. Defouw was born in 1944 in the United States and from his early days was interested in astronomy, which he went on to study at the University of Harvard, obtaining his PhD in 1970, from the California Institute of Technology, with a thesis entitled *Thermal instability and the connective stability of stellar chromospheres.* For two years he participated in a study group at the Institute for Religious Development, led by Willem A. Nyland, a student of Gurdjieff's. Then he spent 10 years as a student at the Gurdjieff Foundation of Colorado. In 2011 he published his book *The Enneagram in the Writings of Gurdjieff* which begins with the following advice to future readers: "I urge prospective readers … not to read this book until they have read *Beelzebub's Tales* and *Meetings with Remarkable Men* at least three times, as Gurdjieff suggests in the 'friendly advice' that appears in the front matter of the former work. To make it easier to exercise the recommended patience, I emphasize my belief that knowledge of the enneagram can be of practical use only to someone who has already attained an unusual level of inner development" (Defouw, 2011: vii). This is a work of high philology about what Gurdjieff wrote and what Ouspensky recorded of Gurdjieff with the purpose of presenting "a unified solution to a number of mysteries connected with his writings and with the symbol that is associated with his teaching, a geometric figure known as the enneagram" (Defouw, 2011: 1).

Chapter 10

Oscar Ichazo: a mix sources

This Enneagram scholar was born, in his own words, "in Roboré, Santa Cruz, Bolivia at seven o'clock in the morning on the twenty-fourth of July, 1931" (Ichazo, 1982b: 73 [Huneeus, 1976]).[176] Of his early education he says: "I had started in a Jesuit school where all the priests were Spanish, very Catholic, very old style. They were extremely rigorous with the Mass every day" (Ichazo, 1982b: 31 [Wilson, 1975]).

He first encountered Gurdjieff's ideas through a group which in the early 1950s, in Buenos Aires, followed the teachings of various masters and traditions, Ouspensky among them. In response to a direct question about the disciplines shared within this group, Ichazo claims, "About two-thirds of the group were Orientals, so they were strong on Zen, Sufism, and Kaballah. They also used some techniques I later found in the Gurdjieff work" (Ichazo, 1982b: 8 [Keen, 1973]).

---

[176] Ichazo has given many interviews over the decades. In this chapter, I cite several, some of which I have traced to their originals, but which are most easily found reprinted in the book, *Interviews with Oscar Ichazo* (Ichazo, 1982b). These include:
1) "A Conversation about ego destruction with Oscar Ichazo" by Sam Keen, *Psychology Today*, July 1973, pages 64-72.
2) "The field of decisions" by Timothy Wilson, 1975.
3) "Observations on Arica" by Antonio Huneeus, 1976.
4) "I am the root of a new tradition" by Dorothy de Christopher, 1981.
Another important interview with Ichazo was carried out by Andrea Isaacs and Jack Labanauskas and published in three parts in *Enneagram Monthly* (1996/1997).

There is one relevant biographical fact that explains Oscar Ichazo's early interest in understanding any kind of phenomena associated with the human mind and body. By his own account, on the 20th of December 1937, when he was six and a half, he had his first, very violent seizure similar to those provoked by epilepsy (Ichazo, 1982b [Keen, 1973]). The attacks recurred every two or three days, just when he was between waking and sleeping. He was in pain, and felt as though he was about to die, and after a time he perceived himself returning to his body and found he was alive. The fear that his next seizure would be his last accompanied him daily, along with the fear that his parents would think him dead when he had only left his body, as he said. From then on he began to investigate what was happening to him so that he could return to normal.

There was a happy coincidence in his life, because —as he says in various interviews— in 1943 he inherited, through an uncle, a library that had been his grandfather's where he was able to read about many things, but he was particularly drawn to the texts on anatomy, physiology and medicine. Later, he learnt martial arts, he trained with sensei Kentaro Ohara, a Samurai, and he was initiated in the ways of Zen meditation. As a teenager he encountered Bolivian indigenous peoples who introduced him to shamanism and the experience of taking ayahuasca. He also tried hypnotism and hatha yoga. At the age of 19, in La Paz, he met a remarkable 60 year old man, who asked him not to reveal his name,[177] who introduced him to the group in Buenos Aires. Within the group, he started out as a coffee boy and later became an active member in the study of techniques for the expansion of consciousness. In 1954 he arrived in Santiago de Chile and two years later, at the Institute of Applied Psychology, he began to give courses, interspersed by long trips between 1956 and 1960.

By his own account, in North Kashmir and southern Iran he studied tantra, and Sufism in the Pamir. Gurdjieff also travelled on this

---

[177] On page 7 of Sam Keen's 1973 interview with Ichazo, reprinted in *Interviews with Oscar Ichazo*.

plateau in Tajikistan. Ichazo claimed that at the end of the 1950s, when he was there, there were three houses called "the monastery" which have since disappeared. "There was real knowledge taught there", he said and continued: "Padmasambhava, the founder of Tibetan Buddhism, came from the Pamir, and if you examine the theories of Padmasambhava, you will see that it's very close to that of the Sufi and Zoroastrian traditions" (Ichazo, 1982b: 133 [De Christopher, 1981]). Ichazo received help during this trip across the plateau of the Pamir Mountains from some Jemaluddin Muslims that he had met in Kabul.

In 1987, tired of hearing and reading different versions of the origin of the symbol he writes, "I don't know what terms I am going to use to tell these people that, in fact, I didn't receive the enneagons from anybody —for saying anybody— or prove me differently. They came to me, 108 in all, as in a vision, showing their internal relations with complete clarity, in 1954 in Santiago, Chile" (Ichazo, 1988: 70). In any case, he had already encountered the Enneagram in the group in Buenos Aires who studied the work of Ouspensky.

We must be clear that Ichazo uses the term enneagon for the symbols applied to different aspects of nature, the cosmos or the human psyche. One of them, the one that is commonly known as the Enneagram of Personality, is, for Ichazo, the enneagon of ego fixation. Speaking more about the vision in which he received the enneagons, he continues, "The enneagons certainly didn't come to me as a coincidence or a casual realization while in my car staring at the stars during a hot summer's night. In fact, they came to me as the result of a long process of investigation, analysis, and careful study of theology, philosophy, and mysticism, and our scientific knowledge of physics, biology, and medicine" (Ichazo, 1988:70). By the time this process of study had intensified for him, he had already encountered, in 1949, the symbol of the Enneagram and the diagrams of Raymund Lull.

After his journeys and his first courses, Oscar Ichazo spent the year of 1964 in voluntary isolation from everything and everyone, entirely alone at his father's house in Bolivia and recounts, "I had an experience there that came without my effort and really surprised me. I felt that this experience was *it* — that I didn't need to learn anything else. I had reached totality" (Ichazo, 1982b: 134 [De Christopher, 1981]).

From 1965 he systematized his ideas and in 1969 he presented his theory of protoanalysis and his doctrine of ego fixations at the Institute of Applied Psychology in Santiago de Chile. Here, he met Claudio Naranjo, who introduced him to the members of the Esalen Institute[178] in Big Sur, California, whom he invited, in 1970, to a 10-month training session in Arica, Northern Chile, where, among other things, he taught the Enneagram.

Fifty seven North Americans attended this training course, "all of them deeply involved in the avant garde methods of psychotherapy" (Ichazo,1982a: 1). He adds that "These people had the tremendous advantage of having already been in too many trips of all kinds: drugs, psychotherapy, and all kinds of things that were around Esalen. At that time Esalen was extraordinarily powerful and extraordinarily serious because the Tibetans were already there; there were proven Zen masters; Rolfing was around. These are things that really count in this culture, that really counted and still count. They discovered a large part of Sufism and a lot of other things. Esalen really played an incredible role" (Ichazo, 1982b: 42-43 [Wilson, 1975]).

The following year he founded the Arica Institute in New York, which has continued to the present, currently with another office in Hawaii, where Ichazo lives. At both, they teach and practice Protoanalytical Theory, system and method that works with different levels of mental structure to reach what these professionals

---

[178] The Esalen Institute was founded in 1962 by M. Murphy and D. Price, Stanford graduates, to carry out interdisciplinary research on subjects that traditional academic establishments do not study. Some individuals who gave courses and workshops there in the 1960s include Gregory Bateson, Abraham Maslow and Fritz Perls.

call anamnesis, which includes self-recall, self-discovery and self-realization.

When he was 60 years old,[179] Ichazo wrote a 49-page document in which he claimed that there was not a single original idea in Gurdjieff's work.[180] To support his theory he ran through the philosophical and spiritual traditions from which he claimed that Gurdjieff and his followers had taken ideas. In the text he flaunted his erudition, showing that he knew the ideas of the Chaldean Magi, Plato's dialogues, the Vedic reminiscences, the doctrine of Stoicism, the Bhagavad Gita, the writings of Aristotle and Plutarch, and the Orthodox Philokalia. He writes this document in response to a letter written by a former pupil of Naranjo's who claims that Ichazo took his system from Gurdjieff and that more recent writers about the Enneagram have given it the scientific bases that it needed.[181]

Reading Ichazo's work, we can immediately perceive that behind his publications from the 1980s onwards, there are decades of study and practice, and the diversity of his sources is verifiable. The Arica School that he founded had, in his own words, a "new ontological position [and therefore] can appropriately be called a new tradition and does not affect any other tradition or discipline. I am not saying the Arica reconciles them. However, from a new perspective they become understandable for us" (Ichazo, 1988: 105).

If we look carefully at what Ichazo started to publish from that time, it is possible to detect the development of his conclusions after a remarkable amount of reading, including some texts about perennial philosophy from different sources.

---

[179] At time of writing, in 2015, Oscar Ichazo is 84 years old and lives in Maui, Hawaii.

[180] *Letter to the transpersonal community* by Oscar Ichazo, 1991. www.arica.org/articles/trletter.cfm

[181] Helen Palmer, "The Enneagram Heresy", distributed among Enneagram students.

Ten years after his work in Arica, Chile, with 57 students including Claudio Naranjo, his discourse was broad and included many different periods of human history.[182] It seems relevant that in his historical account Ichazo places emphasis on authors who, however indirectly, are related with the teachings of Gurdjieff. For example, when he gets to Hegel and in speaking of the dialectical laws, the backdrop is Gurdjieff's Law of Three and Law of Seven. We must remember that Ichazo himself claims to have read the writings of the Armenian teacher,[183] which seems natural considering that Ichazo was born 65 years after Gurdjieff.

In his 1981 conference Ichazo did not mention the Enneagram but he did explore several of its elements. On the one hand he spoke of the three centers of the human being, "So, the analytical point of view comes via the channel of our intellect. The analogical point of view is rooted in our emotions. The empathetical point of view refers to what we speak of as 'intuition' and is connected to our physical body" (Ichazo,1982a: 52-53). And on the other hand, after a brief Oriental incursion to speak of Lao-Tse, the historical Buddha and Tilopa,[184] the Bolivian teacher presented elements that are central to the Enneagram of nine personalities.

"Now, here we can accept the fact that consciousness manifests itself in nine different *systems* which we can separate: the sexual system, the skeletal and muscular system, the gastro-intestinal system, the skin and lymph system, the circulatory system, the

---

[182] See the conference that took place on August 6th 1981 at Alice Tully Hall, in New York: "Between Metaphysics and Protoanalysis" published with the same name and the subtitle "A Theory for Analyzing the Human Psyche" (Ichazo, 1982a).

[183] In a conversation with Alejandro Jodorowsky, Ichazo claims to have read Gurdjieff and his disciples. See p. 277 of Jodorowsky, A. (2010) *La danza de la realidad*, México DF: Random House.

[184] Tilopa (988-1069), is a Mahasiddha, born in Bengal, who develops the Mahamudra level of Buddhism. He is considered the human founder of the Drukpa Karyiud lineage, whose head is now Gyalwang Drukpa.

expression system (voice and facial muscles), the coordination system (cerebellum and medula oblongata), the sentry system (hypothalamus, pituitary and spinal cord), the system of unity (sympathetic ganglia, pineal, and thalamus). And from these nine systems are derived the nine *senses*: smell, kinesthetic, taste, touch, temperature, equilibrium, hearing, vision, voice" (Ichazo, 1982a: 55-56).

The number nine continues to be present, since through these nine senses Ichazo discovers nine basic *structures*: distance, volume, weight, movement, time, past, future, anticipation and idea of self. Through these nine structures he finds nine *domains* that include society and existence: conduct and behavior, rank and authority, work and activity, social interaction, intellectuality, creativity, security and protection, sentimentality and spirituality. "At this point we can observe that the differences between human beings may be described by nine different types of personality which occur when individuals, in early childhood, become deeply attached to one of the domains. We call these clusters of attachments *fixations*" (Ichazo, 1982a: 56).

According to Ichazo, with this understanding we can begin the study of protoanalysis, whose Greek etymology comes from *protos*: first or principal, and *analysis*: dissolution in component parts. In the last part of his August 1981 conference, he explains how to analyze the elements that come into play in each personality type and concludes with the great promise of protoanalysis: "protoanalysis is a proposition for a new theory of the psyche, a theory for self-realization, and also a theory for curing psychic and physical illness, with enormous precision in diagnosis and precision in treatment leading to cure" (Ichazo, 1982a: 65).

There is no doubt that Oscar Ichazo was, in his youth, a great seeker who studied a great variety of traditions and later scrutinized Gurdjieff's legacy. With regard to the history of the Enneagram, what becomes clear from his biography is that he knew the teaching of Gurdjieff before going to Arica for the work sessions with

Naranjo and other colleagues. The symbol had already emerged in the West, Ouspensky's books were already known in intellectual circles. What the symbol did not have yet, was the system that Ichazo calls the nine ego fixations, nor the five enneagons of fixations, passions, virtues, traps and ideas that we find in Ichazo's writings[185]. *This* is Ichazo's contribution, inspired —as he has said himself— by the work of Raymund Lull.

In one interview by Andrea Isaacs and Jack Labanauskas, Ichazo recounts that in the library he inherited from his grandfather he found, in a book by Raymund Lull, the Chaldean seal or symbol of the Enneagram (Isaacs and Labanauskas, 1996/1997). The list of vices, with equivalent virtues, comes from the ideas or dissertations of the Fathers or Doctors of the Roman Catholic Apostolic Church, like Augustine of Hippo or Thomas Aquinas. What Lull does, for mnemonic effect, is place the list in a circumference with the nine-point star. Lull's diagrams present a completely symmetrical star, whereas the symbol of the Enneagram contains a hexad which makes it different. Ichazo's contribution consisted in placing a part of the Christian content in the Chaldean symbol and incorporating the movements that are also present in Gurdjieff's teaching; that is to say studying how conscience can make a change, how, in breaking the mechanical habit of everyday actions, the organism generated mutations in its componentes and can thus take steps towards an evolution of the self. He understood the fixation of hydrogens in the human being through three forces: active, passive and neutralizing. This is what gives his Enneagrams greater power and which gives them the appeal which Naranjo transmitted in his first courses and which may have influenced not a few Jesuits to dedicate their lives to the Enneagram.

The strength of the nine personality types comes, not simply from having placed the vices and virtues in the symbol, but from rooting them in the underlying movement of the Law of Three (or the law

---

[185] See the five enneagons in *Interviews with Oscar Ichazo* (Ichazo, 1982b), pages 15-18 [Keen 1973].

of the three forces of creation) and in the Law of Seven (or the law that restricts creation) taught by Gurdjieff. Ichazo must also have known that the disciples of Gurdjieff used the symbol to place a typology based on the predominance of endocrine glands. For example, in *The Theory of Celestial Influence* by Rodney Collin, published in English in 1954, there is a symbol, with these three types. This is behind Ichazo's enneagons and this is why he so impressed his 57 students from Esalen who first came to his courses in Arica, Claudio Naranjo among them.

In addition to his varied theses, for the purposes of our account, what Oscar Ichazo apparently managed to bring together was the ancient inheritance of the Chaldean Magi, guarded for centuries by the Orthodox Churches in the East, with some redeemable elements of medieval Apostolic Roman Christianity, all in the symbol of the Enneagram.

Oscar Ichazo

Chapter 11

Naranjo, Palmer and the present

Before the 1970s the Enneagram was only known in closed circles and the information about its application in daily life required the teaching of a master.[186] After the training courses imparted by Ichazo in Arica, gradually these opportunities increase and more sources of knowledge become available. Claudio Naranjo was there, a Chilean, born in Valparaíso in 1932. He studied medicine and graduated in 1959, did his psychiatric residency at the University of Chile Psychiatric Clinic, then went on to study varied programmes at the universities of Harvard, Illinois and Berkeley, and joined the Esalen community, in Big Sur, California, as a visiting associate. After meeting Ichazo, in Chile, at the end of the 1960s, he started teaching the personality types using the symbol of the Enneagram in the United States. Initially he shared it with small groups and later he opened his courses to the general public and received students from different areas. As we have already said, some Jesuits priests stand out among his students, and they would soon write about their experiences and share their learning within their communities. Helen Palmer also received information from these courses; in 1988, she would publish one of the most popular and accessible books on the Enneagram (Palmer, 1991 [1988]), which came out six years before Naranjo's own book (1994). Claudio Naranjo founded the SAT programme, based on the name of Gurdjieff's group of friends called Seekers After Truth, a programme which he renewed

---

[186] *Fragments d'un enseignement inconnu*, by Ouspensky was published in 1949 and is followed in 1952 by *Psychological Commentaries on the Teaching of Gurdjieff and Ouspensky*, by Maurice Nicoll. Outside a study group it was difficult to understand and practice the teachings.

and expanded to several countries at the end of the 1980s. Naranjo's teachings have had most echo and gained strength in Spain. The Fundación Claudio Naranjo was founded in April 2007, in Barcelona, with a mission to integrate the proposals of the SAT program and the education system.[187]

What aspects of the Enneagram did Naranjo teach? I leave the answer to Ichazo (in his foreword to Almaas' book): "Naranjo worked mostly with the Enneagram of the Passions which, of course, is the psychological level of the system. Then Naranjo produced excellent psychological insights into the passions and the fixations, and their relationship to the entire psyche. In this way he produced a totally valid perspective of his further inquiries of the nine psychological types or as Naranjo named them appropriately the 'Ennea-Types'" (in Almaas [Ichazo], 1998: vii).

For his main book, Naranjo delves into theories of personality and character by Freud, Reich, Jung, Kretschmer, Sheldon and many others like Abraham, Ferenczi, Klein, Perls, Horney and, of course, Ichazo in order to make a consistent and empirically-founded proposal, something which had not occurred much at that time. In *Character and Neurosis: An Integrative View* he proposes nine personality types whose theoretical background is derived from the cited authors, but also and above all, from Naranjo's search for a theory based on his own practical and experimental work.

Among his most decisive influences he mentions William H. Sheldon, US physician and psychiatrist who explored both the physiological and the behavioral aspects of personality. Naranjo writes, "Sheldon's notion that three dimensions of human temperament are intimately related to the body structures that derive from the original three layers of the human embryo had a profound impact on my understanding of things at that time" (Naranjo, 1994: xxiii). Thus, three body structure types (ectomorphic, mesomorphic and endomorphic) correspond to three temperament groups:

---

[187] For more information see www.fundacionclaudionaranjo.com (in Spanish).

cerebrotonic, somatotonic and viscerotonic, which, in Naranjo's model and others are known as: mental, emotional and visceral.

Naranjo spreads the nine personality types out according to these three types and encloses them in a circle and justifies it as follows, "'the structure of personality traits, when defined by an individual's interpersonal behavior, may best be represented in terms of this circumplex model' (Cooper et al, 1990). This is a circular continuum with adjoining characters being most similar to each other, while oppositions along the circle correspond to bipolarities" (Naranjo, 1994: 14).

There is a flow between the nine types, there are opposites and neighbors, so after describing each one, Naranjo demonstrates the psychodynamic character of his model. In addition, each of the nine types has three sub-types according to the three innate or instinctive reactions depending on the predominance of the sexual impulse, the social impulse or the self-preserving impulse. Thus, Naranjo works with 27 basic personality types, a greater number than any of the previously mentioned authors. One of his most recent books, published in 2012 (in Spanish), is specifically focused on these 27 sub-types and in the prologue he writes: "Although I am already on the threshold of my 80 years, I feel that it is time to leave a written record of some of the subjects that I have reserved, until now, for experiential situations… Through these chapters the reader can form an approximate idea of the 27 sub-divisions of the nine basic personality types, which have already inspired so many books" (Naranjo, 2012:16).

Any well documented history of the Enneagram will include mention Claudio Naranjo.

Another key player in this history is Helen Palmer, who quickly recognized that the teachings should be made public and began to write. She had an academic background and and familiarity with the written word which made it easy to begin. She was in contact with two key 20th century authors: Naranjo and Ichazo.

With the first, Claudio Naranjo, she took a course which immediately inspired her to start exploring everything to do with the Enneagram and write her first book: *The Enneagram. Understanding yourself and the others in your life* (1991). We imagine that this book, first published in 1988, surprised Naranjo, who had at the time not yet published anything about the Enneagram. Six years later, in *Character and Neurosis*, he mentions Palmer to say that her book is the most informative of those published at that time although, he adds, "I would have expected a greater original contribution" (Naranjo, 1994: xxxi). Palmer's second book, *The Enneagram in Love and Work: Understanding your intimate and business relationships* was published in 1993, a year before Naranjo's. In addition to her writing, Palmer began to carry out empirical research and to teach on the Enneagram Professional Training Program. With David Daniels she led panels on the nine personality types and in the Winter of 1994 she founded the International Enneagram Association with a group of the first masters: Beesing, Daniels, Donson, Ebert, Hudson, Hurley, O'Leary and Riso.

Her contact with Oscar Ichazo also deserves a mention, not to add color to this account, but because of the implications of the encounter. He had founded the Arica Institute in 1968. In 1986 he began to write letters to his school. The first collection of letters, written between 1986 and 1987, has been edited as a book and in the later letters, sent in December 1987, we can detect his irritation with the publications of some of Naranjo's students (Ichazo, 1988: 67-107).

In 1991 Ichazo published his 49-page letter[188] in response to a text by Helen Palmer —*The Enneagram Heresy*— which was itself a response or defence against an accusation of plagiarism which Ichazo lodged with the judicial authorities in New York City. In this lengthy text, Ichazo presents together all that he read and studied over the decades to demonstrate the originality of his work and his

---

[188] Letter to the Transpersonal Community (1991), www.arica.org/articles

208

ownership over the knowledge. If it had not become material before a court of law, the content of these arguments would have been interesting in the framework of a debate about research on the Enneagram.

That same year, when the paperback edition of Palmer's book was about to be printed, Harper Collins announced that the book was the subject of a lawsuit initiated by the Arica Institute who alleged that their rights had been infringed. The editorial added a note of clarification in the paperback edition: "Ms. Palmer has developed theories about the use of the enneagram in understanding human personality and its relationship to aspects of higher awareness that are different and distinct from those expounded by Mr. Ichazo" (Palmer, 1991: xvii).

The court hearing took place in a Federal court in New York and continued from early 1991 to mid 1992,[189] eventually deciding in favor of Helen Palmer and her publisher. This episode is relevant because if Ichazo had won, it would have been difficult to publish any other books on the Enneagram in the United States and to have Palmer's books translated into 28 languages, as has now happened.

Palmer has continued to work on deepening her understanding of the Enneagram. In the second half of the 1990s she came into contact with Blake, great exponent of the Gurdjieff-Bennett tradition, when he asked for her opinion on his text *The Intelligent Enneagram*, which she called a "comprehensive sourcebook provid[ing] an overview of Enneagram dynamics, demonstrating a powerful model for enlarging our intelligence in many fields...".[190] There is evidence that she is interested in the original matrices of this knowledge: at the International Enneagram Association's

---

[189] From 9 April 1991 the second circuit of the Court of Appeal refused Ichazo's claim.

[190] Her opinion was placed on the cover of *The Intelligent Enneagram*, 1996 edition.

Global Conference 2015, she proposed that the Law of Three and the Law of Seven were key issues to work on.[191]

This initiative is extremely important because it is an invitation to return to some of the theses of the Fourth Way. These theses would lead many people to move on from the Enneagram of nine personalities to a much broader model that seeks to understand the workings of the Universe.

---

[191] IEA Global Conference program 2015, page 25.

Chapter 12

The legacy of personality theories in the Enneagram

For most people, their first encounter with the Enneagram is what they consider to be a typology of nine personalities; but it is important to be quite clear that the Enneagram is not just one more typology. It is a model of interactions between different natural phenomena and one of them is the human being. A minority of Enneagramists —or at least we know little of them— come to this knowledge from a reading of Gurdjieff and his followers' complete works, where the human typologies are merely one of many subjects they touch upon.

In modern societies where it is common to discredit the *other* for being different, the typology of nine personalities is a very useful entry point, as long as we are aware that the personality type is a mask for the ego which we ought to discard. So, if we know that at all moments in history there have been classifications, it becomes feasible to locate in some of these periods, the elements that contemporary nine-personality-Enneagram authors have drawn from.

In brief and without wishing to disaggregate the elements of each era, we will take a look at studies undertaken throughout history, from the *Corpus Hippocraticum* onwards, in order to demonstrate that, in the West, from the 5th century BCE until the 13th century CE, the basis for classifying temperament and character were the four elements of nature (water, earth, fire and air) and the bodily humors, with some variants, like the addition of the 12 planets by Raymund Lull. This applies in the West, because in the East the elements are considered to be five: the first three, plus metal and wood (air is not considered an element of nature).

The contemporary Enneagram of nine personalities takes up elements that have endured since the time of the Pythagoreans until the 13th century CE, such as the constant reference to the soul, the essence, and the participation of the human in the divine, issues which Juan Huarte still mentions in 1575 and which the Newtonian-Descartian paradigm later displaces, although they do not altogether disappear.

Nineteenth century science, in its determination to measure and quantify everything, gives rise to French, Italian and German morphological theories which classify human beings according to physiological features and the predominance of certain organs in the body. The 20th century Enneagram, which goes beyond the nine personalities, takes into account some of these characteristics, but the more profound authors give the soul and the essence a more important role. If one prefers to leave these metaphysical aspects out altogether that is alright: there are several contemporary authors who have proposed separating the Enneagram from any vestige of spiritual or religious traditions, and have incorporated, instead, some of the ideas of Freud, Klein, Jung, Horney and other representatives of 20th century psychological theory.

The oldest known references to the elements that constitute the personalities come from the kingdoms between the Tigris and the Euphrates. The Chaldean Magi and the Ancient Egyptians spoke of original elements. The Ayurvedic texts confirm that they were also used in ancient India. China has an enormous legacy on the subject, from the beginning of the cosmogonic process, they mention the component elements of the body. Zhou Dunyi, an 11th century philosopher, says, "…and thus, in the midst of this alternation and mutual conditioning and combination of movement and rest, five elements are born and from them the infinite beings" (Lao Tsé [Preciado], 2012). These five elements, as we have said, are water, wood, fire, earth and metal. Their combinations and predominance in bodies give rise, respectively, to wisdom, kindness, love, trust and right, as well as fear, anger, incoherent mirth, excessive reflection and sadness.[192] The theory of the Zhineng Qigong, based on thousand-year old Chinese practices, including Taoism, associates each element with two organs of the body: wood with the liver and the gallbladder, fire with the heart and small intestine, earth with the spleen and the stomach, metal with the lungs and large intestine, and water with the kidneys and the bladder.[193] Then, just as in the Western approximations, the Zhineng Qigong associates each of these with certain behaviors. Thus we can see that the great civilizations of antiquity had already perceived this interconnection between elements and human bodies which amounts to the origin of personality theories.

The legacy of Ancient and Classical Greece allows us to state that several centuries before the common era, there was already an interest in explaining the differences in behavior between individuals. The ancestral starting point for this explanation is the philosophical speculation about the original beginning of everything in existence. They sought, as dictated by the Chaldeans, the four elements of nature: earth, aire, fire and water combined in the human body. Hippocrates is the best known representative of Greek culture on the subject of temperaments and characters, but he is not the only one to write on the subject. There were other contributions both before and after him.

Alfonso Reyes tells us that the *Hippocratic Corpus* "is a collection of medical texts and treaties that cannot be attributed exclusively to Hippocrates, they come from different, often contradictory, sources and where compiled between the 5th and 4th centuries BC" (Reyes, 1982: 163). This compilation includes texts by Thales of Miletus, Heraclitus, Anaximenes, Empedocles, Pythagoras and his disciple

---

[192] From a course on the Idea of Qi, the five movements of Qi (Wu Xing), given by Guillermo Fuentes García on April 18th 2015 in Mexico City.

[193] Pang, Ming (2014) *The Theory of Hunan Whole Entity*, ZQ Educational Corporation. Page 18.

Alcmaeon of Croton, on whose doctrine of harmony between the four elements Hippocrates based his own theory of the four temperaments.

What Hippocrates does is associate certain body fluids (blood, black bile, yellow bile and phlegm) with the four elements of nature (aire, earth, fire and water) to give a name to each of four temperaments: sanguine, melancholic or bilious, choleric or nervous and phlegmatic or lymphatic. He points out, among many other characteristics, the disease that each temperament is prone to. The central feature of the *Corpus Hippocraticum* is its rationality and consistency.

Plato's writings on the subject are eloquent. In the *Timaeus*, or the dialogue that tells the history of the universe until the formation of man, we also encounter the premises to construct a theory of the temperaments. Plato says: "Since there are four kinds which compose the body, earth, fire, water, and air, disorders and diseases arise from the unnatural prevalence or deficiency of these, or from their migration from their own proper place to an alien one; or again, since there are several varieties of fire and the rest, from any bodily part's taking in an unsuitable variety, and from all other causes of this kind... any element that trespasses beyond these limits in its incoming or passing out will give rise to a great variety of alterations and to diseases and corruptions without number" (Plato, 1997 [5th century BCE]: 334). He goes on to describe the bodily humors and the place they occupy in the laws of nature.

Plato and Hippocrates were contemporaries, both take for granted that in the physical constitution of humans there are combinations of elements that contribute to one or other behavior in the world. In his medical practice, Hippocrates is more interested in the imbalances of these elements in order to be able to heal, but both — like many other educated Greeks in the 5th/4th century BCE— know of the existence of various temperaments.

The year after Hippocrates' death, another philosopher was born, on the island of Lesbos, who would study characters and temperaments with attention to the vices and virtues of each. His name was Theophrastus, also known sometimes as Tyrtamus. He came to Athens as a very young man to study at Plato's school and later he became a disciple of Aristoteles. His legacy is broad and varied; he left texts on logic, physics, metaphysics, physiology, pathology, meteorology, zoology, botany, ethics, politics, economics, rhetoric and music. His study of the human characters begins with the words, "I have often in the past applied my thoughts to a puzzling question - one which I think will never cease to puzzle me. Why, when Greece lies under the same sky and all Greeks are educated in the same way, do we not have a uniform system of manners?" (Theophrastus, 2004 [3rd century BCE]: 63). His method, as he describes it, is to observe and record vicious or virtuous behaviors. His objective is that future generations have a summary as a reference point for life and practice. Theophrastus records 30 different characters with more precise psychological features than the four temperaments that Hippocrates had proposed, but they are not as well known as the *Corpus Hippocraticum.*

In the second half of the second century CE, another important figure contributed to the subject: Claudius Galenus, better known as Galen of Pergamon, a prominent Greek physician living in Rome, wrote the most complete work of antiquity on anatomy, physiology, pathology, therapeutics, pharmacy, pulse and the faculties of the soul. He combined these subjects with the ideas of the *Hippocratic Corpus*, a text that he knew almost by heart. A Mexican medical doctor and professor emeritus writes that, "By combining the humoral ideas of Hippocrates with the ancient Pythagorean theories of the four elements, to which he added his own concept of *pneuma* present in all parts, Galen proceeded to explain absolutely everything" (Pérez Tamayo, 1997: 51). Galen described how blood behaves in combination with air; the same occurs with fire and yellow bile, or earth and black bile, or water and phlegm. Health, this physician told his patients, depends on the equilibrium of the humors and the elements in the body. If one of the four elements predominates, the temperament of the person will be influenced by the features of that element.

The criteria for classifying temperament and what we now know as character, vary according to each author, their corresponding discipline or tradition. They are determined, also, according to what each historical period or discipline omits, highlights or discovers. What we would like to draw attention to in this history is how the features of the human types decisively influence the way in which we establish communication with our peers. If I am able to know which aspects of reality are more evident for each personality, I will be better able to capture what the other person is trying to say to me and I will understand which internal universe he (or she) is speaking to me from, even when my interlocutor is not fully aware of it. Similarly, I shall be able to understand those moments of anger or silence that seem inscrutable.

Let us continue with the history to understand where the contemporary instruments for the study of human personality came from; though we should say from the outset that this is not a comprehensive historical reconstruction of human work on the subject, indeed there are approaches and currents that we will deliberately barely mention. The objective here is to give a historical backdrop against which we will be able to highlight the relevance and centrality of the Enneagram, whose trajectory we have presented in the previous chapters.

Evidence of the interest in the study of personality to transcend human limitations have been found not only in Asia Minor and in Greece, but also, "The Muslim alchemists adopted the Greek doctrine of the four elements, and they suggested that a metal could be transmuted by changing quantitatively its elementary constitution" (Mason, 1962: 98). The ancient Arab world was no stranger to this knowledge. In the 11th century Avicenna adopted the humoral theory of disease[194] and the following century Averroes continued working with the hellenistic learning and studied Arab translations of Galen's texts.

In the 16th century there is interesting evidence from scholars focused on the empirically obvious. A French physiologist by the name of Jean Fernel attempted to locate the organ that provokes a specific humor in the body within the framework of Galen's texts and of old Greek humoralism, and thus he hoped to find out how they worked and influenced temperament. Fernel —also known as Fernelius, according to the latinized form of his name— was born in 1497 in Montdidier, in the region of the Somme, northern France, and in addition to his interest in the human organism, he was a mathematician, astronomer and philologer. Like Lull, he was a medieval scholar with one foot in the Renaissance. He gave up individual description and started working on generalizations. His best known work, according to scholars, is titled *Medicina*, "a volume of 630 pages whose *cum privilegio regis* is dated 18th November 1553. It was one of the most read texts on medicine in the 16th and 17th centuries... the first part deals with the elements, the temperaments, innate heat, the humors and human procreation among other subjects, all described in relation to humoral theory" (Pérez Tamayo, 1997: 70).

Fernel does not look into the behavior that derives from each humor, but his contemporary does; Juan Huarte de San Juan, a Spanish physician and philosopher, published in 1575 his *Examen de ingenios para la ciencia* (*Examination of Men's Wits*).[195] In the 16th and 17th centuries this text was carried with great success across Europe, with translations into Latin, French, Italian, English and German. His central thesis was that the differences between people, in terms of their abilities to acquire knowledge, depended

---

[194] Avicenna was Sufi, according to Jean Chevalier in *El Sufismo y la tradición islámica [Sufism and the Islamic tradition]*(1986) Kairós, Barcelona, p.73.

[195] The full text of *Examen de Ingenios* is available on line (in Spanish): http://electroneubio.secyt.gov.ar/Juan_Huarte_de_San_Juan_Examen_de_ingenios.pdf).

on the temperament of each and he described them in their daily life: the sanguine person is cheerful, the choleric is irascible, the melancholic is depressive and the phlegmatic is subdued. According to temperament, he proposed which studies or professions a person should follow. Throughout the book he cites, debates, coincides and disagrees with Hippocrates and Galen.

Huarte de San Juan presents an interesting angle that coincides with some contemporary Enneagram scholars: the relationship between two distinguishable but not separable aspects, personality and essence. This distinction is an ancient, fundamental inheritance which the Newtonian-Cartesian paradigm will inhibit. Personality and essence are a strand that appears in the teachings of Gurdjieff and is explored by several Enneagram schools.

To present his ideas Huarte developed a line of reasoning seasoned with Latin quotations and concluded, "Therefore, we understand, that prudence and wisdom, and the rest of human virtues, are in the soul, and they do not depend on the composure or the temperament of the body, as Hippocrates and Galen thought" (Huarte de San Juan, 1996 [1594]: Chapter V). Later on, in Chapter VII, Huarte concluded that Galen's error was to attempt to discover whether the rational soul, without a body, died or not, when actually this question belongs to a superior science with more precise principles. He raised then, issues that are still debated to the present. There is no consensus on which aspects of our personality are inherited, and which we learn in our early years, and which we carry within us from birth in what Renaissance authors called the essence of the soul. This writer's oeuvre is a commentated compendium on all that has been said on the subject from the Chaldeans until the 1680s.

Every author who has studied issues of character and personality has had to privilege some aspect in order to create a typology. Some have emphasized infancy and childhood experience. Others focus on organic constitution. Some limit their analysis to individual psychological factors. Some place greater importance on the family and the cultural context in which a person develops throughout their life. Some combine different approaches. It is undeniable that the *doxa* (Greek for popular opinion) of the time of writing of any text influences it in a decisive way, be it because the text flows with current thought or battles against it. If, in this context, the Enneagram is significant, it is because of the attempt made — unfinished but certainly greatly advanced— by many schools to include approaches inherited from earlier times and incorporate contemporary contributions without losing congruence.

Juan Huarte de San Juan looked back in time, into the depths of history, to develop a typology of character, but those that came after him, like many of his contemporaries, had to look at those around them, because the 16th century was a era of altered cosmovisions and broken paradigms.   For scholars in every branch of the sciences, looking around them meant taking a stand in the face of conflicting positions and deciding if they were willing to die in the defence of their findings and convictions.

Many changes were established during the course of the 16th century in the West. There was increasing awareness of an individual's creative force and a rupture occurred with the Christian tradition. In the second decade of the century, Martin Luther published his *Ninety-five Theses on the Power and Efficacy of Indulgences*; meanwhile, in Spain, the tribunal of the Inquisition was on the rise. The organization of the state emerged and geocentric beliefs began to fragment. At the same time as scholars sought to recover Greek and Roman classics, they increasingly abandoned supernatural explanations and gradually demanded empirical demonstrations of facts. Concrete man was reconsidered, given new value, with the body as a referent for action. All this would be the substrate of the 17th and 18th centuries, so that the 19th century saw the emergence, within the field of characterology, of the European morphological schools, which focused on physiological descriptions of the human organism.

A group of researchers in France devoted their work, based on their own interpretation of the Cartesian paradigm, to a clinical description of individuals in whom a given organ of the body predominated and the consequent characterological derivations. Two physicians developed typologies that broke with all preceding understanding: "Corman's morpho-psychology is based on the essential opposition between the expansive type and the withdrawn type; the first is cheerful, optimistic, spontaneous, impulsive, with concrete and practical thoughts; the second is pessimistic, reflective, inhibited, with a speculative spirit" (Mueller, 2007: 473).[196] In each case they methodically analyzed all the physiological features of their subjects.

The Italian morphological school undertook more sophisticated measurements, such as of blood, endocrine function, neurovegetative balance or basal metabolic rate. Thus Viola and Pende divide human beings into longilineal and brevilineal and subdivide these groups to distinguish four fundamental types. Germany also has a morphological school, led by Kretschmer, who bases his work on two main types and applies them to human races and historical figures.

These morphological schools share a common paradigm, that of modern science which proposes the separation of the material and the intangible, as well as the accompanying methods, questions and theories. It goes without saying that they focus fundamentally on the physiological; they have a strong influence on academia for several decades, until in the 1940s, William H. Sheldon, a Harvard professor, publishes a book in which, without abandoning morphological typology, he manages to empirically investigate — by means of diligent measurement— the formation of embryonic layers which he correlates with character types. His thesis is based on the development of these layers. For example, if the endoderm (corresponding to digestive tract and related glands) had greater intensity in the formation of the organism, the person will have a viscerotonic character; if the mesoderm (corresponding to muscle,

---

[196] First published in 1960 in French as *Histoire de la psychologie de l'antiquity à nos jours*.

blood and skeleton) predominated at the time of development, the person will have different characteristics of behavior; if the ectoderm (skin, nervous system and brain) predominated, the individual will belong to the cerebrotonic group and their conduct will be different again. Thus Sheldon established the so-called somatotypes.

Sheldon's influence was decisive even outside the field of morphological studies of personality and his theses have been taken up again by those researching the Enneagram in the second decade of the 21st century.[197] One of the most conspicuous contemporary representatives of the Enneagram, Claudio Naranjo, recognized the impact Sheldon had had on his own work (see Chapter 11).

What follows is a brief mention of other schools that have explored the differentiation of personalities, which is important because in the 20th century some contemporary authors who have dedicated their lives to the Enneagram have found parallelisms between their typologies and those of Freud and Jung.[198]

On the subject of characterology, as in other areas he studied, Freud astonished, caused controversy and provoked debate among his disciples and followers. The typology of character he established, according to his theory of psychosexual development, focused on three types of individuals: the oral (psychotic), the anal (obsessive neurotic) and the phallic-genital (hysterical) which correspond to

---

[197] In describing the bodily characteristics of each enneatype, Dr. Jerome Wagner uses some elements from Sheldon's work and others from Ichazo's. For example, in speaking of enneatype 5 he says that according to the Arica tradition of facial protoanalysis, fives have more tension on the right of their mouths and according to Sheldon's ectomorphic body type they have extremely sensitive brains and nervous systems (Wagner, 2010: 360).

[198] This is the case specifically for Don Richard Riso, as he describes in Chapter 14 of *Personality Types: using the Enneagram for Self Discovery* (1996).

the three main stages of infant sexuality.[199] Seeking a correspondence with the nine enneatypes, Don Richard Riso asserts that "If we go through the permutations, the resulting nine personality types are the oral-receptive (corresponding to the Nine), the oral-retentive (corresponding to the Four), and the oral-expulsive (corresponding to the Five); the anal-receptive (corresponding to the Six), the anal-retentive (corresponding to the One), and the anal-expulsive (corresponding to the Two); the phallic-receptive (corresponding to the Three), the phallic-retentive (corresponding to the Seven), and the phallic-expulsive (corresponding to the Eight)" (Riso and Hudson, 1996: 438). Leading writers on the Enneagram of nine personalities, then, are drawing on a historical inheritance of different periods.

Wilhelm Reich, in his first phase, goes further than Freud's theorizations and adds the contributions of others to develop his own theory, "The investigations of Abraham, Jones, Ophuijsen, and others built upon Freud's first work on this subject offer the most complete orientation in this area" (Reich, 1980 [1933]: 210). In his book about the analysis of character, Reich delves deeper and disagrees with Freud but without abandoning altogether the original pattern of oral-anal-genital characters. From 1933 onwards Reich would open new and different lines of investigation that diverge from those of Freud.

Something similar happens to Carl G. Jung, who was 20 years younger than Freud and admired him greatly, considering him, in his own words, to be an an intelligent, shrewd, altogether remarkable and not the least trivial man (Jung, 1989 [1961]: 149).[200]

---

[199] In general, adults tend to fixate their psychic energy in one of the three. Oral individuals can be associated with a receptive personality; anal with a retentive personality and phallic with an expulsive personality.

[200] Four years before his death, in the Spring of 1957, Jung began a series of conversations with Aniela Jaffé, to which he would add unpublished texts and fragments related to their exchanges. Jung did not want these memories to form part of his complete works. He called them *Einnerungen, Träume, Gedanken* and they were first published in English as *Memories, Dreams, Reflections* in 1961.

Jung diligently read everything Freud drafted and was very critical. They had long conversations, after which Jung would evaluate what convinced him and what he could not accept. In his own words: "I can still recall vividly how Freud said to me, 'My dear Jung, promise me never to abandon the sexual theory. That is the most essential thing of all. You see, we must make a dogma of it, an unshakable bulwark.' He said that to me with great emotion, in the tone of a father saying, 'And promise me this one thing, my dear son: that you will go to church every Sunday.' In some astonishment I asked him, 'A bulwark—against what?' To which he replied, 'Against the black tide of mud' —and here he hesitated for a moment, then added— 'of occultism.' ... But that no longer has anything to do with scientific judgement; only with a personal power drive" (Jung, 1989 [1961]: 150). Just two years later, Jung would break with Freud: "In 1912 my book *Wandlungen und Symbole der Libido* was published, and my friendship with Freud came to an end. From then on, I had to make my way alone" (Jung, 1989 [1961]: 206).

Jung developed, in 1921, a theory of psychological types or personalities based on two attitudes of the psyche: extroversion and introversion, combined with what he defines as their four functions: thinking, feeling, sensation and intuition. These combinations give rise to eight personality types, according to the types of relations that the individual establishes with other people and with their own interests. Jung calls this object relations theory. He classifies people into the eight types: Extroverted thinking, extroverted feeling, extroverted sensation, extroverted intuition, introverted thinking, introverted feeling, introverted sensation and introverted intuition. Jung said of this typology that it was enough to note the differences because he was more interested in what unites human beings than in what differentiates them; he is more interested in the soul and its potential than in the limitations of character. In relation to what he had written about psychological types he later said, "The book on types yielded the insight that every judgment made by an individual is conditioned by his personality type and that every point of view is necessarily relative. This raised the question of the unity which must compensate this diversity" (Jung, 1989 [1961]: 207). Jung's psychological types have been the starting point for later modifications. One example is Katherine Cook Briggs' test, creator, along with her daughter Isabel, of what is known today as the MBTI, or the Myers-Briggs Type Indicator, a self-report questionnaire method that describes behaviors but does not go into the motivations behind them, as does the Enneagram.

In his book on the Enneagram, Claudio Naranjo wrote, with regard to Jung's typology, "A project that developed as I produced this book was a systematic explanation of the correspondence of the ennea-types to the psychological types in Jungian typology (the eight types in Jung's original observation and the description of typical respondents to questionnaires based on Jung's concepts)" (Naranjo, 1994: xxxiv).

Jung was convinced that only the process of individuation, central in psychology, could lead to a transformation of the human being, beyond personal differences, as long as issues of the soul were attended to. "The very fact that through self-knowledge, that is, by exploring our own souls, we come upon the instincts and their world of imagery should throw some light on the powers slumbering in the psyche, of which we are seldom aware so long as all goes well" (Jung, 1970: 582). This idea of Jung's is fundamental to understand one aspect of the Enneagram: the subtypes or instincts that accompany each of the enneatypes and which are decisive when the person takes action.[201]

---

[201] Most Enneagram studies do not attempt to decipher or explain the subtypes; according to those who have delved deepest, sometimes they are only mentioned when they become essential for the individual to balance strengths and weaknesses in his (or her) personality. Naranjo's school and the majority of his followers divide the subtypes into three groups, according to the predominant instinctive characteristics: social, self-preservation and sexual. Some authors, like Wagner, prefer to refer to this latter instinct as intimate (2010) and others, like Helen Palmer, call it one-to-one (Enneagram Dot Com, 2009).

Don Richard Riso studied Jung's eight types and found a correspondence with the enneatypes, he even points out that enneatype 3 is described in the Jungian typology although it does not have a separate category.[202] This US author makes a valuable contribution with regard to the lines that connect the nine points of the symbol. He explains that they are connected in a precise order that denotes the direction of integration, which means health and self-fulfillment; the opposite direction would be the direction of disintegration or sickness and neurosis. The former, related to Jung, leads him to write, "From the point of view of the Enneagram, we can see that Jung usually describes some of the traits of the average person of each psychological type, freely ranging around what we would consider to be the Levels of Development. He intuitively shifts to the Direction of Disintegration at the end of his descriptions when he mentions neurotic and psychotic developments" (Riso and Hudson, 1996: 442).

Although Jung ventures into rich and diverse territory, not all of his followers are faithful. The case of one stands out, an Englishman, who graduated from Cambridge and continued his studies in psychiatry and psychology in Paris, Berlin and Vienna. In Zurich he met Jung and remained close to him for 10 years and he became one of the exponents of Jung's work at that time. His name was Maurice Nicoll. In 1921 he encountered the teachings of Gurdjieff and abandoned Jung forever. What did this Cambridge-educated doctor discover that persuaded him to set aside everything he had learnt in his 38 years? Among other things, Nicoll found the Enneagram and he dedicated the greater part of the second volume of his extensive text to it.[203]

---

[202] See section "Jung and the Enneagram" in *Personality Types* by Don Richard Riso (1996).

[203] Maurice Nicoll's five-volume work is titled: *Psychological Commentaries on the Teaching of Gurdjieff and Ouspensky*. They were originally published in London in 1952.

Once Naranjo publishes his work a multitude of authors confirm, apply, refute, complement, simplify and deepen his theories of personality. The interesting thing about those who study him and perceive how his model is constructed, is that they rarely object to the central characterization of the nine types, nor to the forms of communication and action that derive from them.

From Naranjo onwards, research, courses and publications on the enneatypes have multiplied.[204] Great interest in the Enneagram is aroused by the best known aspect which are the fixations of the ego in the nine personality types, an accessible starting point for a system that has an ocean's depth that most people are not interested in.

In the final decades of the 20th century and the first 15 years of the 21st, many non-orthodox psychologists have incorporated the Enneagram of nine personalities to their practice. It has also extended —for better or worse— among people from different academic backgrounds (or none) who find it useful for personal development and work teams.

In the same way, today there are many authors and practitioners of the Enneagram who are convinced that understanding the areas of light and dark in our own personalities is just a first step towards an integral transformation of the person. Following Gurdjieff, they seek a *second conscious shock,* or a second moment in their internal processes to generate a greater degree of evolution of consciousness.

---

[204] At the beginning of the second decade of the 21st century, there are already dozens of books about the Enneagram in at least 10 languages. The quality of these contributions varies from excellent to distorted repetitions of what has already been said.

This is the case for A.H. Almaas,[205] who opens one of his books with a differentiation of two categories of Enneagrams: that of the egoic experience, "reflecting fundamental spiritual ignorance" and that of essential experience "reflecting spiritual enlightenment" (Almaas, 1998: 4). One of his central themes is that the aspects of one's own essence can be revealed if we explore the ego and the personality, with a view to discovering how each of the enneatypes relates to the loss of contact with Being, our essential nature. Here lies Almaas' principal interest: with the help of the Enneagram, our self-comprehension of the loss of contact with Being can be organized simply and systematically. Almaas started working with the ideas proposed by Ichazo and Naranjo about the loss of contact with Being, and went on to develop, through practice, his own findings and his own school.

At the end of the first chapter of *Facets of Unity*, Almaas announces the purpose of his work: "We understand the objectivity of the Enneagram to mean, among other things, that it can be perceived directly by anyone with the necessary capacity, who inquires effectively into the nature of reality. And since it is a true model of reality, one cannot exhaust its knowledge. Knowledge of reality is both unlimited and inexhaustible: Each teaching has a specific way of describing reality and none of these ways exhausts all possible experience. The Enneagram is a structure that facilitates the revelation of truth about Being and about human beings as part of this Being" (Almaas, 1998: 5).

This same writer enters into territories where the answers do not coincide: Are you born with an Enneatype or does it form after birth? We need to update our information about the origin and development of life, not only from the biological perspective, but also —as several Enneagram scholars and practitioners point out—

---

[205] His name is A. Hameed Alí, born in 1944 in Kuwait. At the age of 18 he went to UC Berkeley to study physics and while there he encountered the Enneagram, which he then made his own through practice.

from the perspective of Being.[206] A.H. Almaas gives us his point of view, "The process of the soul's disconnection from its essential nature begins happening very early in life, even before birth. As the disconnection happens, the soul loses its central, most basic, most primary, most primal quality —clear knowingness, clear luminous awareness" (Almaas, 1998: 291). He maintains that the enneatype is determined at birth and, therefore, it is independent of the circumstances of our early life. He knows this is controversial and he admits that there is no data to confirm or disprove it but, in the end, either before or after birth, we lose contact with Being.

In exclusively physiological terms it is useful to be generally aware of the contributions that molecular biology has made in recent years. Many biologists the world over will recognize, and have done for several decades, the limitations of pure genetics to explain the laws of heredity. In the 1980s two Chilean biologists, Humberto Maturana and Francisco Varela, both with Harvard PhDs, proposed that the smallest unit of life could not be characterized exclusively on the basis of material components. There is a process of constitution of identity which begins in a network of metabolic productions; this refers to the self-production of the living organism at the cellular level (a process they called autopoiesis) but it does not take place only in terms of its physical-chemical structure but also in relation to it as an organized unit. This is biological phenomenology, that is to say that the human being is not the source of all biological order; we have to take into account that human organisms give rise to other organisms with different properties to those of the parents. Maturana asserts that, "all biological phenomena occur as a result of the individual realization of living organisms" (Maturana and Varela, 2004: 11).

Connected to the Enneagram, this theory about living beings supports the individual nature of human behavior, without

---

[206] A.H. Almaas, a writer who distinguishes the Enneagram of ego-fixations from the Enneagram of basic experience that reflects spiritual illumination, proposes the Enneagrams of Virtues and Holy Ideas.

overlooking the decisive influence of the environment in which an individual is born. Maturana writes, "At the moment of conception, the genetic constitution of the organism determines a range of possible ontogenies, within which the history of interactions with the environment will carry out one, in the process of epigenesis" (Maturana, 2004: 103). For one ontogeny to take place, of all those possible, is to live an enneatype with its genetic origin and its interaction with the surrounding environment. But contemporary biologists go even further, they propose other dimensions of human evolution apart from the genetic and epigenetic. In addition to these two, Jablonka and Lamb[207] have researched two more dimensions: behavioral and symbolic, which enrich the possibilities for structural change in a given organism, independently of its genetic inheritance.

The important thing about the Enneagram model is that, once an interested person finds his or her type and subtype, they understand the features of their personality and also those of the people they relate to daily or sporadically. Understanding them makes one more tolerant and more able to capture not only the particulars of their communication with others, but also to identify their potential, complementary contributions to collective actions.

---

[207] Jablonka, Eva and Lamb, Marion (2006) *Evolution in four dimensions. Genetic, Epigenetic, Behavioral and Symbolic Variation in the History of Life.* London: MIT Press.

Chapter 13

The Gurdjieff-Bennett-Blake
legacy for the process of communication

Gurdjieff's mistakes have also been taken advantage of to broaden the reach of the Enneagram to unsuspected quarters. Anthony Blake was ten years old when Gurdjieff died; but, thanks to his contact with John Bennett, he has been able to penetrate the aspects he considers most important in the older man's philosophy. Bennett introduced him not only to Gurdjieff's work but also to his own and their dialogue on these subjects lasted until Bennett's death. Afterwards, Blake worked with Elizabeth, Bennett's widow, to organize the publication of his work and seek new interpretations and applications for his teacher's oeuvre.

Blake realized something that now seems obvious, but which Gurdjieff's disciples may have thought was simply part of the master's method: they could not debate amongst themselves. Blake writes, "Of course, working in groups was always part of the Gurdjieff method, but it had not allowed speaking together and its potential for thinking together" (Blake, 2009: 1).

Ignoring or missing opportunities for dialogue on transcendent subjects and common tasks seemed to Blake a waste, especially because, as he wrote, "through dialogue I discovered an access to mind that led me into the world of group analysis and a way of 'working on oneself' that complemented Gurdieffian methodology" (Blake, 2009: 1). He was able to carry out the task of complementing Gurdjieff's and Bennett's work in a profound and creative way, thanks to the influence of another professor of his at Bristol University: David Bohm, author of *Quantum Theory*, published in 1950. Bohm also wrote *On Dialogue* (2004), a book of incalculable value about the nature of collective thought, which Blake would incorporate into his work. He draws on Bennett for his experience with patterns of thinking and the discipline of "systematics", a modern equivalent of Pythagorean thinking based on whole numbers and used to study the content and structure of meaning.

With this inheritance from his teachers, and a systematic and empirical approach to work, Blake writes *The Supreme Art of Dialogue: Structures of Meaning* about the patterns and flows that have their origin in the construction of meaning (2009). Twelve years earlier he had published *The Intelligent Enneagram*, the book that best penetrates the nature and possibilities of the symbol. What we perceive is an amalgam of the Enneagram and quantum mechanics not only to explain the nature of the processes of communication but also to offer empirically proven collective work methods to carry out creative and globally useful projects.

In his introduction to *The Supreme Art of Dialogue*, Blake says that in time he came to understand that working on oneself was not an entirely private affair, but that it was intricately involved in relations with others. This begins with the use of the symbols that we learn from our earliest infancy, that is to say with language and the forms of body language that go with it.

The Enneagram of nine personalities, which Blake does not participate in (at least not in his more recent texts), has polished the characteristics of each enneatype and has managed, after decades of observation and practice, to point out how each one communicates. We must take into account that the basic personality corresponds to a form of the ego, to a mask that the person was obliged to adopt to survive the hustle of social life and relations with others. So we must begin by getting to know that mask, our own and —if they allow us— those of the people that we usually live and work with.

This is where the contributions of the various studies about the nine personalities have a natural cross over point with Blake's proposals on dialogue. He finds, beginning with Bohm's work, that people can be considered to be molecules of meaning that relate to one another under certain conditions. Before we get into the details, it is worth remembering something that, in terms of communication, happens to us every day.

The ways in which people express their feelings and thoughts comes both from what we have learnt, and what we have inherited genetically or epi-genetically, and sometimes also from what is lodged in our sub-conscious. We are not all made the same, nor have we experienced the same circumstances. There are times when someone is saddened because of the harshness of another's words, when that other only spoke that way because it is the manner in which he (or she) learned to speak or defend himself. Perhaps each person's enneatype and circumstances intertwine in such a way that some people cannot build bridges for fluid communication.

In conversations with the people closest to us, there is usually no ill intent or desire to set a distance between us. So what emerges in that act of communication, is what each one of them is in that precise moment of interaction or when they discharge some withheld tension. The forms of communication are much more varied because each of us has an ocean's depth within us. Each one of us is unique and unrepeatable, but at the same time we are not all that original. There are patterns that repeat, personalities that are so alike that it is easy to point out their common features, although each exercises their own with individual traits and from their own particular biography. This is where the Enneagram of nine personalities could play an initial role in Blake's proposal. In order to start to build new common meanings, as he suggests, it is enormously useful to first master the blind spots that each of us has in our manner of establishing verbal and visual contact with others.

Why not suggest someone study the communicational characteristics and the types of actions in some other system that is not the Enneagram?

Essentially, for one reason: the Enneagram symbol forms the basis for the interactions between different personalities and in it are inscribed the various levels of evolution for each enneatype; this symbol is, in itself, a method that unites ancient wisdom with modern research. It is a method which is not limited to the paradigm of a certain period, but rather which articulates common elements of different eras and which aims towards the highest possible levels of consciousness.

The symbol of the Enneagram indicates the path or method that each person should follow to reach what they wish for. The etymology of the word *method* leads us directly to the word path: μέθοδος, *methodos*, which is made up of οδος (path or journey) and μετα (after or change).[208] In the symbol we have a route laid out for us which does not stop at any personality type for each human being, not only because of the abundance of sub-types that allow specificity and completeness, but also because it leads towards an awakening of human potential.

Usually the methods used at a certain time are rooted in the paradigm within which they were first articulated, in the epistemology that sustains them. At this point we can turn to the inescapable Kuhn, who writes of paradigms: "These I take to be universally recognized scientific achievements that for a time provide model problems and solutions to a community of practitioners" (Kuhn, 1970: viii). The Enneagram breaks with the norm because the people doing science 500 years before the Common Era —who were left out of the paradigm of the moment during the Age of Enlightenment— have re-emerged in the present. Their general acceptance seems unlikely, for now, given the

---

[208] The Greek prefix, μετα, means both further or after and change. Either meaning applies to the sense of *method* that is implicit in the Enneagram.

dispersion of knowledge in so many sciences and disciplines and given the systems of evaluation that are common today within each speciality.

Theories about human communication and the study of language have made some superb contributions to our understanding of coinciding with one another, to capture the other's meaning and to express ourselves without being misinterpreted. There are, however, some aspects that have not been thoroughly explored and which would be even more helpful to understand the act of communication. That *something* that has barely been mentioned by scholars is the specific way in which each type of character or temperament expresses their own way of seeing the world and acting within it. For some people, the emotions predominate and their manner of speaking is very different to those who have a strong intellect or who use very few words and almost no gestures. Enneagram practitioners would say that the former belong to the emotional triad and the latter to the cerebral triad. In the form of expression, there is a latent message that can be activated (or not) when received by a receptor who, in turn, has an innate sensitivity (or insensitivity) to certain stimuli. Character and temperament are an almost forgotten variable in the study of human communication.

Achieving full understanding that can translate into efficient and lasting action is extremely complex. Transmitting information is simple, as is broadcasting it. The problem lies in the re-semantization that the listeners apply to the original expression. Each person constructs and decodifies messages according to their own components, their particular biography, their lifestyle; that is to say, according to their enneatype. This is the source of the many misunderstandings and confusions that impair human communication.

Although we all have elements of all the enneatypes, there is one which kicks in automatically at times of crisis, utmost confidence or unexpected changes. It is the base-enneatype, which can present, as we have said, three forms or sub-types, depending on its dominant instinct. This gives us the range of 27 different possible personality types. In addition the two enneatypes either side of the base-type also influence it and are called "wings". This gives us 54 possibilities. But if each wing also has three possible dominant instincts, the permutations become 162 different possible personality types and if we add to this the particular life histories of each individual, the variation is exponential. Therefore no-one can be labelled as a fixed enneatype, but it is possible to identify certain basic features of the nine original enneatypes.

Several contemporary authors of the Enneagram of nine personalities have described how each enneatype communicates. Some, like Ginger Lapid-Bogda, recognize different aspects of the act of communication; the enneatypes are studied both as emitters and receivers of a message. She explains, for each enneatype, some typical elements of body language when expressing an idea, their blind spots when speaking to others and the receiver distortions that operate when they are listening to another person (Lapid-Bogda, 2004: Chapter 2). David Daniels and Virginia Price present several characteristics of each type. They identify style of communication as one of the most important of these characteristics. They point out which stimuli make each enneatype respond defensively and they also propose ways that others can support each enneatype in these situations (Daniels and Price, 2009: 20-54). In his second book on the Enneagram,[209] Jerome Wagner presents the principles that explain the workings of personality with the background motivations and values that make up the vision each type has of the world. He then goes on to describe how these dynamics work for each of the nine types. Within these dynamics we find the details of the nine approaches individuals use in the act of communication (Wagner, 2010: Part 2).

---

[209] The first is: *The Enneagram Spectrum of Personality Styles: an Introductory Guide* (also published as *An Introduction to the Enneagram. Personality Styles and Where You Fit*), 1996.

These three books together provide us with a rich and versatile panorama which is worth studying in detail. There is one more author, with 22 years of empirical experience, who has written a brilliant summary of the same thing with the additional advantage that he goes directly to the point of what is most relevant for each type. He is Roberto A. Pérez, author of the diagram titled *Communication*,[210] in which he describes the attitude of each personality type when communicating, as follows:

- **Type Ones: preach, teach.** Focus attention on behaviors and not motivations. Judge instinctively.

- **Type Twos: advise.** Prefer to speak in private and share advice within the context of a conversation.

- **Type Threes: promote themselves.** Focus on selling their ideas and initiatives, great persuasive skills.

- **Type Fours: complain.** All verbal expression is insufficient to transmit the complexity of their internal world. They adopt other forms of expression.

- **Type Fives: give speeches.** Determined to explain things and understand them. Need logical and analytical reasons.

- **Type Sixes: blend into the group.** Take a cautious and prudent attitude; their form of expression reveals doubts and fears.

- **Type Sevens: tell anecdotes.** Focused on lively and fascinating accounts, often captivating.

- **Type Eights: imperative.** Focused on confrontation and the pressure to get to the truth, in a convincing and energetic tone.

- **Type Nines: vague.** Give each thing the same attention, express themselves serenely and without emotion (Pérez, 2015: 39).

---

[210] Roberto A. Pérez, *Manual de Eneagrama, Tomo I, Version 08.13*, page 39, distributed at a course in Rosarito, Baja California, Mexico, January 27 - 29th 2015.

The location of a person in a specific type is not permanent since processes of integration of consciousness can take place within each enneatype. Consciousness is understood as an element of the essence of a person which can cause substantial changes in the way that person communicates. One objective it to go beyond a masked form of communication. The features we mention here are those of an average person, who is neither integrated nor disintegrated, someone who has not considered how to drop the mask that has served them for years. Even so, an average enneatype can contribute the advantages of its form of communication when working in a team.

Anthony Blake has imagined what could have been achieved at Gurdjieff's school if he had allowed his disciples to talk amongst themselves. The thought-processes generated would have prevented the dissolution of the group. With this in mind and with various theoretical and practical acquisitions, he began his own work.

Without abandoning the Enneagram symbol, and using Bennett and Bohm's contributions, Blake offers us the experience that he acquired from the 1970s until 2008, when he published the first version of *The Supreme Art of Dialogue*. In the beginning he explains that Bohm was strongly influenced by his therapist Patrick de Mare, who had, in turn, studied analysis with some of S.H. Foulkes' groups.[211] As a result of his experiences with groups, Bohm proposed that in order to achieve real dialogue we need a group that is neither too big, nor too small, but medium sized, made up of around 17 people. Blake would later stress the importance of the medium sized group and give it as a requirement to guarantee the essential characteristics of a dialogue, which are:

---

[211] S. H. Foulkes was a German medic, psychiatrist and neurologist, author of numerous texts on group psychotherapy including *Therapeutic Group Analysis* (1964), UK: George Allen & Unwin. He was Norbert Elias' psychoanalyst and invited him to take part in an interdisciplinary group whose results were published in *Psychiatry in a changing society* (1969).

"It begins from 'ignorance'

It establishes mutual equality between the participants

It requires the recognition of each person as a subject, not an object

It operates in the present moment

It is creative

It requires a diversity of points of view

It produces a unity that cannot be predicted or aimed for" (Blake, 2009: 11).

By dialogue, Blake understands a freely circulating conversation, not directed to the future, but to the present moment, with a diffuse structure which allows the emergence of the speaker. It requires the suspension of everyday habits and the assumptions of discourse. If there is adequate variety in the medium-sized group, meaning will emerge between the known and the unknown but it cannot be observed, it requires participation in order to achieve the basic structure for the construction of meaning. Observation, says Blake, separates the observer from the observed, whereas in participation there are only paths to be opened, and no models to apply.

Blake assures us that the Enneagram allows us to symbolize the process of construction of meaning shared through the triangle that we find within the circumference. The stretch from the 9 to the 3 represents the first process, which is the articulation of each part of the meaning. The second process, which goes from 3 to 6, corresponds to the organization of that meaning at a higher level. The third process begins at the 6 and takes place with the creation of the final meaning, at the 9, which can be expressed in the form of narrations or symbols. The lines of the hexad describe how the varied elements that come into play are related to one another with an inner meaning. All this is one part of Blake's theoretical and practical contributions, which deserve further study. It is clear that for communication, as in other areas, the Enneagram encompasses many as yet uncharted territories.

Epilogue

There was a time to attempt to recover histories, and I tried. The time has come to accept that *this* search through the past has come to an end. I am handing over the baton. I hold on to the only thing that exists: the present. Let those who come later travel, search in the archives, compare sources and answer historical queries.

For my part, I would like to be reborn, although there are many in my generation who believe the time to die is nigh. I am making another attempt, without closed models, without routes firmly traced by others, paying attention to the egoic stumbles of all the ages, setting myself the mission to study and practice what Blake and Almaas propose in their books.

It is time to see myself in the other, to open dialogues with others, to be with those who are different, with those who I have said I do not understand. Building community is the project; a community which weaves together the best of our differences, starting from a shared objective. Faced with the disappointments of all that surrounds us, we need to step away from our own centre and feel the pleasure of reciprocal exchange with others.

If a part of all this was achieved in the past, there is nothing to stop us from re-inventing the present.

Mixcoac, Mexico City, January 16th 2016

Cited bibliography

ADDISON, HA (2006) *The Enneagram and Kabbalah: Reading Your Soul*, Jewish Light Publishing.

ALGAR, Hamid (1976) The Naqshbandi Order: a Preliminary Survey of its History and Significance, *Studia Islamica,* No. 44: 123-152, Paris: Maisonnueve & Larose.

ALMAAS, AH (2000 [1996]) *Luminous Night's Journey. An autobiographical fragment,* Boston & London: Shambala Publications.

ALMAAS, AH (1998) *Facets of Unity - The Enneagram of Holy Ideas*, Shambhala Publications.

ALMAAS, AH (2004) The Inner Journey Home. Soul's Realization of the Unity of Reality, Boston: Shambhala Publications.

ARANDA PESCADOR, Carlos (2013) Aproximación al Origen del Pensamiento de G.I. Gurdjieff: las Raíces Musulmanas, Tesis doctoral, Facultad de Filología, Universidad Complutense de Madrid.

AUSEJO, Elena (2004) La cuestión de la obra científico-matemática de Ramón Llull, *Revista de la Sociedad Española de Historia de las Ciencias y de las Técnicas*, Volumen 1: 2121.

BAKHTIAR, Laleh (2013a) *Rumi's Original Sufi Enneagram*, Institute of Traditional Psychology, Chicago.

BAKHTIAR, Laleh (2013b) *The Sufi Enneagram. The Secrets of the Symbol Unveiled*, Institute of Traditional Psychology, Chicago.

BAKHTIAR, Laleh (2013c) *Sufi Enneagram, Spiritual Sign*, KAZI Publications, Chicago.

BAUDINO, Abdul Karim (2014) *El Eneagrama Sufi*, Rosario, Argentina: Huwa Ediciones.

BEESING, M, NOGOSEK, RJ, O'LEARY, PH (1984) *The Enneagram: a Journey of Self Discovery*, Dimension Books Inc, New Jersey.

BENNETT, JG (1973) Gurdjieff : Making a New World, London: Turnstone Press.

BENNETT, JG (1974) *Witness: the autobiography of John G. Bennett,* Omen Press, Tucson Arizona.

BENNETT, JG (1975) *Gurdjieff: a great enigma*, Coombe Springs Press.

BENNETT, JG (1983) *Enneagram Studies*, Bennett Books.

BENNETT, JG (2013) *The Masters of Wisdom,* Estate of J.G. Bennett. Kindle Edition.

BERGADÁ, María Mercedes (1950) El aporte de Francisco Suárez a la Filosofia Moderna, *Actas del primer congreso Nacional de Filosofía.* VOLUME III, Universidad de Córdoba, Argentina. Full text available online: http://www.filosofia.org/aut/003/m49a1921.pdf

BERGOGLIO, JM (2013) *Address to the Leadership of the Episcopal Conferences of Latin America during the General Coordination Meeting*, delivered on 28.07.2013 at Sumaré Study Center, Rio de Janeiro. Available online http://w2.vatican.va/content/francesco/en/speeches/2013/july/documents/papa-francesco_20130728_gmg-celam-rio.html (consulted March 2016)

BERLIN, Isaiah (1998 [1949]) *Personal Impressions*, The Hogarth Press, London. Kindle Edition.

BERLIN, Isaiah (2000) *Three Critics of the Enlightenment: Vico, Hamann, Herder*, Princeton University Press.

BLAKE, AGE (1996) *The Intelligent Enneagram*, Boston & London: Shambhala Publications.

BLAKE, AGE (2009) *The Supreme Art of Dialogue. Structures of Meaning,* Charles Town, West Virginia: Du Versity Publications.

BOHM, David (2004) *On Dialogue*, New York: Routledge.

BRIANCESCO, Eduardo (1986) La exploración del mal moral en el último Tomás de Aquino, *Teología*, periodical of the Theology Faculty of the Pontificia Universidad Católica Argentina, Num. 47. (Full text available online: https://dialnet.unirioja.es/servlet/articulo?codigo=2524139)

CASSIN, Elena et al. (1982) *Los Imperios del Antiguo Oriente,* Tomo I, Madrid: Siglo XXI de España Editores.

CASSIN, Elena et al. (1983) *Los Imperios del Antiguo Oriente*, Tomo III, Madrid: Siglo XXI de España Editores.

CHOURAQUI, André (1991) *La historia del judaísmo*, México, D.F. : Publicaciones Cruz.

COLLIN, Rodney (1984) *The Theory of Eternal Life*, Random House.

COLLIN, Rodney (1997 [1954]) *The Theory of Celestial Influence: Man, the Universe, and Cosmic Mystery*, Arkana, Penguin Books (Full text available online: http://www.baytallaah.com/bookspdf/95.pdf)

COLLINS, Randal (1998) *The Sociology of Philosophies: A Global Theory of Intellectual Change*, Harvard University Press.

COOPER, AM, FRANCES, AJ, and SACKS, MH (1990) *Psychiatry, Volume I, The Personality Disorder and Neurosis*, Basic Books, NY.

DANIELS, D and PRICE, V (2009) *Essential Enneagram: The Definitive Personality Test and Self-Discovery Guide* (Revised and updated), Harper Collins.

DEBUS, Allen (1978) *Man and Nature in the Renaissance*, Cambridge University Press.

DEFOUW, Richard J (2011) *The Enneagram in the Writings of Gurdjieff*, Dog Ear Publishing, Indianapolis.

DESCARTES, René (1995 [1649]) *Les passions de l'âme*, Texte integral, Classiques Francais.

ELIAS, N (1994) El retraimiento de los sociólogos en el presente, in: *Conocimiento y Poder*, Madrid: Ediciones de la Piqueta.

ELIAS, N (1998) The Changing Balance of Power Between the Sexes in Ancient Rome, Chapter 11 in Elias N, Mennell S, Goudsblom J, *On Civilization, Power and Knowledge: Selected Writings*, University of Chicago Press.

EMPEREUR, James (1990) *The Enneagram and Spiritual Direction: Nine Paths to Spiritual Guidance,* Bloomsbury Academic.

EMPEREUR, James (2000) *El Eneagrama y la Dirección Espiritual*, Prologue by Maite Melendo, Bilbao: Editorial Desclée de Brouwer.

Enneagram Dot Com (uploaded June 2009) *Enneagram types and subtypes with Helen Palmer* (video) From https://www.youtube.com/watch?v=D86IVsoiqTE

EVAGRIUS PONTICUS (1972) *The Prakticos and Chapters on Prayer*, translation and introduction by John Eudes Bamberger, Kentucky: Cistercian Publications.

FABRE, CÁRDENAS and BORJA, coord. (2014) *La Compañía de Jesús en América Latina después de la Restauración*, México: Universidad Iberoamericana Ciudad de México y Pontificia Universidad Javeriana.

FARA, Patricia (2009) *Science. A Four Thousand Year History*, New York: Oxford University Press.

FERNÁNDEZ, Álvaro (2011) *La Teúrgia de los Oráculos Caldeos. Cuestiones de Léxico y de Contexto Histórico*, PhD Thesis,

Granada, España: Universidad de Granada, Department of Greek and Slavic Philology.

FRAGER, Robert and FADIMAN, James (2005) *Personality and Personal Growth (6th edition)*, Pearson Education, New Jersey

GARCÍA, Rolando (2000) *El Conocimiento en Construcción. De las Formulaciones de Jean Piaget a la Teoría de los Sistemas Complejos*, Barcelona: Gedisa.

GARCÍA MARTÍNEZ, F (1996) *The Dead Sea Scrolls Translated: The Qumran Texts in English*, translated by Watson WGE, Brill/ Eerdmans Publishing Company.

GILBERT, Adrian (2002) *Magi*, Montpellier VT: Invisible Cities Press.

GÓMEZ DE LIAÑO, Ignacio (1998) *El Círculo de la Sabiduría. Diagnóstico del Conocimiento en el Mitraísmo, el Gnosticismo, el Cristianismo, el Maniqueísmo.* Madrid: Siruela.

GÓMEZ DE LIAÑO, Ignacio (2001) *Athanasius Kircher. Itinerario del éxtasis o las imágenes de un saber universal*, Madrid: Siruela.

GONZÁLEZ URBANEJA, PM (2008) El teorema llamado Pitágoras. Una historia geométrica de 4000 años, *Sigma Revista de Matemáticas*, No. 32 www.hezkuntza.ejgv.euskadi.eus/r43-573/es/ contenidos/informacion/dia6_sigma/es_sigma/adjuntos/ sigma_32/8_pitagoras.pdf consulted 17/02/2016

GRANADA, Miguel (1994) Agostino Steuco y la perennis philosophia, *Daimon, revista de Filosofía,* No. 8, Spain: Universidad de Murcia. Online journal: http://revistas.um.es/ daimon/article/view/13361

GURAIEB, José (1976) *El Sufismo en el Cristianismo y el Islam.* Buenos Aires: Editorial Kier.

GURDJIEFF, GI (2010 [1963]) *Meetings with Remarkable Men*, Martino Fine Books [also online http://www.holybooks.com/wp-content/uploads/Gurdjieff-Meetings-with-Remarkable-Men.pdf]

HART, G (1997) *Egyptian Myths* University of Texas Press

HEGEL, Georg Wilhelm Friedrich (1974) *Lecciones sobre la Filosofía de la Historia Universal*, Madrid, Ediciones de la Revista de Occidente.

HELFFERICH, Adolph (1858) *Raymund Lull und die Anfänge d. Catalonischen Literatur*, Berlin: Springer.

HUARTE DE SAN JUAN, Juan (1996 [1594]) *Examen de ingenios para la ciencia [An Examination of Men's Wits]*- with a preliminary note by Mariela Szirko, *Electroneurobiología*, 3 (2): 1-322 (full text in Spanish available online http://electroneubio.secyt.gov.ar/ Juan_Huarte_de_San_Juan_Examen_de_ingenios.pdf)

HUXLEY, Aldous (1947) *The Perennial Philosophy*, Chatto and Windus, London

ICHAZO, Oscar (1982a) *Between Metaphysics and Protoanalysis. A theory for analyzing the human psyche*. New York: Arica Institute Press.

ICHAZO, Oscar (1982b) *Interviews with Oscar Ichazo*, New York: Arica Institute Press.

ICHAZO, Oscar (1988) *Letters to the School*, New York: Arica Institute Press.

ISAACS, Andrea and LABANAUSKAS, Jack (1996/1997) An interview with Oscar Ichazo by Andrea Isaacs and Jack Labanauskas, *Enneagram Monthly*. Part I: November 1996; Part II: December 1996 and Part III: January 1997. Business WorldPress Themes. Portola Valley, Ca. (Full text available online at http:// www.enneagram-monthly.com/setting-the-record-straight.html consulted 11/02/2016)

JUNG, CG (1989 [1961]) *Memories, Dreams, Reflections — recorded and edited by Aniela Jaffé* (trans. Richard and Clara Winston), Vintage Books

JUNG, CG (1970) *Civilization in Transition*, Volume 10 of The Collected Works, Princeton University Press

KARAMUSTAFA, Ahmet T (2007) *Sufism. The Formative period*, Berkeley, CA : University of California Press.

KUHN, Thomas S (1970 [1962]) *The Structure of Scientific Revolutions*, International Encyclopedia of Unified Science, University of Chicago Press

KÜNG, Hans (2011) *The Catholic Church: a short history*, Hachette

LAPID-BOGDA, G (2004) *Bringing Out the Best in Yourself at Work: how to use the Enneagram system for success*, McGraw-Hill Education

LAO TSE (2012) *Tao Te Ching. Los libros del Tao*, edited and translated into Spanish by Iñaki Preciado Idoeta, Presentation by María Teresa Román, Madrid: Trotta

LAPORTE J-M (2010) *A Christian Transposition of the Enneagram: With Paul of Tarsus and Ignatius Loyola*, online http://orientations.jesuits.ca/ennea%20spexx.pdf

LÓPEZ FÉREZ, Juan Antonio (2009) Filón de Alejandría: Obra y Pensamiento. Una Lectura Filológica. [Philo of Alexandria: work and thought. A philological approach], *Sythesis*, Vol. 16: 13-82. (Full text available online: http://www.memoria.fahce.unlp.edu.ar/art_revistas/pr.3937/pr.3937.pdf)

LOYOLA, Ignatius of (1914 [1548]) *The Spiritual Exercises*, translator: Fr Elder Mullan, S.J. Published online by ixtmedia.com, the Digital Catholic Bookstore http://www.companionofjesus.com/se-mullan.pdf

MADIROLAS, Eduardo (2005) *El Camino del Árbol de la Vida, vol I. Un Curso de introducción a la Cabalá Mística*, Barcelona: Equipo difusor del libro.

MADRIGAL, Santiago (2014) *Los Jesuitas y el Concilio Vaticano II: Meditación Histórica en el Bicentenario de la Restauración de la Compañía de Jesús*, Madrid: Universidad Pontificia de Comillas.

MAJERCIK, Ruth (1989) *The Caldean Oracles, Text, Translation and Commentary*, Netherlands: E.J.Brill.

MARTIN, DR (1966) Below the Hindu Kush, *Documents on Contemporary Dervish Communities: A Symposium*, Collected, edited, and arranged by Roy Weaver Davidson, London: The Octagon Press, pp. 22–24. Now available online http://www.cosmopolis.com/files/sarmoun-brotherhood.html

MASON, Stephen F (1962) *A History of the Sciences*, Collier Books.

MATURANA, Humberto and VARELA Francisco (2004) *De Máquinas y Seres Vivos. Autopoiesis: la Organización de lo Vivo*, Buenos Aires: Editorial Universitaria y Grupo Editorial Lumen.

MATURANA, Humberto (2004) *Desde la Biología a la Psicología*, Buenos Aires: Editorial Universitaria y Grupo Editorial Lumen.

MEIER, JP (1994) *A Marginal Jew: Vol 2: Mentor, message, and miracles*, Yale University Press.

MOORE, James (1993) *Gurdjieff, a Biography, the Anatomy of a Myth, Great Britain*: Element Books Limited.

MUELLER, Fernand-Lucien (2007) *Historia de la Psicología*, México: Fondo de Cultura Económica.

NARANJO, Claudio (1994) *Character and Neurosis: An Integrative View*, Gateway Books.

NARANJO, Claudio (2012) *27 personajes en busca del ser*, Barcelona: Ediciones La Llave.

NEEDHAM, J (2000) *Science and Civilisation in China - Volume 6: Biology and Biological Technology, Part VI: Medicine* (with collaboration of Lu Gwei-Djen and edited by Nathan Sivin), Cambridge University Press.

NICOLL, M (1996 [1952]) *Psychological Commentaries on the Teaching of Gurdjieff and Ouspensky*, Vol. 2, Weiser Books. (Full text available online http://selfdefinition.org/gurdjieff/maurice-nicoll-directory/Nicoll-Psychological-Commentaries-Gurdjieff-Ouspensky-Vol-2.pdf)

NOTT, Charles (1990 [1961]) *Teachings of Gurdjieff. A Pupils Journal*. London: Penguin Group.

NOTT, Charles (1984 [1969]) *Further Teachings of Gurdjieff. Journey Through This World*. Maine: Samuel Weiser.

ORAGE, AR (1930) *Psychological exercises & essays*, Farrar & Rinehart, New York.

OUSPENSKY, PD (2001 [1949]) *In Search of the Miraculous - Fragments of an Unknown Teaching*, Mariner Books. (Full text available online at www.gurdjieff.am/in-search/index.pdf [10.12.2015])

OUSPENSKY, PD (2008) *Conscience: the Search for Truth*, Morning Light Press.

PALMER, Helen (1991 [1988]) *The Enneagram. Understanding Yourself and the Others in Your Life*, New York: Harper Collins.

PALMER, Helen (1995 [1993]) *The Enneagram in Love and Work: Understanding your Intimate and Business Relationships*, HarperOne.

PANG, Ming (2014) *The Theory of Hunan Whole Entity*, ZQ Educational Corporation.

PANIKKAR, Raimón (2006) *Paz e Interculturalidad. Una reflexión filosófica*, Barcelona: Herder.

PÉREZ, Roberto A. (2015) *Manual de Eneagrama, Tomo I, Version 08.13*, given out at a course offered 27 - 29 January 2015 in Rosarito, Baja California, Mexico.

PÉREZ TAMAYO, Ruy (1997) *De la Magia Primitiva a la Medicina Moderna*, México: Fondo de Cultura Económica.

PICO DELLA MIRANDOLA, Giovanni (1486) *Oration on the Dignity of Man (De hominis dignitate)*. (Full text available online: https://ebooks.adelaide.edu.au/p/pico_della_mirandola/giovanni/dignity/)

PLATO (1997 [1935 translation]) *Plato's cosmology: the Timaeus of Plato*, Translation with a running commentary by F. M. Cornford, Hackett Publishing Company, Indianapolis, Indiana.

PLOTINUS (2009 [3rd century CE]) *Amor, Belleza, Daimon*, México: Editorial Me Cayó el Veinte.

PUECH, Henri-Charles (1982) *Las Religiones Constituidas en Asia y sus Contracorrientes*, México: Siglo XXI.

REDONDI, Pietro (1990) *Galileo Herético*, Madrid: Alianza Editorial.

REICH, Wilhelm (1980 [1933]) *Character Analysis*, translation into English by Vincent Carfagno, Farrar, Straus and Giroux, New York.

REYES, Alfonso (1982) *Obras Completas*, volumen XVIII, México: Fondo de Cultura Económica.

REYES, Alfonso (1983) *Obras Completas,* volumen XIII, México: Fondo de Cultura Económica.

RISO, DR (1993) *Enneagram transformations: Releases and Affirmations for Healing Your Personality Type*, Houghton Miffling Harcourt

RISO, DR (1995) *Discovering Your Personality Type: The New Enneagram Questionnaire*, Houghton Mifflin Company, NY

RISO, DR and Hudson, R (1996) *Personality Types: Using the Enneagram for Self-Discovery*, Mariner Books

RISO, DR and Hudson, R (1999) *The Wisdom of the Enneagram: Complete Guide to Psychological and Spiritual Growth for the Nine Personality Types.* Bantam USA.

ROHR, R and EBERT, A (2001) *The Enneagram: a Christian Perspective*, (trans. Peter Heinegg), The Crossroad Publishing Company, NY

ROSSI, Paolo (2006) *Logic and the Art of Memory: The Quest for a Universal Language*, Continuum, New York

SANDERS, NK, translator (1973) *The Epic of Gilgamesh*, Penguin Classics

SCHÄFER, P (1992) *The Hidden and Manifest God: Some Major Themes in Early Jewish Mysticism,* translation into English by Aubrey Pomerance, State University of New York Press.

SCHOLEM, G (1995 [1946]) *Major Trends in Jewish Mysticism*, Schocken Books NY.

SHAH, Idries (1999) *The Sufis*, Octagon Press.

SHIRLEY, John (2004) *Gurdjieff: And Introduction to His Life and Ideas*, Penguin, NY.

SVIRI, Sara (1993) Hakîm Tirmidhî and the Malâmâtî Movement in Early Sufism, in L. Lewisohn (ed), *Classical Persian Sufism from its Origins to Rumi*, KNP Publications, London and New York 1993, 583-613. (full text available online http://www.goldensufi.org/a_ss_malamati.html)

TEILHARD DE CHARDIN, Pierre (1966) *The Vision of the Past*, Collin.

TEILHARD DE CHARDIN, Pierre (1980) *The Heart of the Matter*, Harcourt Brace Jovanovich.

THEOPHRASTUS (2004 [3rd century BCE]) *Characters*, translation into English by James Diggle, Cambridge University Press.

YATES, Frances A (1982) *Lull & Bruno - Collected Essays*, Routledge and K. Paul.

YATES, Frances A (1983) *Renaissance and Reform: The Italian Contribution - Collected Essays*, Taylor & Francis.

WAGNER, Jerome (1998) *The Enneagram and the Spiritual Journey*, Chicago: The Midwest Ministry Development Service (full text of briefing available on line http://www.midwestministrydevelopment.org/pdf/Enneagram.pdf)

WAGNER, Jerome (2010) *Nine Lenses on the World: The Enneagram Perspective*, Evanston, Illinois: Nine Lens Press.

WEISMANN, Itzchak (2009) *The Naqshbandiyya. Orthodoxy and Activism in a Worldwide Sufi Tradition*, New York: Rutledge.

WILTSE, Virginia and PALMER, Helen (2011) Hidden in Plain Sight: Observations on the Origins of the Enneagram, *The Enneagram Journal*, Vol. IV, Issue 1, July 2011.

ZERMEÑO, Guillermo (2003) Libros jesuitas incautados y proscritos. In: *Artes de México*, No. 68: 61 - 68.

ZWEMER, Samuel (1902) *Raymond Lull: First Missionary to the Moslems*, Funk & Wagnalls Company

www.ingramcontent.com/pod-product-compliance
Lightning Source LLC
Chambersburg PA
CBHW071721120626
46550CB00001B/336